A Companion to the
Shakespearean Films of Kenneth Branagh

A COMPANION TO THE SHAKESPEAREAN FILMS OF

KENNETH BRANAGH

by Sarah Hatchuel

BLIZZARD PUBLISHING

Winnipeg • Niagara Falls

First published in the year 2000 in Canada and the United States by
Blizzard Publishing Inc.
73 Furby Street, Winnipeg, Canada R3C 2A2.

Distributed in the United States by General Distribution Services,
4500 Witmer Industrial Estates, Niagara Falls, NY 14305–1386.

Cover photo courtesy of Renaissance Films.
Cover design by Otium.
Printed for Blizzard Publishing in Canada by Kromar.

5   4   3   2   1

Blizzard Publishing gratefully acknowledges the support of
Canadian Heritage, the Manitoba Arts Council, and the Canada Council to its
publishing program.

Canadian Cataloguing in Publication Data

Hatchuel, Sarah.
   A companion to the Shakespearean films of Kenneth Branagh
   ISBN 0-921368-89-5

I. Branagh, Kenneth. 2. Shakespeare, William, 1564–1616—Film and video
adaptations. I. Title.

PR3093.H38   1999   791.43'0233'092   C99-920126-3

To my grandfather,
Edmond Ganansia

Contents

Acknowledgments

This Companion would not have been the same without some people I would like to thank deeply here:

Russell Jackson, fellow of the Shakespeare Institute and Kenneth Branagh's textual adviser, for receiving me so kindly in Stratford and explaining how he works with Branagh and the other actors.

Patrick Doyle, music composer, for giving me such insights into his creative process.

Pierre Berthomieu, Professor of cinema at the University of Sorbonne Nouvelle and Bordeaux III, for sharing with me his documents and thoughts in view of the publishing of his book on Kenneth Branagh's cinematography. The chapters on the cinematic adaptations owe him a lot.

Pierre Iselin, professor at the University of Sorbonne Paris IV, for directing my academic research.

Peter Atwood, my editor, for giving priceless advice.

Jude Tessel for being such a wonderful proofreader, in such a short time.

Ngoc Vu for organizing the Internet Mailing List devoted to Kenneth Branagh and for compiling the Kenneth Branagh Compendium on the Net. She allowed me to communicate with people from around the world and gained access to great information. Thanks also to Ellen Armstrong and Marilyn Mosher for the "Branagh Frequently Asked Question" site on the Internet. It was a precious help for my research.

The librarians of the Shakespeare Centre and the Shakespeare Institute in Stratford-upon-Avon for guiding me in my search for articles, videotapes and slides.

Kevin De Ornellas (Queen's University of Belfast) and Dr. Nathalie Vienne-Guerrin (University of Rouen), whose insights will heavily influence future publications.

And, finally, thanks to my family and friends (particularly Isabelle Gonzalez, Anne-Marie Simonpieri, Nada Ismaïl, Nicolas Louvet, Natacha Moenne-Loccoz and Caroline Wilmot) who saw my enthusiasm for Shakespeare grow with the years.

Foreword

My first "Shakespearean" experience was watching the BBC Shakespeare series on television. I was eight years old and the plays were broadcast in France every Sunday. It left me with no memorable feeling except boredom, which you can expect from a child when she is forced to watch a long play with subtitles for a whole afternoon. I then firmly decided: Shakespeare was not for me.

Ten years later, I was studying management and economics at college. And, on the twelfth of February 1991, I saw the movie *Henry V* by Kenneth Branagh. The shock was violent and visceral. I was stirred by the vision of it, the sound of it. The images transported me into the story. The words, their music, moved me deeply. The power, the violence of what was said, along with the harmony and beauty of that rhythmic language, was almost ravishing. All was there: words, action, mud, blood. And Patrick Doyle's music backing Shakespeare's verses caressed them, enveloped them so well that one could believe it had always been with them, inside of them. From the words, music rose. From the music, words were born. I was experiencing one of the best movies in my life. Kenneth Branagh's performance was epic and lyrical but at the same time showed us the doubts of a lonely and human king.

When the film ended, I was both hooked on, and reconciled with, Shakespeare. In the following days, I saw the movie twice again and began to read the play, to learn some passages from it, and then to know the whole part of Henry V and the Chorus. I decided to apply to a summer Shakespearean acting course at the London Academy of Performing Arts and finally spent the summer of 1991 studying Shakespeare's works through an actor's eye: speech, movement, text, fencing, improvisation. All that experience helps me still to understand how directors and actors work.

But life is life. And after this brief—but intense—artistic break, I went on with management. Yet, all through those years, I kept appreciating Shakespeare's works. A new world had opened before me, and I had plunged into it with a thirst for literary, poetic, and cinematic emotions.

As much as 1991 belonged to *Henry V*, the subsequent years belonged to *Hamlet*. During a 1992 stay in London, I fell by chance upon the full-text BBC radio version of *Hamlet*, co-directed and played by Branagh. After Laurence Olivier's movie, this was only my second exposure to the play, and I did not need any cinematic images to realize that this play was *the* play. The natural acting and the clear delivery brought forth mental images with an incredible easiness. Slowly but surely, *Hamlet* took the place of *Henry V* in my heart. All climaxed in the spring of 1993 when I saw Branagh play Hamlet on stage. At last I could see the play come to life and, so great was the actors' power and improvisation, each night was like taking a new course in Shakespeare.

In 1998, Branagh announced the creation of a new film company, the Shakespeare Film Company, which will be devoted exclusively to the production of Shakespearean movies. Branagh has just completed a film version of *Love's Labour's Lost*, and is planning to produce *As You Like It* and *Macbeth*. Now then, is the occasion for us to examine what his commitment to the works of Shakespeare has brought us. So far, I believe his 1996 film *Hamlet* may be considered the accomplishment of his cinematic career. The richness of its visual imagery as well of the range of emotions it delivers reflect Branagh's artistic development over the years and a considerable part of this book is devoted to this particular adaptation. Having reached with *Hamlet* a filmic maturity that seems to close the first phase of his career as a movie director and end the first cycle of his Shakespearean movies, it felt the right thing now to write a book on Kenneth Branagh's work.

Although this companion is the extension of an academic work defended at the University of Sorbonne, it is not intended to be a pure academic, scholarly book, as it is unashamedly infused with deference and gratitude to Branagh's works. It is more the accomplishment of a six-year journey, an intellectual as much as an emotional journey, and is meant for anyone who is interested in Shakespeare, film and theatre. Branagh's Shakespearean body of work has unexpectedly changed the way people all over the world feel about and react to Shakespeare. I felt the need to study this exceptional change in reception and to answer some of Branagh's harshest critics. Through this work, I have not attempted to plumb the soul of Branagh's mystery. I have looked simply for understanding how this particular talent has made Shakespeare so accessible to a new generation, conveyed all the lyricism, power, and everlasting modernism of such plays as *Henry V*, *Hamlet,* and *Much Ado About Nothing* to a generation that is used to rejecting the classics.

To gather information for this companion, I went to the Shakespeare Centre in Stratford-upon-Avon to view the Royal Shakespeare Company video archives. In March 1997, I talked to Dr. Russell Jackson, fellow of the Shakespeare Institute and Branagh's textual adviser; and, in April 1997, I interviewed Patrick Doyle, Branagh's music score composer. I worked with Branagh's movie scripts, press material, and written or broadcast interviews of Branagh and his collaborators, as well as scholarly, theatre, and film reviews in libraries in Stratford (Shakespeare Centre, Shakespeare Institute) and in Paris (British Council, library of Sorbonne, library of Sorbonne Nouvelle, library of Nanterre, National Library Department of Arts and Entertainment). I saw the Royal Shakespeare Company production of Adrian Noble's 1984 *Henry V* on video at the Shakespeare Centre—which keeps the archives of the RSC—and I attended in person Noble's 1992 *Hamlet*—which I subsequently re-watched on tape at the Shakespeare Centre. For the productions I haven't seen—the Renaissance Theatre productions, for instance—I have relied on the company programs, on press material, academic reviews, photographs, and on the documentary *Discovering Hamlet*, featuring the rehearsals of the 1988 RSC *Hamlet* directed by Derek Jacobi. Very recently, I also attended a special screening in London of Branagh's new film *Love's Labour's Lost*.

In this book, I quote Branagh and his collaborators frequently so they can give their own artistic point of view on their work and what they wanted to convey. As often, I quote the theatre, literary, and film critics in order to analyze the reception of the different productions.

The movies under specific examination in this book are *Henry V* (Renaissance Films, 1989), *Much Ado About Nothing* (Renaissance Films, 1993), and *Hamlet* (Fishmonger Films, 1996), all directed by and starring Kenneth Branagh. His stage and radio roles also discussed are *Henry V* (Royal Shakespeare Company, directed by Adrian Noble, 1984), Benedick in *Much Ado About Nothing* (Renaissance Theatre, directed by Judi Dench, 1988), *Hamlet* (Renaissance Theatre, directed by Derek Jacobi, 1988), *Hamlet* (Renaissance Theatre in collaboration with BBC Radio Drama, directed by Glyn Dearman and Kenneth Branagh, 1992), and *Hamlet* (Royal Shakespeare Company in collaboration with Renaissance Theatre, directed by Adrian Noble, 1993). This work has thus three objectives: to study why and how, in Branagh's movies, the delivery of Shakespeare's language and the direction of actors have reached such a high level of clarity and naturalism; to compare the three Shakespearean movies to the theatre productions that preceded them, in order to point out the major influences of the theatre on Branagh's movie work; and to analyze the movies in terms of their textual and cinematic adaptations in order to spot what has contributed to their popularity, and to understand how they fit into our post-modern era.

This book does not intend to judge Branagh's works and assess his critical choices in any way. It will attempt to point out facts and analyze a body of films which are there for us to see. Nor does it intend to evaluate the fidelity of Branagh's movies to Shakespeare's plays, as the question of being faithful or unfaithful to a dramatic text becomes tricky when a change in medium is concerned. Rather, this book intends to reveal the theatrical influences, textual changes, recurrent structures, and codes which have made Branagh's movies what they are. In brief, the aim of this book is not to say "this is good or bad, it should have been like this ..." but rather "This is how it is. Let's try to discover why."

I do believe that Branagh's instinctive vision of Shakespeare is indeed interesting and that his approach has often reflected—and been as coherent as—an academic one. It is no doubt thanks to Kenneth Branagh that so many Shakespearean films are produced nowadays. And his work may have even influenced the way theatre companies are now tackling Shakespeare with a fresh, natural, and intelligible language and approach.

Introduction
Shakespeare Revisited

In the course of a few years, Shakespeare has become one of the most fashionable script writers in the world of movies. Since 1989, numerous Shakespearean adaptations have appeared on screens around the world: Franco Zeffirelli's *Hamlet*, Oliver Parker's *Othello*, Trevor Nunn's *Twelfth Night*, Adrian Noble's *A Midsummer Night's Dream*, Ian McKellen's *Richard III*, Al Pacino's *Looking For Richard* and Baz Luhrmann's *Romeo+Juliet*. John Madden's *Shakespeare in Love*, which presents an imaginary period in Shakespeare's life, has also been hugely successful with its screenplay by Tom Stoppard inspired by several plots of the plays, notably *Romeo and Juliet*.

This renewal can be credited to Kenneth Branagh's *Henry V* and his follow-up *Much Ado About Nothing* which grossed twenty-two million dollars at the box-office in the U.S. and was made with a budget of only eight million. Producers now are much less afraid of investing in a Shakespearean adaptation. Branagh's *Henry V*, first released in autumn 1989, in fact ended a fallow period for Shakespearean screen adaptations, which began in 1971 after Roman Polanski's *Macbeth*.

Yet, if we look at the past, there has always been an urge to merge Shakespeare and movies. In fact in 1899, only four years after the invention of motion-picture films, Shakespeare's *King John* was filmed for the screen. And this trend of importing Shakespeare's stories and words into a more realistic environment has developed, it seems, since the English Restoration in 1660. Theatre actors-producers, from David Garrick in the late 1700s to Henry Irving in the late 1800s, have felt this same desire to stage Shakespeare in impressive and spectacular sets, using lighting, stage machinery, and mechanical devices to increase the impression of realism. Branagh clearly situates himself in this trend, and pursues it further through the medium of cinema. Our time is much more literal and visual than Shakespeare's time: if, during Shakespeare's day, people said they were going to "hear" a play, today we say that we are going to "see" a play. Over the centuries, there has been a huge transfer from ears to eyes, and Kenneth Branagh clearly adapts Shakespeare's plays to the modern situation.

In an eleven-year career in the movies, Branagh performed and directed three Shakespearean adaptations: a history play (*Henry V*, 1989), a comedy (*Much Ado About Nothing*, 1993) and a tragedy (*Hamlet*, 1996). A fourth will be released very soon: a musical adaptation of *Love's Labour's Lost* (2000). Branagh also appeared as Iago in Oliver Parker's 1995 *Othello*; this movie will not be discussed here, even though Branagh was a powerful and original Iago in it—the film belongs to its director Oliver Parker.[1]

Kenneth Branagh's Shakespearean movies occupy a very peculiar cultural position. As Shakespearean works, they participate in an "elite" culture, often rejected by the young. Yet, by their well-paced and sensuous cinematic treatment, they participate in the world of Hollywood movies, often scorned by scholars.

In September 1993, *Sight & Sound* stated:

> For those in the middle classes brought up on that streak of puritanism which thinks that anything culturally serious must be painful, Branagh's approach is trivializing. But it depends on where you're coming from. To those who wouldn't usually go near a theatre, Branagh might seem intensely serious. . . . What looks like vulgarity and mediocrity (both repeated insults in the repertoire of Branagh-bashers) to someone bookish or expert in film may feel like an entry into high culture to someone else.

Branagh's intuitive and romantic approach has often been attacked by academic, theatre, and film critics. Branagh has been accused of using easy effects, suppressing any subtlety in the plays, and remaining too traditional. His camera moves have been received as disorganized, frantic, and nauseating. His ambitious activities of director, actor, and writer have given him a reputation for arrogance and egocentricity. However, despite all that can be said, good or bad, about Kenneth Branagh, his movies have contributed to the renewal of Shakespeare on the big screen and made Shakespeare accessible to a new, younger, more popular audience, who, without Branagh, would never have discovered the Bard's works.

Kenneth Branagh is a theatre actor turned movie director. The countless theatrical influences he has been subject to helped him gain confidence and develop his filmic visions. However, in his screen adaptations, these theatrical influences have not been translated into a slow pace or the still shots proper to the filmed theatre. Branagh's adaptations feature some big theatrical effects—let's think here of *Henry V's "Non nobis"* sequence, *Hamlet's* "My Thoughts Be Bloody" scene, or *Much Ado About Nothing's* opening overture. But the big effects are never stagey; Branagh uses theatricality to make the drama stands out, but he also loves for the story to ring in the most natural way.

His taste for romantic lyricism, slow motion, great melodies, and twirling camera moves has divided the critics, and made Branagh either loved or hated. This difference in reception culminated when *Hamlet* came out in February 1997 in England: while *The Observer* stated: "A hit, a hit, a very palpable hit . . . Visually, the movie is constantly impressive,"[2] *The Sunday Telegraph* complained, "Blond bombshell can't keep his mouth shut . . . I was bored out of my skull."[3]

If Branagh has made Shakespeare fashionable and popular for Hollywood producers and young people, he has removed it partly from the scholars; and some people, especially in England, bash his work without being aware of the enormous, worldwide impact its original, illuminating, and emotional approach to Shakespeare has had. A first approach which then can be deepened, enriched, and inspire vocations in the movies, theatre or teaching.

Branagh provides us an emotional entry into culture. His films go beyond the division between popular and elite culture by showing the audience how much Shakespeare is our contemporary, how much his works are human, bloody, carnal, sensual, and magically poetic. Michael Skovmand says in his introduction to the book *Screen Shakespeare*:

> Without doubt, Branagh's *Henry V* and *Much Ado About Nothing* have revitalized the domain of Shakespearean film. In secondary and higher education they are of great value as accessible, contemporary interpretations of exemplary clarity and charm.

Surprisingly, many young people have come to Shakespeare through Branagh's non-Shakespearean films, particularly *Dead Again* and *Mary Shelley's Frankenstein*. These two films feature universal themes which are themselves very "Shakespearean": love, death, destructive and creative powers. For *Dead Again's* apocalyptic finale, Branagh and

Patrick Doyle, his composer, added a chorus in which we can hear Othello's speech "It is the cause, my soul" (Act V, scene ii).

Since 1989, Branagh's cinematic work follows, consciously or not, a ternary cycle: Shakespearean adaptation, thriller, then modern comedy. Yet, despite the diversity of genres, his body of work has remained very coherent, with each non-Shakespearean film influencing his Shakespearean movies and vice-versa. This commitment to other genres has annoyed some film critics who prefer to categorize filmmakers; but it has also conveyed a kind of subliminal message to the public: since a Shakespearean film is only one film among others in Branagh's own filmography, it may also be considered as a movie among others by the public. It proclaims that a Shakespearean film can be as entertaining as a thriller or a contemporary comedy. The casting of popular and famous actors such as Jack Lemmon, Robin Williams, Michael Keaton, and Charlton Heston also helps to convey that Shakespearean adaptations are entertaining, ordinary movies.

Branagh's adaptations remain very traditional. Branagh does not scan entire plays searching for fashionable messages; he prefers a straightforward approach. Interviewed on his vision of *Much Ado About Nothing*, he replied: "I'm the patron of a youth company in Swindon which has just done it with the returning soldiers as GIs, with a very particular social milieu. That's fine. It's just that every time you do that, you always pay a price, you always cut at least one bit of the play."

His merit has been to make Shakespeare's language clear and natural. When Branagh's theatre company, Renaissance Theatre, produced *Much Ado About Nothing* on stage, the language sounded so unaffected some people believed it had been improvised. This impression was repeated when *Henry V* was released: some spectators thought the cue "O, here comes your father," (Act V, scene ii) whispered by an embarrassed and surprised Henry to Katherine, had been re-written or invented for the occasion.

Young people thus have discovered the plays with modern rhythms and inflections and without declamatory acting. Critics and scholars have often felt they were seeing the plays for the first time. Movie critic Roger Ebert remarked: "As Kenneth Branagh delivered the St. Crispin's speech [*Henry V*, Act IV, scene ii], I was emotionally stirred even though I had heard it many times before. That is one test of a great Shakespearean actor: to take the familiar and make it new."[4]

Branagh makes Shakespeare appear epic, lyrical, and emotional through images and music, while remaining faithful to the spirit, poetry, and meaning of the text. For Frank Occhiogrosso,

> The single most memorable feature of [*Henry V*] is the sheer excitement of it. The rhythmic pounding of the music, the resounding delivery of Henry's great speeches, and the blending of effects in service to Shakespeare's sublime verse make for the exhilaration that movies only at their best supply. [This movie] stamps itself indelibly upon the visual imagination of the viewer.[5]

In his book on Branagh's cinematography,[6] Pierre Berthomieu studied the themes we can find recurring in all of Branagh's movies: man lost in infinite space, man overtaken by creative or destructive forces; the power as well as the insignificance of theatre; the religious impulse; broken harmony. These themes, acknowledged by Branagh in an interview with Berthomieu, are interwoven in all his Shakespearean films. In fact, these movies present Shakespeare's text through the prism of Branagh's imagination and his personal themes. Sometimes, these echo themes present in Shakespeare's plays, but they often add a dimension, not present in Shakespeare, which gives a new context and resonances to the words.

According to actor Richard E. Grant,

> So many actors talk of taking Shakespeare to the people, but Branagh does it. He could have been a stalwart star of the [Royal Shakespeare Company]. Instead, he used his own money to set up his company, to get Shakespeare away from the big companies and into the actors' power again. If you bring greater excitement, and people, into the theatre, then that's what counts.[7]

Yet how has Kenneth Branagh achieved such a strong impact on Hollywood, on actors, directors, academics and on the public's appreciation and understanding of Shakespeare? How has he brought Shakespeare to the attention of a new generation? These are precisely the questions we intend to answer in the following chapters.

One answer lies in the clarity and naturalness of his acting, his vocal ability, and his method of directing actors. This will be addressed in Chapter Two, "Delivery and Direction."

A second answer can be traced to Branagh's theatrical roots. He has always worked through each play on stage before adapting it on film. These theatrical experiences have profoundly influenced his films and have given him the opportunity to identify the passages and scenes in the script that a movie could clarify, simplify, or illustrate. This will be the subject of Chapter Three, "The Theatrical Influences on Kenneth Branagh's Movies."

Branagh also makes Shakespeare's plays accessible through subtle changes in the text and to the story: through line cutting or reassignment and the addition of a subtext, usually through interpolated sequences. Chapter Four, "From Shakespeare's Text to Branagh's Script," will deal with these textual changes.

Another answer lies in Branagh's cinematography, on his choices of lighting and colours, of camera angles and moves, and the way he chooses to illustrate some words with literal images. His cinematic discourse will be thoroughly analyzed in Chapter Five, "Images, Action, and Movement." Branagh's cinematic choices are very successful at bringing meaning and accessibility to the movies, as he has never lost sight of the fact that he was making movies in the tradition of Hollywood.

But the first answer to these questions is a very simple—almost obvious—one. Branagh started such a revolution in the modern Shakespeare world because he felt the urge do so. He *consciously* set out to change Shakespeare's place in the popular imagination.

Notes

1. In an interview with Charlie Rose, when Branagh was asked about a textual cut in *Othello*, he answered: "I didn't direct this. I just played my role. You should ask the guy that shot it" ("Charlie Rose," PBS, Dec 1995). Moreover, Branagh has no previous theatre experience with that play except for an amateur production in which he played Cassio when he was sixteen.
2. Philip French. "A hit, a very palpable hit." *Observer*, 16 Feb 1997.
3. Anne Bilson. "Blond bombshell can't keep his mouth shut." *Sunday Telegraph*, 16 Feb 1997.
4. Roger Ebert. Review of *Henry V*. *Chicago Sun-Times*, 15 Dec 1989.
5. Frank Occhiogrosso. "Branagh's *Henry V*," a film review. *Shakespeare Bulletin*, Spring 1990.
6. Pierre Berthomieu. *Kenneth Branagh: Traînes de feu, rosées de sang*. Paris: Editions Jean-Michel Place, 1998.
7. Quoted in Richard Corliss. "Branagh the Conqueror." *Time International*, 13 Nov 1989.

Chapter One
Kenneth Branagh's Mission of Accessibility

In May 1993, American journalist Charlie Rose interviewed Branagh:

> Rose: Do you have this mission to somehow, either in theatre or in film, make Shakespeare come alive to all those people who unlike you have not yet felt the passion, the humour and the drama that it offers?
>
> Branagh: I do feel a kind of mission, yes. I don't think it's a question of him coming alive. Because he is alive. But, in my case, I have a very vivid memory of having been forced to read *The Merchant of Venice* aloud at school. I was thirteen or fourteen and I might as well have been reading the telephone directory. It made no sense at all. And then another teacher made a connection with *Romeo and Juliet*. He asked: "What is it all about?" There was a stunned silence and he said: "Sex, it's all about sex!" So, to fourteen-year olds with lots of hormones whizzing in confusion around their systems, that was a kind of the beginning of a key.[1]

Branagh's sense of mission reveals itself to be linked to his own unhappy experience with Shakespeare when he was an adolescent. Moreover, when Branagh was still a student at the Royal Academy of Dramatic Art, a tour of *The Merchant of Venice* was organized for the London high schools. The student company was met with deep boredom and dangerous hostility. In *Beginning*, the autobiography he wrote at the tender age of twenty-eight to pay for the first offices of his theatre company, he says: "For the first time I confronted an audience who talked loudly all the way through and threw things."[2]

This experience was decisive in Branagh's later decision to make Shakespeare more popular and accessible through the productions of his own theatre company, Renaissance Theatre, founded in 1987 with David Parfitt, and through his movies. What he told Charlie Rose in 1993 is a case in point:

> You must be satisfied artistically with yourself but you have to want to reach people. Your piece of art is only completed when somebody watches it. Now, if you know that the work you're working on already has this intimidation factor, you'll do everything you can to get that out of the way so you can get it across to people.[3]

In 1991, Branagh confided his favourite working experience to French actor Gérard Départdieu. He told the story of a performance of *A Midsummer's Night Dream* by Renaissance Theatre in 1990 in front of black teenagers brought by their coach for a "cultural afternoon."

> Before we came on stage, they were so loud that we could no longer hear ourselves. They shouted and threw things . . . But the wonderful thing is that we managed from time to time to reach a complete silence. A fantastic, electric silence . . . All of a sudden, thanks to the truth of a scene, the truth of an actor, the truth of an emotion, they were under the spell completely . . . and then everything started again. It was like a barometer that told us instantly when we got the thing and when we had lost it.[4]

This is one of Branagh's favourite performances and it reveals his desire to convey Shakespeare to people who maybe would never have had the opportunity to appreciate it. In the many interviews at the release of *Hamlet*, Branagh confided several anecdotes of his encounters with young American suburbanites. He was entranced by the natural way in which he could talk of recent Shakespearean adaptations as if they were ordinary films.

This motivation to carry Shakespeare's emotion to young people who should not enjoy it in the first place can be traced back to Kenneth Branagh's Irish working-class origins.

Ireland and Movies

Kenneth Branagh was born in 1960 in Belfast, Northern Ireland, in a moderate Protestant non-literate, working-class atmosphere. His father was a carpenter who did not think much of books, and his mother raised the children and occasionally worked in shops. "My values were influenced by a completely working-class background until I was in my teens," Branagh said. "This allows people to believe me when I say, 'Listen, honestly, I think you're going to enjoy this Shakespeare play'—more than if I'd gone to Eton or Oxford."[5]

Until nine years old, Kenneth Branagh lived in a popular street of the town, in a warm environment in which everybody knew and helped each other. Branagh's passion, his romantic enthusiasm, has its roots in Celtic culture; his ambition as well as his need for activity would come from his Protestant up-bringing. In *Beginning*, he admits: "I have always suffered from original guilt. About everything. I don't know whether it's a peculiar part of the Irish inheritance, but it's a powerful and motivating force in me."[6]

As a child, Branagh used to sit and listen to the "crack," Irish slang for "gossiping and telling stories about the family and friends." According to Branagh, "There would be large family get-togethers. It was people making their own entertainment. . . . They had a natural sense of pace—when to pause, little rhetorical flourishes. They were fireside actors. . . . It was an oral tradition that needed an audience. And a lot of music."[7]

Young Branagh thus was acquiring the talent of a storyteller and comic actor early. Yet, it is without doubt his uprooting that led this embryonic actor to turn finally to the theatre and eventually to the movies.

In 1969, the "troubles" in Northern Ireland intensified. Branagh's family chose to emigrate to England and settled in Reading, one hour from London. Young Branagh suffered a lot from this uprooting and loss of identity. At a time when English soldiers died in Belfast, it was not always easy to be a young Irish boy in England, even if you were a Protestant. Branagh's first acting part was, in fact, to stay Irish at home and sound English at school. In Branagh's autobiography, we read:

> For as long as I could, I kept up the double life, but my voice gradually took on the twang of suburbia. However I still sounded different, and was very careful when the subject of English casualties in Ulster came up at school. It was another stage in the painful process of learning when to keep my mouth shut.[8]

It was through the theatre productions he participated in at school that Branagh began to discover a way out, a legitimate way of expressing and re-inventing himself, a way of smoothing over his feeling of belonging nowhere.

He spent a rather lonely adolescence, searching for theatre reviews and books, reading, and watching TV series and movies. A fan of old Hollywood movies, especially musicals and gangster movies, Branagh entered the world of illusion with delight. He gives a revealing answer in an interview in 1993 in Cannes. The journalist was playing a word association game and, to the words "real life," Branagh replied immediately, "movies."

Until sixteen, Branagh had never had any contact with Shakespeare, except for some famous films by Olivier and a TV adaptation of *Hamlet* with Richard Chamberlain in the title role. Yet, at sixteen, Branagh saw Derek Jacobi play Hamlet in Oxford. He spoke in 1993 of that quasi-mystical experience:

> When I felt the power of live theatre and was caught up in the power of words, it acted upon me in a way I couldn't put my finger on except that the little hair at the back of your neck would rise and you'd think: I don't know what it is but it's different, it's got me going and it's just touched me like music would touch you, there's a deeper chord struck by this great poetry.[9]

His first encounter with Shakespeare was an emotional shock, a sensory experience, almost a musical sensation, and not an intellectual or literary discovery. Branagh has wished to convey this same magical and powerful experience to an audience who think Shakespeare is an incomprehensible dusty monument. In September 1993, *Sight & Sound* stated clearly: "He persists, like many an autodidact who hasn't been to university or film school, in celebrating the potential for self-discovery in Shakespeare or in the classics."

The Irish working-class background of Kenneth Branagh never encouraged him to discover Shakespeare by himself. Unlike his contemporaries from the upper class, he was never socially *supposed* to love Shakespeare. Even his father thought books were useless. Therefore, when Branagh saw a Shakespearean play on stage and found it a source of exciting emotions, he not only discovered the power of Shakespeare's words but also that those emotions *could* be experienced by people who, like himself at the time, were not expected to understand Shakespeare—even less be caught up by his work. This discovery can easily explain Branagh's deep-felt ambition to present Shakespeare in a way that can disarm preconceptions and lead all people to connect with the language. At sixteen, Kenneth Branagh decided to become an actor, and what followed was a whirlwind of success. At eighteen, he obtained the only regional scholarship granted to a student of art and entered the Royal Academy of Dramatic Art. At twenty-one, he began his career as a TV actor and starred in success-ful West End plays. At twenty-three, he entered the Royal Shakespeare Company (RSC) in which he became the youngest actor ever to play Henry V.

From the Royal Shakespeare Company to the Renaissance Theatre Company

One might expect that, for a young actor, entering the famous Royal Shakespeare Company would represent a kind of fulfillment. For Branagh, it was far from so. The saddest part of his autobiography, *Beginning*, describes the atmosphere of disillusion and bitterness reign-ing within the RSC in 1985.

> The idealism I had felt on joining the RSC had been severely eroded[...]. Part of the problem was that the system raised ex-pectations which were sure to be disappointed.[10]

Moreover, he found the actors' workload simply infernal. The ac-tors had to perform in five plays each season which, according to him, prevented a real artistic quality from being achieved. The RSC was too big a machine, and the financial stakes too high. The directors were obliged to make quick decisions about the concept and approach, the setting and costumes, for a play very early on, without asking the actors' opinions. In 1985, within the RSC "fringe" shows, Branagh wrote and directed the satirical comedy *Tell Me Honestly* about the working and communication habits of the RSC. He left the company at the end of the season.

In this departure, there was a desire to return to a more straight-forward vision of the plays. For some time, the English theatre had chosen to play Shakespeare in modern costumes. The plays were performed as Freudian dreams or elaborate metaphors: *Romeo and Juliet*, for example, reflecting the Israeli–Palestinian conflict. Branagh wished to return to the roots of the plays and emphasize the language and the story.

In 1986, he decided to put his perception of theatre into practice by directing and acting in his own low-budget production of *Romeo and Juliet*. The atmosphere during the rehearsals was as mad and unbridled as in his later film *In the Bleak Midwinter*. Only fifteen actors played all the parts, which gave birth to some odd incongruities such as Mercutio being restored to life as Friar Lawrence. The public welcomed the production warmly. The critics were more divided. But Branagh's idea was coming to life: he was going to create his own theatre company, a company in which the actors would participate in the artistic, technical, advertising, and financial aspects of the productions, a company which would escape from the cult of the director and his traditional "concept," a company which would convey Shakespeare to a public of all ages and all backgrounds.

Branagh explained his motivations:

> I left the RSC because of the desire to communicate. The drive has a lot to do with my own background, coming from a non-theatrical, non-literary background. . . . When I left the RSC, part of my reaction was to pursue the same kind of work, the classical repertoire, made available to people who might not otherwise go see it. In this case by travelling around Britain to theatres and to cities that might not otherwise see three Shakespearean plays in repertoire with the same company, a young company not telling them Shakespeare was good for them but being excited by the fact that they were excited. By conveying and carrying the torch of that enthusiasm, saying: listen, we don't know these plays in great details. We're telling them as if the plays were being discovered for the first time, for that's how we feel about them. We're not going to assume that you've seen the plays before or that you know that famous essay about it or this famous book about it. We're just going to say: What a great yarn *Hamlet* is.[11]

In 1987, with a friend David Parfitt, Kenneth Branagh created his own theatre company. He called it Renaissance, a name which reveals his deep yearning for renewal, as well as the company's youth. It also reflected the new vigour invading English theatre at the time: young actors like Ralph Fiennes, Colin Firth, and Daniel Day-Lewis were on their rise; Michael Bogdanov and Michael Pennington had initiated the English Theatre Company which toured England—and the world—with its famous productions of the War of the Roses plays (*Richard II*, *Henry IV parts 1 and 2*, *Henry V*, *Henry VI parts 1, 2, and 3*, and *Richard III*).

No public subsidy was granted to Renaissance Theatre. If Branagh regretted the lack of financial security, he enjoyed nevertheless the independence and freedom to be able to decide where and when to produce a play.

Renaissance's intention was to surprise the spectators, to disarm them with a natural, real, clear, and simple way of acting. The company was composed of young actors, most of whom were still inexperienced. By approaching the plays for the first time, they brought a freshness to their part. Thus the style of Renaissance attempted to be in tune with its audience, the majority of which consisted of people unfamiliar with Shakespeare's works. Their tours included Birmingham, Belfast, Dublin, Bath, Brighton, Manchester, Newcastle, and Leeds. Branagh was coming back to his twofold roots of Irishman and English-provincial. Renaissance plays had so much success that Branagh received enraged letters from people who could not buy a ticket! These passionate reactions have, without doubt, encouraged Branagh to bring Shakespeare from the theatre to the movie medium, to satisfy as many people as possible.

Renaissance's first season featured three very different plays: *Public Enemy*, a thriller written by Branagh which tells the story of a young Belfast man obsessed with James Cagney movies and falling into a murderous madness; *The Life of Napoleon*, a one-man show by comedian John Sessions; and *Twelfth Night*, which Branagh directed without acting in it. The reviews were raves. The production was appreciated for its naturalism, clarity, and strangely disillusioned vision of the play.

In 1988, for Renaissance's second season, Branagh asked famous, experienced Shakespearean actors to come and direct *As You Like It*, *Much Ado About Nothing*, and *Hamlet*. Branagh talked Judi Dench, Derek Jacobi, and Geraldine McEwan into directing one production each and passing the torch of their experience on to the younger actors of the company. This way of working exemplifies Branagh's approach to working in the theatre:

> I love that sense of theatre being handed down, through the generations, from Irving, who was seen by Olivier, who was seen by Hopkins, who was seen by me.[12]

And . . .

> I'm in love with the romance, the continuity of acting, the idea
> that there are only eight generations of players back to the Globe
> Theatre.[13]

From Renaissance Theatre to Renaissance Films

Given the success of Renaissance Theatre's productions, Branagh
thought it was time to move to another medium, a medium which
could reach more people and still bring them some accessible Shakespeare. Russell Jackson, Branagh's textual adviser, told me that Branagh
chose to adapt Shakespeare to the movies rather than television because of the emotional impact provided by the big screen. On TV, it
would be difficult indeed to film a man lost in a big epic landscape:
you just wouldn't see him.

He thus created a subsidiary to Renaissance Theatre, devoted solely
to making movies: Renaissance Films. Branagh would continue to
produce and direct plays, but with Renaissance Films he was also
dedicating himself to making film adaptations which could be watched
and re-watched by people around the world.

Branagh's enriching experience acting the part of Henry V at the
Royal Shakespeare Company had convinced him that a truly popular
film could be made of *Henry V*. The plot was linear and easy to follow,
and the film could combine a political story, a thrilling adventure,
and an exciting battle. Moreover, the character of the king could be
made much more interesting and deeper than Olivier's 1944 movie
portrayed, and the war sequences could be made so much harsher.
There was, of course, the problem of finding the money to finance
the project.

Back in 1987, when Branagh was in search of funds to produce
Renaissance Theatre's *Twelfth Night*, Stephen Evans, a financial broker
interested in the arts, read articles about Branagh and Renaissance in
the newspapers, and decided he could be of some help. He met with
Branagh and offered his collaboration. From this time onwards,
Stephan Evans as the financial broker, David Parfitt the manager, and
Kenneth Branagh the artistic visionary, worked hand in hand to make
the dream of Renaissance come true.

To finance *Henry V* in 1988, Evans brought some friends into the
deal and eventually secured a contract with the BBC which advanced
£2 million for the shooting.

Furthermore, Branagh had the necessary perseverance and charisma to approach and attract famous British actors—some with whom he had already worked, like Derek Jacobi and Judi Dench. The passionate belief he had in his film persuaded them that the project could actually work and they agreed to participate in the adventure. In fact, Branagh's enthusiastic sense of "mission," his ability to organize things and obtain the needed human and financial ressources, as well as his capacity to persuade people to join him, persisted through the years to come, and each time he has embarked on another Shakespearean adaptation, he has called on these abilities.

Thus, on the set of *Henry V*, on the second day of shooting, when Branagh appeared majestically as the young Henry V, entering through that huge dark door, it not only announced the arrival of the king but also the birth of a film actor and director.

Before 1988, in fact, Branagh had acted in only two small movies, *High Season* (directed by Claire Peploe, 1985) and *A Month in the Country* (directed by Pat O'Connor, 1986). He had *never* directed a film before *Henry V*, not even a short one. His only directing experience had been in theatre, with the satirical play *Tell Me Honestly* in 1985, *Romeo and Juliet* in 1986, and both *The Life of Napoleon* and *Twelfth Night* in 1987.

His movie *Henry V* principally focuses on the king's youth and inexperience. Branagh told the *New York Times*: "I feel the play is about a journey toward maturity."[14] And maybe the film reflects its director's *own* journey towards maturity. At twenty-seven, attempting to realize his film project, Branagh could closely identify with the twenty-seven-year-old Henry's attempt to achieve a similarly bold project against all odds. In his autobiography, Branagh regularly compares himself to Henry.

Henry V was Branagh's first movie and the money was very difficult to raise. Until the very last moment, the shooting remained in doubt. Like Henry with his soldiers, Branagh had to hide his doubts about his ability to direct a film from the crew and actors. Branagh confides in *Beginning*: "I seemed to be consumed with obsessive anxiety." On the last day of shooting, what Branagh told his team was utterly revealing: "A disaster it might be, but a singular one. Everyone was glad to be here. We few, we happy few." This theme was repeated by the press at the movie release: "Branagh took on much the same odds as Henry did at Agincourt . . . The actors beamed like the happy few, ready to cry God for Kenneth" (*Sunday Times*, Sep 10, 1989); "He has marshalled his forces as well as Henry led his army" (*The Observer*, Oct 8, 1989); "There is already something of the spirit of Henry's happy few in the cast and crew behind the camera . . . every member of this film unit would go to the wall for Kenneth Branagh" (*Daily Mail*, Nov 18, 1989).

Maybe Branagh was able to convey Henry's emotions so precisely because he was under the same conditions of pressure. Emma Thompson once confided: "Ken was so exhausted and stressed out I had to cradle him in my arms after the day's filming." In *Beginning*, Branagh tells about how tiring the shooting of the battle scene was: "I went home exhausted and somehow defeated, and for no good reason burst into tears. I felt as if I had come back from the war."[15] The speed with which *Henry V* was filmed (only seven weeks of shooting while Olivier took eight weeks just to shoot the battle scene) has contributed to the rhythm of the film. Moreover, compared to his 1984 stage performance, Branagh has created a Henry much more dense, powerful, and reflexive.

A Career on Stage and Film

The film *Henry V* was certainly an event in Kenneth Branagh's career but it did not prevent him from returning to the stage in the following years.

After the shooting and the post-production of *Henry V*, he was already back in the theatre, directing and performing in two Renaissance Theatre productions of Shakespeare plays: *A Midsummer Night's Dream* and *King Lear*. He took the two plays around the world, in a tour which culminated in Los Angeles in 1990. Hollywood was not so far away, indeed . . .

In 1991, Branagh received a script by Scott Frank and decided he wanted to film it. The movie was *Dead Again*, a romantic thriller with supernatural overtones, telling the intertwined stories of two couples, both to be played by Kenneth Branagh and Emma Thompson. Branagh was attracted to this twisted story of love and murder, moving from the past to the present. It gave him the opportunity to pay homage to the films of Alfred Hitchcock and Orson Welles, which he had watched and revered as a child.

In 1991 and 1992, Branagh alternated again between the stage and the movies in an incredible whirl. He directed a production of Chekhov's *Uncle Vanya* starring Richard Briers for Renaissance Theatre, and shot the movie *Peter's Friends*, a comedy *à la* Woody Allen about a group of friends gathering for the New Year and assessing their lives.

Branagh next appeared as Coriolanus in another Renaissance production directed by Tim Supple for the Chichester Theatre Festival, just before filming his adaptation of *Much Ado About Nothing* in Tuscany. He then went back to the stage and played Hamlet for the Royal Shakespeare Company from December 1992 to April 1993. But while acting in the theatre every night, he was already preparing his next movie, a new Hollywood version of *Frankenstein*, with the large budget of $40 million and to be produced by Francis Ford Coppola. Branagh was to direct and star in it, alongside Robert de Niro who played the creature.

As he was working more and more on his own, Branagh decided to part from Renaissance. The company ended its theatrical activities and concentrated on producing movies: from 1995 onwards, it notably produced *The Madness of King George*, Trevor Nunn's *Twelfth Night,* and *The Wings of the Dove*.

Mary Shelley's Frankenstein turned out to be a powerful, romantic, energetic movie, which divided the critics and the public. But the experience no doubt aesthetically influenced his 1996 film of *Hamlet*, in which shots of misty and snowy plains recall images and scenes from *Mary Shelley's Frankenstein*. Moreover it is no surprise to hear Branagh comparing both films: "[The script of *Frankenstein*] was sent to me as I was rehearsing a production of *Hamlet*, and it seemed to me that the two things were linked. Hamlet and Victor Frankenstein are each obsessed with death. Hamlet's whole story is a philosophical preparation for death; Victor's is an intellectual refusal to accept it."[16]

Although *Mary Shelley's Frankenstein* eventually made a profit, it left Branagh somehow longing to return to his roots and movies of smaller scale. In 1995, he filmed his own script *In the Bleak Midwinter*, a comedy shot in black and white about a group of amateur actors putting on *Hamlet* for Christmas in a small village.

In the Bleak Midwinter is perhaps Branagh's most personal film. He does not act in it but the whole movie reflects his love for both Shakespeare and the acting profession. We see the actors forming a family, creating a real harmony and unity. The film is partly autobiographical and it is easy to recognize aspects of Branagh's personality in the character of Joe Harper, the director of the play within the film. Through Harper, Branagh gives us some insights into his own directing skills, as we shall see in the following chapter. While this companion will not devote entire sections to this movie (even though it contains some scenes from *Hamlet*, it is not a Shakespearean adaptation in the strict sense of the word), *In the Bleak Midwinter* shows the enthusiastic and passionate *process* of performing Shakespeare. It reveals Branagh's artistic sensibilities, his own obsession for *Hamlet* and his desire to adapt it on film:

> People have asked me why I'm doing *Hamlet* and I often say all the answers were contained in *In the Bleak Midwinter*. These answers include: I don't know. I have to. It's marvellous. It's ridiculous. It's meaningful. It's meaningless. And it's funny.[17]

Although one can notice some similarities between the sequences of the play within the film and the 1996 film of *Hamlet*—notably the extensive use of smoke which anticipates some misty shots in the film—*In the Bleak Midwinter* mainly contrasts with Branagh's subsequent *Hamlet*. It is shot in black and white, while *Hamlet* will use bright and vivid colours. It presents a gloomy version of the play, while *Hamlet* will clearly depart from that tradition.

Branagh had vainly tried to raise money to make a film adaptation of *Hamlet* since the success of his *Henry V* in 1990. But producers were reluctant to finance the production of a play with such a "bleak" reputation. Furthermore, Franco Zeffirelli had just released his own version at the time, more or less a remake of Laurence Olivier's Freudian interpretation, with the tremendous asset of Mel Gibson in the title role. Branagh therefore had to delay the filming of his own *Hamlet*: he had to find the money and wait for the moment when the public was ready to accept another version of the play on film. Castle Rock Entertainment—which distributed *In the Bleak Midwinter* and produced Oliver Parker's *Othello* in which Branagh played Iago—finally agreed to finance Branagh's *Hamlet* in 1995. Therefore, when in *In the Bleak Midwinter*, Joe says: "I see [*Hamlet*] as a very *dark* play," he expresses what many potential investors pronounced to justify their refusal to finance a four-hour *Hamlet*. In answer, Branagh's film is set in a surprising world, full of light and extravagance, where everything is in excess: food, alcohol, sex. Even Horatio, the serious and wise scholar, cannot help but draw out a small bottle of alcohol and drink from it avidly after the ghost's first apparition.

The budget of *Hamlet* was only $18 million, which is very low for a movie of this length and scope. This meant there was much economic pressure on some spectacular takes, like the confetti scene and the approach of Fortinbras' army: they could only be shot once.

Branagh's 1996 *Hamlet* is the result of a twenty-year dream, sixteen years of theatre experience and eight years of film preparation. Branagh put into it everything he learned in the theatre and the movies: "I played it just late enough to get away with playing it and still put in everything that I know and had learned from previous experience," he said.[18]

This experience, in the theatre and the movies, has enabled Branagh to produce a Hamlet for the nineties, one who restores a balance between the man and the soldier, thought and action. This *Hamlet* also represents his artistic accomplishment: "This film is simply the passionate expression of a dream. A dream that has preoccupied me for so many years. I cannot really explain that either. The reasons are in the film. The reasons are *the* film."[19]

After *Hamlet*, the climax of his career so far, Branagh stopped directing for a while and just enjoyed the pleasure of acting in other directors' movies and learning from their techniques. He played the main parts in Lesli Glatter's *The Proposition*, Robert Altman's *The Gingerbread Man*, Paul Greengrass's *The Theory of Flight*, Woody Allen's *Celebrity*, Danny Boyle's *Alien Love Triangle*, Barry Sonnefeld's *Wild Wild West* and Michael Kalesniko's *How to Kill Your Neighbour's Dog*.

At the end of 1998, Branagh created the Shakespeare Film Company, devoted exclusively to the productions of Shakespearean adaptations, and announced he would direct *Love's Labour's Lost*, *As You Like It*, and *Macbeth*. *Love's Labour's Lost*, just completed, has been shot as a musical, in the tradition of the Fred Astaire and Gene Kelly, including famous songs by Cole Porter, Irving Berlin and George Gershwin, thus continuing Branagh's mission to film Shakespeare's texts in an entertaining and highly accessible way.

Notes

1.   An interview with Charlie Rose, broadcast on "Charlie Rose," PBS, May 1993.
2.   Kenneth Branagh. *Beginning*. London: Chatto & Windus, 1989, p. 63.
3.   An interview with Charlie Rose, May 1993.
4.   A meeting between Kenneth Branagh and Gérard Dépardieu organized by *Studio* magazine, published in *Studio,* Jan 1991.
5.   Quoted in Dinitia Smith, "Much Ado About Branagh." *New York*, 24 May 1993.
6.   Kenneth Branagh. *Beginning*, p. 58.

7. Quoted in Dinitia Smith, "Much Ado About Branagh."
8. Kenneth Branagh. *Beginning*, p. 24.
9. An interview with Charlie Rose, May 1993.
10. Kenneth Branagh. *Beginning*, p. 159.
11. An interview with Charlie Rose, May 1993.
12. Quoted in Mark Lawson, "More than an actor." *Independent*, 9 May 1987.
13. An interview with Charlie Rose, May 1993.
14. *New York Times*, 8 Jan 1989.
15. Kenneth Branagh. *Beginning*, p. 236.
16. Quoted in Graham Fuller, "Interview with Kenneth Branagh." *Interview*, Nov 1994.
17. Quoted in David Gritten, "Why is Kenneth Branagh starring and directing a 3-hour version of Hamlet?" *Los Angeles Times*, 2 Jun 1996.
18. Quoted in David Clark, "Blond Ambition." *What's On*, 12 Feb 1997.
19. Kenneth Branagh. *Hamlet: Screenplay, Introduction and Film Diary*. London: Chatto & Windus, 1996, p. vii.

"the action to the word, the word to the action"
—Hamlet, III.ii

Chapter Two
Theatrical Influences on Kenneth Branagh's Movies

Branagh's three films, *Henry V, Much Ado About Nothing,* and *Hamlet,* and his decision to launch Renaissance Films represent a new stage in his mission to make Shakespeare accessible. Yet, we should not forget that all three of those Shakespearean films have a strong place in Branagh's theatre life.

Branagh played the part of King Henry V in 1984 for the Royal Shakespeare Company in Adrian Noble's production. He played the part of Benedick in Judi Dench's 1988 production of *Much Ado About Nothing* for Renaissance Theatre. As for Hamlet, he played the role in 1980 during his last year at the Royal Academy of Dramatic Art, in 1988 directed by Derek Jacobi for Renaissance Theatre, in 1992 for a BBC Radio version, and again in 1993 directed by Adrian Noble for the Royal Shakespeare Company. These theatre experiences were precious help in the developement of his cinematographic vision, but Branagh's general approach to Shakespeare, a familiar and accessible delivery and direction, also has its roots in his theatre experience.

Delivery and Direction

Branagh has explained his desire to make Shakespeare's language sounds as familiar as possible to a '90s ear:

> One of the things that has always challenged me, inspires me, and makes me enthusiastic about working with Shakespeare is the attempt to make it sound as natural as possible. I've always been anti-declamatory. The very best Shakespeare in acting for me is when it's just people—people walking and talking like people do. But the extra juice you get is this dramatic poetry.[1]

As early as the opening prologue of *Henry V*, the first lines of Branagh's first film, Derek Jacobi's Chorus welcomes the audience in the most unaffected way. Branagh adds this direction in his screenplay: "The manner is conversational, friendly, intimate. He welcomes us with the clarity and warmth of a great storyteller."[2] The Chorus is there to guide the viewers into a new universe, that of Shakespeare. Emma Thompson, speaking the lyrics to "Sigh No More, Ladies" at the beginning of *Much Ado About Nothing*, is similarly conversational and intimate.

Interviewed for *Plays & Players* in 1985, while still at the RSC, Branagh gave his opinion on the way to "say" Shakespeare:

> Acting Shakespeare begins with understanding the character, not with saying the words in a particular way. I loathe the concept of verse speaking. . . . The verse must not be separate from the character. . . . The emotion and the vocal delivery are inseparable. So it follows that if you've found the character, if you feel in your gut what he feels, then you must be speaking the part. The character and the emotion is the truth, the guide. Nothing else.[3]

This actor's confidence, as well as an atmosphere of confidence between the director, the actors, and the crew is essential to making a Shakespearean screen adaptation sound the most natural. Interviewed on the set of *Henry V*, Branagh confirmed:

> We're sticking to the verse, but it will have something of the way we speak English today. That's why I've surrounded myself with a first-class cast and crew. Knowing all the people working with me can do their jobs standing on their heads gives me confidence and makes it easier for me to create my vision of this play.[4]

One of Branagh's longtime collaborators is the composer Patrick Doyle. Born in Scotland in 1953, Patrick Doyle studied at the Royal Scottish Academy of Music and Drama and wrote his first score for a stage musical in 1978. He both acted and composed music for TV until he joined Branagh's Renaissance Theatre Company in 1987. He composed the incidental music for *Twelfth Night*, *Much Ado About Nothing*, *As You Like It*, *Hamlet*, *Look Back In Anger*, *King Lear*, and *A Midsummer Night's Dream*. In 1989, Doyle composed the film score for *Henry V* which launched his career as a film composer. Since then, he has composed almost all the scores for Branagh's movies.

Music, in a film, is an essential conveyor of emotion and tone and Patrick Doyle's music helps the audience better understand Shakespeare's language. "Shakespeare is a strange language and the music can help an audience which is unfamiliar with it grasp the significance of the lines. It can tell you when to be scared or when to be moved but it should always communicate through the subconscious,"[5] says Doyle. "In Shakespearean films, the music has to really underline a lot of dialogue. It has to find its way in and out of those fairly famous speeches. It's always a tricky thing knowing how to capture the essence of a speech or the essence of a moment. There tends to be more music in Shakespeare pictures because it does help the audience along a bit. The music helps to tell them: This is a very important point, this is the twist of the story, listen carefully."[6]

Doyle has a gift for melody and knows how to write melodies that are at the same time simple, wonderfully moving, accessible, and memorable. "Ken likes to have strong melodies. He asks me to be as melodious as possible,"[7] Doyle says, and in a note introducing the *Hamlet* soundtrack album, Branagh pays homage to his composer: "In this score Patrick Doyle attempted the most difficult of things for an artist—simplicity. . . . I think he has succeeded superbly well."[8]

The working collaboration of Doyle and Branagh has proved extremely fruitful. Unlike other directors, Branagh spends much time discussing the music with his composer. Given their same enthusiastic, passionate, and intuitive personalities without doubt the two men developed a form of automatic understanding. It is no surprise to hear Doyle say: "I know before he hears [a tune], I know he'll like it. And if I don't like it, then he always knows."[9]

For *Much Ado About Nothing*, Branagh wanted to cast British actors with little screen experiences and American actors with much more movie experience, but less experience in Shakespeare. The difference in attitude and accent would make for complementary styles and an original approach to the play. According to Branagh, the aim was to make "a Shakespeare film that belonged to the world."

Branagh has always been an admirer of the natural, reckless, and bold American style of acting. He thought this would serve the impulsive and giddy actions of the characters' in *Much Ado About Nothing*.

When he approached the American actors Denzel Washington (Don Pedro), Keanu Reeves (Don John), Michael Keaton (Dogberry) and Robert Sean Leonard (Claudio), Branagh told them he did not want any artificial Shakespearean voices. The actors would play their part with their own accent but would have to study the text technically. Branagh did not see this deliberate choice of American actors as a betrayal of or a departure from Shakespeare; on the contrary:

> With *Much Ado*, there are lots of lines in there that are so contemporary sounding that it could have been written yesterday. And if you combine that with our desire to deliver it as naturalistically as possible, a combination of being very technically assured so you hear every word, you hear every consonant, but it's spoken like we're talking now rather than me suddenly turning into Shakespeare-speak. . . . I wanted a combination of techniques and disciplines and characters, and for the sound of the piece to be different. Academic experts all argue that the Elizabethans would have sounded much more like a modern American or Ulster accent, with a hard "r." It seemed to me that the kind of music of the play would be well served by a difference, a visceral quality that the play demands. So that when it does get nasty, it has a kind of rough quality to it.[10]

To help the American actors gain confidence, Dr. Russell Jackson participated in both the rehearsals and the shooting on location in Tuscany.

Russell Jackson, fellow of the Shakespeare Institute in Stratford, first became involved in Branagh's works when Branagh asked him to participate in Branagh's own production of *Romeo and Juliet* in 1986. They had known each other from Branagh's time at the Royal Shakespeare Company in 1984 when Branagh often visited the Shakespeare Institute to talk to the students.

On the films, Russell Jackson works as Branagh's extra eye, as Branagh is frequently both acting and directing. Jackson helps each actor become aware of the rhythm of the text, where he or she should pause, breathe, etc., and he points out the repetitions, the alliterations, the places where a character's vocabulary gives clues to his personality. He explains the literal meaning of some sentences and suggests ways of delivering them. Always in view is the aim to breathe spontaneity, naturalness, and freshness into the language while respecting its poetry. For Russell Jackson,

> Once you have the general drift, a lot of the prose speeches are clear enough, and, like the verse, they respond to a golden rule

of Elizabethan writing: find the antitheses—so many of the lines include a "not this, but that" pattern, and often if the audience can hear that, the rest follows more easily. Sometimes in the verse an upward inflection at the end of a line or a tiny pause in the middle makes the sense clearer, like a lens suddenly pulled into focus. . . . The audience should enjoy the dialogue and believe that these characters speak this way because that's how they feel—not because they're in something called "Shakespeare."[11]

For *Hamlet*, Branagh went so far as to cast actors from England, America, France, Russia, and Scandinavia. "I've always believed Shakespeare is for everybody," he said, "so we cast it colour-blind, accent-blind, and nationality-blind."[12]

Moreover, this universal approach to casting increases the audience for the film. As Russell Jackson says: "You can attract people, saying 'come and see what Robin Williams can do in a Shakespeare movie.'"[13]

According to Richard Briers, a famous English TV comic, converted by Branagh to a theatre, and then a film, actor: "Ken's got the general's gift of being the man you automatically follow. His instructions are clear, and he's positive he's right."[14] Other actors who have worked under Branagh's direction have been fascinated to see how much he could mould them and draw out a performance they did not feel capable of themselves.

For Kate Winslet (who played Ophelia in *Hamlet*) "Kenneth Branagh is the most amazing director I've ever worked with. He gets hold of your soul, puts his fist down your throat, gets into your guts and just stirs until [your performance] gets thicker and thicker and so rich."[15]

In Renaissance Theatre's second season Branagh watched other actors direct and succeed in staging accessible and intelligent productions. This confirmation of his decision to invite actors to direct probably gave Branagh confidence to pursue that direction himself. Branagh understands his actors and he knows what practical indications may help them reach the core of their character. Moreover, what perhaps differentiates him from other actors-turned-directors is that he has continued acting, even after achieving success as a director. Acting seems a necessary activity to Branagh, maybe one that allows him to unwind more than the demanding and more rigid role of director.

Very aware of the acting process, he recognizes that the director's task does not consist in merely commenting on the text:

What surprised me in directing is how much of it is people management, assessing personalities and beginning to realize that it's
not actually what you say necessarily about a line in a play or
about a character. It's about judging the mood of the actors that
day when they walk on the set or before they walk on the set and
even the day before.[16]

Then, in a declaration that could have been said by Joe Harper, the
hero of his movie *In the Bleak Midwinter*, he added:

Directing came from watching actors. I've been very interested in
actors. I love actors because we're our best friends and our worst
enemies all at once. What actors do is both insignificant and
tremendously brave and important. We can be the vainest, silli-
est stupid people and we can be the most courageous fantastic
important influences. Actors are chronically underestimated and
the director can see and encourage and, with the right rapport,
can produce great things.[17]

For Jack Lemmon (Marcellus in *Hamlet*), "Ken allows [the actors]
to bring their feelings and their interpretation to the part and then
will make suggestions—a little more here, a little less there. Like all
good directors, he has the security to allow other people to bring what
they've got to offer."[18]

Branagh is also supported on the film set by another "second eye."
Hugh Cruttwel, the former director of Royal Academy of Dramatic
Arts, began coaching Branagh as a young actor and has been with
him through almost all his performances. Hugh Cruttwell's role is to
assure that the performance of Branagh the actor does not suffer too
much from the responsibilities of Branagh the director. He also helps
the other actors with their character search.

In fact, on his movie shoots, Branagh has always tried to recreate
the family feeling he achieved within Renaissance Theatre. From the
beginning of his career, Branagh has worked with more or less the
same core group of actors and crew to create the atmosphere of confidence and solidarity he considers essential to conveying his artistic
vision on screen. In 1993, he confided:

We worked in a family situation, with actors and film crew that
I've worked regularly with. Because I believe in that. A string
quartet doesn't really play well together until they have about five
years of practice. And I believe the benefits of an ensemble, not

exclusively working together, but building up a body of work and a rapport, can mean that when you get to the next big project that requires everything and everybody to be working at their best pitch, it can really pay dividends.[19]

Unlike many film directors, Branagh thinks rehearsal sessions before a shoot are not a waste of time. They allow him to point out the more difficult details and work them through without the pressure of shooting . . . or the cost of several takes. According to him, "Rehearsals break down everyone's nervousness. It is a place to establish a trust and rhythm with the actors. . . . For me, it is like putting a flame under things to get them hot, but not quite to the boiling point."[20] Even before the shooting of *Hamlet*, Branagh asked his actors to know their parts by heart from beginning to end, just like in the theatre. Prior to filming they did a complete run-through of the whole play so that, when they began filming and would have to perform their scenes out of order in front of the camera, they would have a feel for where their characters were in their personal stories.

Branagh also organizes discussions and improvisation sessions to explore the atmosphere and environment in which the characters will grow and evolve. For *Much Ado About Nothing*, Branagh asked the following questions: How long have the soldiers been away? How violent was the war? How many times have they visited Leonato's house before? To what extent do the soldiers know one another? How old are they? How long do they expect to live? And so on.

Branagh insists on finding the motivation of each character: "When I was training to be an actor at the Royal Academy of Dramatic Art, this question of *Why?* was something that Hugh Cruttwell constantly urged me to consider. The *how* of creating a piece of art always comes second. It's the *why* that will get you to the truth of a character."[21] This obsession with the *why* can be found again in *In the Bleak Midwinter*. The director in the film, Joe Harper, advises his actors thus:

> I think we have to worry a little less about the exterior of these characters, clothes and walks and accents, et cetera, and concentrate a little more on each individual's needs, their drives. What is it they want and need. Why they do what they do. Not "how." The how will take care of itself if we ask always, why, why, why?[22]

Branagh the director encourages the actors to create personal backgrounds for their characters. For Branagh, this "back-story" is essential to convey a character to the audience, especially in the movies. According to him, "the audience won't know specifically my off-screen history for Benedick—his upbringing, his family, his likes and dislikes—but I hope that with this history firmly in my mind, they will at least intuit part of it, feel a depth to the character beyond what he says and does."[23]

Branagh has succeeded in the transition from theatre director to movie director by using precisely the same direction techniques he used with actors on stage. This determination to achieve a realistic and natural style of acting is one of the essential factors in the accessibility of his Shakespearean movies. Film, even more than theatre, requires a clarity and naturalness of speaking in order to be credible. In a film, it is easier for an actor to communicate intimate emotions. There is no need to project his or her voice and the actor is free to give a more controlled and subtle performance. The audience can then enter the character's mind more easily. In fact, if theatre works on the level of demonstration and projection, cinema works on the level of intimacy and identification. Branagh's conviction that Shakespearean lines should be spoken with crispness and with a freshness of tone fits perfectly the medium in which he now works.

Branagh's skill as an actor, his ability to direct his cast and take advantage of the intimate, emotional medium of film no doubt contribute to the impact his movies have had on the renewal of Shakespeare on screen. We should now take into account the experience Branagh acquired in playing each part in the theatre before taking on any film adaptation.

In the following sections, we shall first deal with the theatrical influences on *Henry V*, then move on directly to the theatrical influences on *Much Ado About Nothing* and, finally, to those influences on *Hamlet*. We shall return to each movie to analyze Branagh's work on the script and his screenplays, and, of course, his work with the camera in both the textual and cinematic chapters later in this book.

Henry V: The Influences of Adrian Noble

Branagh talks of a "marination process."[24] Each filmic vision has developed and matured over three or four years between the end of the theatre run and the film shooting: from 1985 to 1988 for *Henry V*; from 1988 to 1992 for *Much Ado About Nothing*; and from 1993 to 1996 for *Hamlet*. According to Branagh, "In all my screen adaptations of Shakespeare my intention has been to illuminate things I always wished had come across more strongly on stage."[25]

Cinema is able to overcome the limitations of the stage, to tell a story without any spatial limitations. In the cinematic medium, it is possible to develop the exterior as well as an interior dimension of the plays. In a movie, one can use exterior shots to add an epic element to the story, as well as go deep inside the characters' minds with intimate close-ups. It seems that Branagh uses film not necessarily because he absolutely wishes to do a film version of a given play but because film enables him to produce the version most faithful to his original vision.

Branagh has used his stage experiences to overcome the chasm which often exists between theatre and cinema. Michael Skovmand underlines:

> [Branagh]'s approach is that of finding the right *cinematic* equivalent of a primarily *theatrical* concept. . . . [He] takes us beyond filmed theatre into a species of audiovisual Shakespeare which, at its best, seems to combine some of the most attractive elements of both worlds: the Shakespearean world of words and the cinematic world of motion and spectacle. Indeed, Branagh's approach to filmed Shakespeare is a move away from the often tortured preoccupation with what are seen as radical differences between theatre and film, and a welcome reminder of how much film and theatre actually have in common.[26]

In his introduction to the script of *Henry V*, Branagh thanks Adrian Noble "whose magnificent RSC production of *Henry V* was an inspiration for this film version" and points out: "When I left the RSC in 1985, after playing the part for nearly two years, I was already producing a mental 'storyboard' for the movie version."[27] Branagh also confided that his first filmic vision of *Much Ado About Nothing* occurred during the stage performance of *Much Ado About Nothing* directed in 1988 by Judi Dench:

> One night during Balthasar's song "Sigh No More, Ladies," the title sequence of the film played over and over in my mind: heat daze and dust, grapes and horseflesh . . . The men's sexy arrival, the atmosphere of rural Messina, the vigour and sensuality of the women, possessed me in the weeks, months, and years that followed.[28]

Likewise, playing Hamlet more than three hundred times on stage and noticing how the lighting and setting could be adapted to help a theatre audience see what is important were catalysts for Branagh's mental storyboards for the film version.

  Notably, Branagh's longtime collaboration with Patrick Doyle began with their stage productions. Unusual for a film composer, who generally comes in when the shooting is over, Doyle participates in the day-to-day shooting of the movie, and often as an actor too. He played the soldier Court in *Henry V* and the musician Balthasar in *Much Ado About Nothing*. This involvement early on in the film production gives Doyle the opportunity to see the actors work and attend the daily rushes. According to Doyle, it gives him "a unique insight into the characterization, construction, and requirements of the film."[29] The "Ophelia" theme in the *Hamlet* score thus came to him during the shooting after seeing Ophelia (Kate Winslet) read Hamlet's letter in front of Claudius, Gertrude, and Polonius.

  Having been an actor has been essential for his ability to capture in his music the mental shifts in the characters and the story. His most beautiful pieces indeed have a purely diegetic source: they are born from the story itself. The orchestration of the *"Non nobis"* sequence in *Henry V* begins with a common soldier singing within the story itself. The final dance in *Much Ado About Nothing* begins with the characters singing and the music coming out from their own instruments. And the night theme of King Henry V is only an extension of a diegetic tune played on a pipe by a soldier in the scene. Doyle's music is rooted in the story and this is due perhaps to his countless experiences in drama.

  Henry V was Branagh's first film as a director. *Henry V* also was the first film score written by Patrick Doyle. The challenge of writing music both accessible and powerful, but that would not swamp the text, was huge. According to Doyle, "the music shouldn't win over the drama. It must back the film and help it. As much as possible it must not invade the screen"[30]; "in the theatre, the music links a scene to another, while in a film it underlines, intensifies, the dialogue and the action."[31]

  Doyle does not conduct the orchestras during the recording of his music. He prefers to stay in the booth with the director and producer to concentrate on adapting the music to the film images. He did, however, direct the orchestra for the big chorus of "Sigh No More, Ladies" at the end of *Much Ado About Nothing*, because the song had been recorded live during the shooting and the studio music had to follow precisely the rhythm of the words.

Yet in *Henry V*, although Doyle's music intensifies the dialogue as a film score should, it keeps its theatrical aspect, regularly marking the play's transitions. Music highlights the move from the private sphere of the low-lifers and Princess Katherine to the public sphere of the French and English royal courts. Each departure for war, for another conflict, for another battlefield, is backed by music, as in Adrian Noble's 1984 theatre production.

Branagh's experience in the theatre has fine-tuned his storyteller instinct. This has helped him enormously in his cinematographic work. In 1993, he revealed:

> When you work in the theatre, you have a very clear obligation to tell a story because you can't tell the audience I want you to look there. In movies, you can cut from that, to that, to that and you can't look anywhere else. Whereas in the theatre, you have the whole space. You have to be very *aware* of how to tell a story.[32]

The influences of the stage productions on the movies, on their performance, direction, costumes and setting, are essential to understand how Branagh gained the necessary experience to make his successful Shakespearean films, but of course, one should not forget the dialectical aspects of such a process. Branagh's Shakespearean films are accessible because their director did not forget his theatrical roots, took advantage of the fact he had been involved in the plays on stage before and could spot out what the cinema could extend or clarify. But at the same time, the films are accessible because Branagh chose to *depart* from the plays and adapt Shakespeare's works to the screen, using the very means and possibilities of the cinema.

In the film adaptation of any literary work, there are of course some differences from the original theatre productions, which are governed essentially by circumstances (budgets, casting, schedules, etc.), but we shall try to focus here on the intentional choices of Branagh only.

Henry V was directed by Adrian Noble in 1984 for the Royal Shakespeare Company for the first time in ten years. The production lasted a little more than three hours, with only minor textual cuts. Branagh, at age twenty-three, played the title role. Rehearsals went on for nine weeks—much longer than the average time. This allowed the actors to collaborate on the artistic vision of the play and their performance choices. As Branagh disclosed to *Plays & Players* in 1984: "What you see on stage is very much a collaborative effort between the director, designer, and all the members of the cast."

Indeed, in his film version of *Henry V*, Branagh follows Adrian Noble's direction as much as he departs from it. Except for the Chorus, the characters are played in nearly the same way: the king is both earnest and cruel in the two productions; Exeter is the same protective and brutal uncle; Montjoy, the French herald, becomes an admirer of Henry in both; the low-lifers convey the pain and suffering of war. Adrian Noble's 1984 RSC production was influenced greatly by the Falklands War which occurred only two years before. Without explicitly referring to the Falklands, Noble treated the bloody conflict of the play in a harsher way than previous productions, stressing its brutality and the soldiers' distress. The global vision of the stage production has also been transfered to the movie: we witness the same inner doubts troubling a very young and inexperienced king; we are presented with more or less the same ambivalent feelings towards war and the same sacrifices it demands of the king; we witness the same army suffering in difficulty and pain under the oppressive rain. In fact, Branagh's theatrical experience in 1984 almost worked as a rehearsal for his 1989 film.

For example, on the stage, the clergymen were not the shallow fools of Laurence Olivier's 1944 movie, but great politicians. The convoluted Salic law speech (Act I, scene ii) was an honest explanation of the French crown succession; and the irony in Canterbury's line, "so, it is as clear as the summer's sun" was intentional. Branagh repeats these same directions in his movie: the clergymen are again calculating politicians, the Salic law speech is meant to explain an intricate political situation and the irony of "the summer's sun" intentionally makes the nobles laugh.

Exeter, portrayed on stage by the charismatic Brian Blessed, played an important function in the theatre production, acting as Henry's shield and weapon, and executing the killing orders when the young Henry was too moved to make the necessary sacrifices. Exeter also supported Henry in the difficult moments and physically held him when he was exhausted. In the movie, Branagh's Henry is strongly attached to his battle comrades, especially to the fatherly figure of Exeter, whose part is played again by Brian Blessed. When the town of Harfleur is yielding, Henry collapses exhausted in Exeter's arms.

The king's old friends—the low-lifers—were played on stage in 1984 generally as comedic characters, but without success according to the reviews. Yet, Adrian Noble linked the low-lifers to the pain and fear of war. In the departure scene at Mistress Quickly's (Act II, scene iii), Nym delivered "I cannot kiss, that's the humour of it" with a grave and desperate tone. A white curtain was raised at the back of the stage and a huge door was opened on darkness, like an anticipation of misfortune and terror. In his 1989 movie, Branagh removes most of the comic allusions, but keeps this sad and realistic side to the low-lifers, who leave for war reluctantly. The enormous doors may also have influenced Henry V's spectacular first entrance in the film.

Designer Bob Crowley's stage effects and Robert Bryans' lighting, though extremely bare, were effective and overwhelming. For the siege of Harfleur (Act III, scene i), a wall with three ladders rose at the back of the stage and released the choked, retreating English soldiers onto the stage amidst foggy smoke and lighting. This pessimistic vision of their initial retreat is also taken up in the movie. Branagh's "Once more unto the breach" is much more desperate than was Olivier's, and Branagh's Henry is less confident in his ability to bring his troops back to attack.

On the stage, however, Branagh shouted "Once more unto the breach" from the top of one of the three ladders before throwing himself backwards in the air and falling into his men's arms. This bold and powerful moment, adapted from a theatre exercise to develop trust between actors, infused into the atmosphere of fear and defeat a feeling of daring and nobility. In the movie this move becomes Henry's arrival on a rearing horse, with fire and explosions in the background. Again, both the thrilling and dangerous aspects are emphasized.

In the play, the battle scenes were directed without any actual fighting but as a martial ballet with huge banners, coloured lighting, lots of smoke and thundering music. Any scenic greatness was reserved for the French, who were played as serious characters and not the weak and impotent fools in Olivier's film. On the eve of the Battle of Agincourt (Act III, scene vii), the French rose in twinkling armour on a gilded platform with comfortable chairs, and in complete contrast to the English "horrid ghosts." This difference was amplified by the costumes as well. The English wore grey clothes, with no specific shape or ornament while the French displayed ostentatious fifteenth-century velvet garments. Just before the battle, the French leaders were suspended high on a platform, looking down at the weak English army.

This staging without doubt inspired the low-angle shot in the movie in which the French scrutinize the English army from the top of a hill on the morning of the Battle of Agincourt. In the film, the contrast between the French and the English is also stressed by clothes and comfort—the French have a spacious tent while the English sleep outside—but also by music: we hear the French soldiers laugh and play loud music while the English play a plaintive melody on a pipe.

Noble's 1984 production presented on stage the execution of Bardolph, which is merely reported in the text (Act III, scene ii), making it the transition between the victory at Harfleur and the looming dangers of Agincourt and a key scene in the play. It became an emotional peak just before the intermission and contained the most spectacular stage effect in the play: the whole English army was lined up at the back of the stage under a big canvas protecting themselves from a pouring rain. In the movie, this stage effect is conveyed by a series of shots showing the exhausted English soldiers as they trudge painfully in the rain and the mud, and fording rivers with heavy burdens on their backs.

In the theatre production, before his execution Bardolph was carried by force down stage right, while Henry stared at him from the opposite side of the stage. Bardolph kneeled down, throwing imploring glances at Henry. There was a complete silence for ten seconds. Then, with great effort, Henry looked to Exeter who was standing behind Bardolph, and addressed him a slight nod. Exeter garotted Bardolph and strangled him. The strangling was slow and horrible: bulging eyes, bloody saliva, the sound of a breaking neck. The king vainly tried to withhold his tears. When he was released, the dead Bardolph remained on his knees, head down. Only at this moment did Henry declare: "We would have all such offenders so cut off."

This theatrical moment struck Branagh deeply. In *Players of Shakespeare 2*, he remarks:

> The joyous camaraderie of the company led to wonderful revelations, as when we discovered *en masse* the power of having Bardolph executed on the stage in front of the king. The first time we played it in rehearsal was thrilling. For me it shed a whole new light on Henry's loneliness.[33]

It is no surprise, then, that Branagh includes the execution of Bardolph in his 1989 movie, this time with a hanging instead of a garotting. Nevertheless, the terrible cracking noise of the neck can still be heard, which gives a disturbingly realistic touch to the sequence. The ten seconds of silence in the stage production is replaced with a flashback in which Henry takes the time to recall his old friend. The film insists again on the effort the king must make to order the killing. Henry's following speech is clouded with tears.

In the stage production, Henry was performed as a very young and attractive character who matured during the play and learnt the terrible price of war.

When preparing for his stage role, Branagh came to the conclusion that the king was "an intensely private man . . . forced to live completely outwardly . . . under pressure from all sides. . . . All the responsibility of kingship which he takes so very seriously keeps all such human emotions contained, but all the more charged and dangerous. When such qualities are released we see them at their extremes."[34] In his first scene on stage, during the meeting with the clergymen and the nobles, Branagh played a very reserved king, almost clumsy and showing little of his emotions. The choices in performance and direction stressed both the youth and isolation of Henry. Critic Irving Wardle described Branagh in that first scene as "a cold, quiet figure, watching and listening and giving nothing away"[35] and then suddenly exploding in "paroxysms of psychotic rage" during the tennis balls speech (Act I, scene ii). In his 1989 movie, Branagh delivers the same speech in a harsh rising anger, with a looming fear of the powers he is releasing. Christopher Ravenscroft, taking up the part of Montjoy he had played on stage, throws Henry a glance that is astonished, admiring, and distrustful at the same time.

Branagh made this ability to break into volcanic anger a key to his 1984 stage performance. In the traitors scene (Act II, scene ii), Henry burst into an enraged agony. He thrust Lord Scroop, his former "bedfellow," to the ground and then took him in his arms. In the 1989 movie, Branagh thrusts Scroop onto a table in a quasi-sexual assault and gently caresses his face while reciting the list of his treasons. The pain of loss, betrayal, and abandonment again can be clearly felt.

During the night before the Battle of Agincourt, when the disguised king talks with the three soldiers (Act IV, scene i), Henry's arguments seem very weak compared to the sharp truths of Williams, one of the three soldiers. This effect is amplified by the king's assuming a Welsh accent, which makes him even more a stranger to the three men. Branagh felt that Henry's answers were far from satisfactory: "I finally came to the conclusion that Henry answers no question in that scene and the 'Upon the King' soliloquy emerges because of the terrible certainty of what Williams has said."[36] The king's doubts, isolation, and loneliness as well as his huge moral and political responsibilities were reflected in the "Upon the King" speech (Act IV, scene i).

"Upon the King" was delivered on stage as a measured, grave, and lonely meditation; "O God of battles" was a desperate appeal; and "O not today!" was a real shout of anguish. Henry fell on his knees and, almost hysterically, began to recount all he had done to obtain forgiveness for his father's doubtful acquisition of the crown. In "and all things stay . . . for me," Branagh wanted to convey "the dark dread of a man who would expect to go to hell and for whom the place was an absolutely real concept."[37]

This passage very much influenced the way Branagh performed it in 1989. In the movie, "Upon the King" is also a lonely meditation; "God of battles" is a desperate plea; and "all things stay . . . for me" is delivered with fear and reluctance. As Susanne Fabricius said insightfully, "The film is just as much about overcoming fear as about winning a war."[38] The only notable change was the absence of a Welsh accent, perhaps to reduce the distance between the king and his soldiers, or not to puzzle an international audience.

Moreover, in the stage production, Branagh delivered "Upon the King" in a spotlight. The entire stage was dark, only Henry was lit. The lighting conveyed Henry's loneliness, but also focused on his tortured mind. This intense focus can be found in this scene in the film in Branagh's use of close-ups. In fact, the close-up is a way to "enter" a character's mind and feel his emotions better than can be done in the theatre, where the actor is physically distant from the audience. Branagh clearly took advantage of the change of medium to convey what he wished "had come more strongly on stage."

As early as 1984, Branagh's Henry was extremely religious. In his comments on his approach to King Henry V, Branagh wrote: "I made clear my firm belief in the *genuine* nature of Henry's humility and piety. . . . He is a *genuinely* holy man and it seemed to me ridiculous to play him as some one-dimensional Machiavelli."[39] All through the play, Branagh took advantage of each opportunity to stress Henry's piety. "May I with *right* and *conscience* make this claim?" (Act I, scene ii) was a sincere, divine invocation and not a mere royal formality.

Branagh and Noble decided from early on that "the many paradoxes in the character [of Henry] should be explored as fully as possible. That we shouldn't try to explain them." And Branagh kept repeating: "Do not judge this man, place him in context—*understand*." The genuinely religious side of the king thus was placed side by side with his ruthlessness: "I agreed that the man who threatens such violence before the gates of Harfleur was a professional killer of chilling ruthlessness."[40] Michael Manheim, writing about the film, sees the same complexities: "He is the Henry for our time basically because along with his ingenuousness, sincerity, and apparent decency—he is also a ruthless murderer. Branagh's characterization radically divides our sympathies."[41] Branagh's Henry V is modern because of these very paradoxes.

In the cinema, with the possibity of moving the camera closer, the inner feelings of the king can be disclosed to the public in a more emotional way than on stage.

However, two significant differences between the stage production and the film are worth examing for their effect on the presentation of the character of Henry V.

In 1984, Adrian Noble used an omnipresent and ironic Brechtian Chorus, played by Ian McDiarmid, to counterbalance any feeling of glory in the play. The Chorus wore a costume a critic compared to a pilot's jacket, making him the audience's contemporary, not Henry's. In Branagh's 1989 movie, Derek Jacobi's Chorus wears a long black coat, also directly addressing the modern viewers. The two Choruses thus immediately introduce themselves as our guides. Yet their resemblance stops here.

The two characters—Henry and the Chorus—were in a structural opposition and the reviews talked much of this bipolarity in the stage production. According to James Loehlin, "the dissonance between McDiarmid's knowing, cynical observer and Branagh's very earnest young king was one of the keys to the effectiveness of the production. . . . It was open to both anti-war and patriotic interpretation."[42] McDiarmid's Chorus especially laughed at "Now all the youth of England are on fire" and insisted on the greed of "crowns imperial, crowns *and* coronets, / Promised to Harry and his followers" (Act II, Prologue). To emphasize their opposition, in a brilliant *coup de théâtre*, Henry and the Chorus bumped into each other, looking at each other in an astonished awareness. The public watched with delight the world of fiction clash with the world of "fictionalizing."

In Branagh's movie, this irony disappears: the dramatic action is never compromised by the Chorus despite his numerous interventions. The worlds of the Chorus and Henry remain distinct.

Derek Jacobi's Chorus in the 1989 movie neither disturbs nor problematizes anything. Rather, he brings rhythm and coherence to the action and, above all, contributes to making the king an attractive and appealing character. In his script, Branagh thus describes Henry's entrance on the eve of the battle:

Now, beside a cart, we see the Chorus, in the camp. He continues.

CHORUS
O, now, who will behold,
The royal captain of this ruined band

We cut to see Henry enter shot in close up and follow him as he makes his way through the camp, meeting with some of his soldiers.

[. . .]

CHORUS
A largess universal, like the sun,
His liberal eye doth give to everyone,
Thawing cold fear, that mean and gentle all,
Behold as may unworthiness define,
A little touch of Harry in the night.

We now cut to Henry, standing beside his two worried brothers.[43]

The Chorus' voice is tender and admiring. Jacobi is introducing the king's entrance while the camera films Henry near his brothers, comforting them. Peter Donaldson well assesses the situation when he says:

Jacobi's successive appearances gradually lose their critical edge and cease to serve the purposes of Brechtian distantiation as the film moves toward less-guarded approval of Henry and his cause. . . . His affection for the king ("this star of England") is evident; and the ironies of the Epilogue are those of mortality and mutability, not social critique.[44]

In that, Branagh radically deviated from Adrian Noble's theatre production.

After the Battle of Agincourt, Adrian Noble continued to establish his non-romantic vision of war by emphasizing Henry's order to kill the French prisoners. After delivering "The French have reinforced their scattered men" (Act IV, scene vi) along with a trumpet blast, Henry gave the order to execute the prisoners in a calm and determined tone. Then, "Give the word through!" followed in a powerful and vicious shout. It was clear that Henry was not retaliating for the French slaughter of the English boys as he was not yet aware of it. Immediately, the Chorus drew back the rear curtain to reveal the slaughtered boys. This sudden juxtaposition gave the impression that Henry was in some way responsible for that bloodshed.

Branagh has completely removed this execution order from his movie.

Yet we should not hastily analyze this decision to cut the order to kill the prisoners, and Branagh's decision to protect his character's morality. One should not forget the long-standing controversy in Shakespearean criticism over Henry V's character, especially at this moment in the play. Does the king display one of the most cruel aspects of his personality by ordering the killing? Or does he do the right thing in order to gather more men—who won't be required to look after the prisoners any more—and therefore win the battle? In removing the line, Branagh removes this question from this particular moment in the film, but he hasn't removed it from the film entirely. Henry has already faced this kind of question at several other moments in the movie, specifically in moments which Branagh voluntarily included in his film: the rejection of Falstaff, inserted as a flashback and imported from *Henry IV, part 2*, the decision to send Lord Scroop—who was his bedfellow—to death after the conspiracy scene; the interpolated sequence in which we actually *see* Henry order the hanging of Bardolph—who used to be one of his best friends. Moreover, in the cinema, the spectacle of Agincourt becomes very realistic. We don't imagine the horrors, we *see* them. In fact, if Branagh has removed the line referring to the killing of the prisoners, he certainly hasn't removed the questions surrounding the King's ambiguity.

Now, let us return to the 1984 production of the play and to the end of the Battle of Agincourt and subsequent events (Act IV, scenes vii and viii). After the battle, the king's reaction in front of the carnage, "I was not angry since I came to France / Until this instant," already was an enraged outburst in 1984. Branagh flew at a French prisoner and was about to kill him. But he got hold of himself and released him with frustrated tears. This action showed the futility of revenge and redeemed the king for the execution of the French prisoners earlier on, but has not been included in the film. It is meaningless to redeem the king for executions he has not ordered.

When Montjoy enters after the battle, Henry thrust him violently to the ground, on the pile of dead bodies. "What means *this*, herald?!"

was a furious and threatening yell, clearly referring to the killing of
the English boys. This same scream and action have been repeated in
the movie: Henry pushes Montjoy off his horse and thrusts him into
the mud.

On stage, when the herald admitted the English victory, an almost
dubious Henry kneeled down and whispered: "Praisèd be God, . . .
and not our strength for it." The exhausted soldiers then threw their
weapons on the ground in a loud metallic sound. This made for a
very effective theatrical moment, mentioned in several reviews. Henry
tried to stand up while asking for the name of the castle but collapsed
in Exeter's arms. He painfully walked down stage to deliver the line
"Call we this the field of Agincourt." As Fluellen praised the Welsh-
man's qualities, Henry laughed and wept. Still crying, he took Fluellen
in his arms for the line "For I am Welsh, you know, good country-
man." The tears and exhaustion with which Henry received the news
of his victory extended Noble's dark treatment of war. This post-battle moment of doubt, relief, of embracing, weeping, and laughing,
has remained unchanged in the 1989 movie.

This release of emotions between Henry and Fluellen when the
two men proudly display their Welsh origins is enhanced without
doubt by Branagh's Irishness. As Peter Donaldson notices, "Henry's
emotional range, along with his deep, slightly mad 'Welshness' can
only be fully expressed when he has achieved success in his more
self-controlled role as English warrior-king,"[45] in the same way that
Branagh could openly reveal his Irish origins after having succeeded
within those eminently British institutions RADA and the RSC. In fact,
it is amusing to note that Branagh cut out many allusions to the captains' different nationalities but he has kept Gower's cue, "The Duke
of Gloucester . . . is altogether directed by an Irishman," a wink to
viewers who are aware of the film director's origins. He has also kept
the Irishman Macmorris's outraged question, "What ish my nation?"
which must have haunted Branagh in the same way.

In the 1984 stage production, the intensely moving moment between Henry and Fluellen was followed rather awkwardly, according
to the critics, by the gloves episode (Act IV, scene viii). Likewise, the
comedy of Fluellen's lines on Alexander the Pig during the reporting
of the English boys' slaughter earlier on (Act IV, scene vii) had also
undercut the dramatic atmosphere of that scene. You indeed could
expect Branagh to suppress all the text of those two scenes and save
only a mere visual moment of the gloves scene.

In 1984, gravity returned very quickly when the soldiers gathered around their king to hear the list of dead. Henry seemed incredulous and shocked by the French number of dead. He delivered "Davy Gam, Esquire" with a hint of personal grief and made a long pause in "of all other men / But . . . five-and-twenty." Branagh faithfully repeats this sequence and this delivery in his movie. His Henry is as much bewildered, sorrowful, and relieved.

At the end of the "list of the dead" scene, in the theatre, the soldiers went slowly backstage singing a "*Non nobis,*" while the Chorus drew a curtain through the proscenium. During the Barbican run of the play in London, the lower part of the curtain was covered with names written in a medieval style. Those names were suggestive of the Vietnam Memorial in Washington, D.C. This whole sequence again showed the cost of war without denying the warriors' humanity and heroism: the moral and political tone recalled Oliver Stone's movie *Platoon.* In the film some years later, Branagh's cinematic translation delivered the "*Non nobis*" in his famous travelling shot to which we will often return in this book.

The challenge to go from the exacerbated and conflicting emotions at the end of Act IV to the frivolous courting of Katherine in Act V is enormous. In the 1984 stage production this transition was very moving and subtle. Just before the beginning of the courting scene, some men in silhouette entered behind a transparent curtain and began to light candles around the dead on the battlefield, creating a tableau of deep waste and mourning. When the audience was transported to the French court of Act V, the moving and terrible sight remained on view all through the courting scene.

In the movie, Branagh inserts a flashback into the political discussions preceding the wooing scenes in which all the dead people with whom we have become familiar through the course of the film—the boy, Falstaff, Bardolph, York—appear one last time to haunt the king and remind him of the human cost of war.

In fact, the transition, which was very effective on stage, is less successful in the movie. In theatre, it is much easier to overcome the the hurdle of literalness and draw on the stage's ability to make present two distinct realities simultaneously. The presence of the transparent curtain during the last scene could convey at the same time the terrible human cost of war *and* the unemotional post-war negotiations. In the cinema, a much more realistic medium, it is difficult to use the design in a metaphorical and emotional way, or to present in the same place two situations which happened at different moments in time. But the acting also changed in these transition scenes, from the theatre production to the film, and this change attempts to compensate for the inability of the cinema to juxtapose the consequences of war with the wooing scenes.

The 1984 courting scene (midway through Act V, scene ii) started with a very embarrassed Henry, swallowing his first "I love you" in a guilty tone: he was just too aware of how much it did not ring true. "Clap hands and a bargain" was a desperate attempt to get out of a difficult situation as quickly as possible. Those two sentences made the theatre audience laugh out loud. Likewise, Henry's answer to Katherine's "Is it possible dat I sould love de ennemi of France?" was not threatening at all but delivered as if it was a genuine point in favour of the king: "For I love France so well I will not part with a village of it." The reply set big laughs and even some applause going. Branagh also transformed "by my honour, in true English, I—[pause]—love . . . thee" into a memorable moment. The king discovered his love at the same time as he was admitting it. When Katherine refused to kiss him because of French manners, he delivered "Oh, *Kate*" in a tone of amused frustration, as if saying: "Oh, come on, Kate . . ." Just after the kiss, he suddenly rushed away from the princess when the French king appeared in the room again. "Here comes your father," whispered in a guilty, conspiratorial tone, like a teenager caught red-handed, received the greatest laughter in the play.

Katherine was performed as an adolescent taking advantage of her charms. You could feel that she was rather interested in this young and attractive Henry. Yet, she did not seem to be aware of the political stakes of the courting, even though the negotiating French and English nobles remained backstage in view of the spectators.

In Branagh's 1989 movie, the scene is presented in a slightly less comedic mode. The princess, played by Emma Thompson, is a tougher prey to catch. She is much more aware of the political action behind the courting, compensating for the fact that the spectators no longer see the negotiations between the nobles. The mere casting of Emma Thompson in the part, an actress who was no more an adolescent and who is usually known in England for her regular support for feminist issues, may also explain the fact that the scene could not be played as it had in the stage production.

As in the earlier stage production, Branagh's Henry is a lover with a deep respect of the woman in front of him. He sincerely sought

Katherine's respect and affection, listened carefully to what she said and charmingly struggled with the French words. Michael Manheim, quoting one of his female students, wrote: "Whereas Olivier's Henry is the lover every man would like to be, Branagh's is the lover every woman would like him to be."[46] Despite his obvious power over the princess, he remains convincing when he suggests that it is still possible for Katherine to make a choice. He genuinely insists on the conditional mark in "thou hast me, *if* thou hast me, at the worst! And thou shalt wear me, *if* thou wear me, better and better." In fact, the possibility to choose is literally staged: Katherine has a space to move around and away from Henry. Laurence Olivier's Katherine, in contrast, was held firmly in place and could not rebel against what was happening to her.

The part of Queen Isabel, wife of the French king, was cut out entirely in the theatre production; so it is in the movie. The final blessing speech meant to bring peace to the two nations is given, in both theatre and film versions, to Henry—with a simple change of pronouns, "your" becoming "our." This has the consequence of presenting Henry V as a more sympathetic figure in the end. In fact, the entire last scene shows us a king whose sins have been wiped clean. We shall return to this discussion of the sympathetic portrayal of the king in the next chapter, on Branagh's textual adaptations..

On stage, the Chorus's last speech reintroduced Adrian Noble's twofold vision of the play. At the final "Amen," the characters froze in a motionless tableau while the light faded. The backstage candlelit carnage thus was made even more visible. A spotlight isolated Ian McDiarmid who delivered the Chorus's last verses slowly and gravely. The modern and weary point of view re-appeared in his ultimate ironic tone: "they lost France and made our England bleed / Which oft . . . our stage . . . hath shown."

The movie also ends in a motionless tableau. The Chorus delivers the same prophetic lines but with a genuine regret for this too short moment of glory. In fact, it is in his treatment of the Chorus that Branagh's film most diverges from the Adrian Noble's 1984 production. In contrast with McDiarmid, the Chorus played by Derek Jacobi never conveys any irony.

However, as we said before, the dialectical aspects involved in the process of influence should not be forgotten. The reason why the film version is also very accessible is precisely because Branagh found cinematic ways to depart from Adrian Noble's production and *emotion-*

ally extended some sequences, through flashbacks, realism, and music. Branagh's film presents us with a realistic, muddy, bloody battle which extended Noble's theatrical vision of war as a terrible human waste. With flashbacks, Branagh extended the interpretation of an earnest *and* cruel king: we behold his past when he was still a prince—which creates a subtext and gives his character real depth—but, at the same time, we see him reject his best friend Falstaff. In fact, we end up seeing Shakespeare's play through the prism of Branagh's imagination and personal themes.

Much Ado About Nothing:
The Influences of Dame Judi Dench

In 1988, Renaissance Theatre Company began its second season. Branagh had met Judi Dench in 1986 on the shooting of a television adaptation of Ibsen's *Ghosts* and was convinced that great actors had not only the ability to transmit their experience to younger actors but also to direct and present their unique vision of a play. Judi Dench had never directed a play before and she was not sure she was competent enough to do it. But Branagh, enthusiastic and passionate about this project, succeeded in convincing her to direct *Much Ado About Nothing*. With Branagh in the role of Benedick, the play toured in regions of the U.K. before being staged in London. Several of its actors (Jimmy Yuill, Richard Clifford, Edward Jewesbury, and others, including Branagh) appeared four years later in Branagh's film version.

Judi Dench's ambition was above all to tell a story. Critic Martin Hoyle noticed: "The company's touch is confidently traditional: intelligent, clear, and kindly."[47] The atmosphere of the play was "sunny,"[48] "swift and breezy."[49] And, according to Branagh, the production was "robust in tone, [rough] and [sexy]. It's hot-tempered Italianate qualities distinguish it from the more obvious 'Englishness' of [*As You Like It* and *Hamlet*]"[50]

Some choices in the play direction are clearly taken up in Branagh's 1993 film version.

Judi Dench explained her vision of the play: "when I directed *Much Ado* I knew that I wanted the play to be set in Italy, and that there should have been a war the men were coming back from. . . . I wanted the men's world and the women's—which is also the household's—to be quite distinct."[51] In his 1993 movie, Branagh also stresses the military side. In the opening of his script the soldiers arrive on horse-back, raise their arms in unison, and give a warlike shout. For Branagh, it was important to present Don Pedro and his men as soldiers whose time spent away from a deadly war is precious. The audience can therefore better understand Claudius's intense and almost immediate love for Hero.

The feminine and masculine worlds are also very distinct in the film. As everyone rushes to the villa for the welcoming scene, the men and women are shot running towards each other until they eventually join in the villa courtyard in a chess-like position, men on one side, women on the other. In the stage production, men wore white, buttoned, military-style jackets, tight trousers and high black boots. Women wore white loose muslin dresses with girdles below the breast. Phillys Dalton, the costume designer on the film, was very much inspired by these garments. We can identify in the film the same costume style from an indefinite period: long white dresses for the women (but this time cinched at the waist), even more militaristic garments for the men still with high black boots and tight trousers.

For the stage production, Jenny Tiramani conceived a Mediterranean set of a stylish Sicilian villa complete with a loggia and small trees in pots. The warm lighting was reflected by a large white canvas spread on the stage. The setting evoked "a timeless lovers' Ilyria of white sunshine."[52] According to Michael Ratcliffe, "[the play] restores elements often missed in recent years: the lyrical affections and energies of the young, above all, complicatedly in love."[53]

The movie also features a sunny Italian villa for its setting—shooting took place at Villa Vignamaggio, a huge villa in Tuscany, and the former house of Lisa Gherardini Giocondo, the "Jocund"—and the film also takes up these energies of the young. For Richard Alleva, Branagh "has made *Much Ado* into *A Midsummer Day's Dream*, and the lovers behave as they do because they are dazzled by sunlight, exhilarated and exhausted by heat, blinded by the physical beauty of flowers and flesh, and always at least a little pixilated from being young, alive, and accepted."[54] Just before the film release, Branagh said: "I wanted to show a primitive passion in which the characters live and love under the sun . . . The sun changes your thoughts and the rhythm of your actions."[55] In fact, the movie is heat, wine, grapes, and sensuality. And as in the stage version, the set and costumes do not restrict the story to a definite period but are there to free up the imagination.

In the first scene of Judi Dench's stage production, the characters of Leonato's household were idle, lying in the garden. Leonato was playing with a jigsaw puzzle, the women were resting in the sun or leaning against the walls, sometimes throwing languishing glances to see if the men were about to arrive. Branagh's movie opens in almost the same way. The family and friends of Leonato are picnicking in a field near the villa. Beatrice recites "Sigh No More, Ladies" perched in a tree. Friar Francis plays the guitar. Men and women are lying in the grass drinking wine and eating grapes.

Like Emma Thompson in 1993, Samantha Bond's 1988 Beatrice showed clearly that Beatrice's heart had once been broken by Benedick. Martin Hoyle noticed that "the quiet emphasis of Beatrice's lines on Benedick's former winning of her heart 'with false dice' raises the possibility of previous attachment and hurt."[56] Samantha Bond played Beatrice as an independent and passionate woman, looking for a lover with the same strong personality and spirit as herself. Her "merry war" with Benedick was sexually motivated, which made Nicholas de Jongh say: "The stratagems to bring them together are . . . designed to bring two cautious and reticent people together."[57] In the movie, it is obvious that Benedick (Branagh) and Beatrice (Thompson) are attracted to each other. In their first scene together, Beatrice throws insisting glances at Benedick. Then Benedick does the same, gazing at Beatrice in the outdoor gallery upstairs, he tells Claudio "There's her cousin, and she were not possessed / with a fury, exceeds her as much in beauty as / the first of May doth the last of December."

Emma Thompson and Branagh suggest in their performances of Beatrice and Benedick "former lovers who had been genuinely hurt by their first encounter, which perhaps occurred at the tender age of Claudio and Hero in the play."[58] In Branagh's movie, the young lovers are indeed about twenty years old, while Beatrice and Benedick, easily ten years older, are at a point where they could remain convinced bachelors for life. As soon as the movie begins, this previous romance that ended in hurt shows through in Emma Thompson's performance. Her "You always end with a jade's trick. I know you of old" is delivered in a sad voice, almost to herself, as if she were revealing her secret love to the camera. According to Branagh, under the ironic and witty facades they have built to protect themselves from their emotions, are hidden two of the most romantic characters in all of Shakespeare's plays.

Without withdrawing any comic elements from the Beatrice–Benedick relationship, Judi Dench allowed the darker side of the play to stand out. Hero's rejection at her wedding (Act IV, scene i) was tragic: Claudio and her father dragged her violently to the ground. In the movie, Claudio's angry outburst is stressed even more by the camera moves and numerous cuts to the other characters' different reactions. The canopy collapses like Claudio and Hero's hopes for happiness. Leonato again takes his daughter by the hair and drags her to the ground. This emotional and destructive moment contrasts dramatically with the scene that follows.

On stage, the disastrous episode of the wedding allowed Beatrice and Benedick physically to come into contact, and suddenly all their defences fell. Val Sampson witnessed: "I've rarely heard a theatre so silent during their tender love scene."[59] This discovery of love sprang up after a whirlwind of hatred. Judi Dench had indeed given equal importance to the plots of both Hero and Beatrice. In the movie, this scene in which Beatrice and Benedick admit their mutual love inside a small chapel is equally touching. When it was staged in 1988, that same scene made Vincent Canby say: "Because it is such a surprise amid the tumult, it has an emotional impact I've never before experienced in Shakespeare, on stage or screen."[60] The theatre production as well as the movie choose to enhance the tragic and public moments in order to make the soft and private moments stand out.

In the 1988 stage production, Claudio was performed as a very young, attractive man. Nicholas de Jongh noted: "James Larkin's superlative Claudio justifies the rejection and his cruelty by playing him as a true romantic hero, tense, feverish, gripped by passionate suspicions, quite out of his control."[61] And Branagh told Jeff Dawson in 1988: "They [Claudio and Hero] just have that innocent thing about them, so you can believe that Claudio can be as irrational as he is and that he can fall in love with that instant kind of abandon and he can also behave appallingly over that wedding scene. Youth explains some of the silliness of the behaviour."[62] Without doubt the film has been inspired by this performance. As in the 1988 stage production, Branagh chose in 1993 to situate Claudio and Hero at the beginning of their twenties in order to supply a coherent explanation for their behaviour. In Branagh's film, Robert Sean Leonard plays Claudio as a man who is experiencing his first feelings of love, a passionate youth who is genuinely and deeply hurt by Hero's alleged unfaithfulness.

Unlike Claudio, Branagh's Benedick has always proved his greater maturity. In 1988, critic Paul Taylor could already notice: "Rather than explode into anger when his friends try to revive their callous horse-play after Hero's 'death' [Act V, scene i], Branagh's astonishingly mature Benedick immobilizes them with his subdued, sorrowing gravity."[63] This moment can be found almost unchanged in the 1993 movie. In his script, Branagh writes:

> A stone-faced *BENEDICK approaches on horseback. . . . Without warning he grabs CLAUDIO roughly by the face and thrusts him to the wall.*[64] (my emphasis)

On stage, the gulling of Benedick [Act II, scene iii] was treated in the most comic way possible. Leonato delivered his cues with the emphases of a bad actor and he dried up on Don Pedro's question "Why, what effects of passion shows she?" In his 1993 script, Branagh will also stress the same funny aspect of the scene:

> *LEONATO is completely stumped.*
>
> *Exterior / FOUNTAIN / Day*
> *LEONATO now in a cold sweat. Panic setting in on DON PEDRO and CLAUDIO. The star performer is letting them down.*
>
> LEONATO
> What effects, my lord? She will sit you . . .
> you heard my daughter tell you how.[65]

Nicholas de Jongh thus described the end of the gulling scene in 1988: "Branagh's Benedick . . . gradually breaks from reticence and caution to falsetto outbursts of astonishment that he has truly been selected. [His] performance interestingly shows up the way in which the soldier transforms himself into a human being."[66]

And in Branagh's script we can read:

> BENEDICK
> The conference was sadly borne.
> They have the truth from Hero.
>
> *He stops for a moment to say the miraculous thing.*
>
> BENEDICK
> Love me?
>
> *Thinks.*

BENEDICK
Why, it must be requited.[67]

Branagh has transformed "Love me!" into a question and delivers it in a rising high-pitched voice and in a tone of genuine surprise, just like in the 1988 play.

For Critic Michael Billington in 1988: "Mr. Branagh . . . has the music-hall comic's instinctive sense of timing: arguing himself into love, he concludes 'the world must be peopled' leaning on the last word with just the right vanity."[68] In 1993, Branagh again produces the same intonation.

Yet, it is amusing to note that, unlike in the play, Branagh's Benedick does not shave to please Beatrice. Is it because as a critic wrote when *Dead Again* was released: "with a beard, you cannot see that Branagh has no lips in close-up"?

In 1988, the Dogberry scenes were already, according to Nicholas de Jongh, "gross in a way that scarcely consorts with the emotional subtleties."[69] In 1993, Branagh will agree with Michael Keaton on the way to play Dogberry: "[he] should be not only a verbal but a physical malaprop."[70] Dogberry's verbal eccentricities are therefore extended in the film by physical eccentricities: when leaving Leonato for the last time, Dogberry respectfully takes Leonato's hand but kisses his own hand; when he gallops with Verges on imaginary horses, he first "rides" in the wrong direction; while ordering the guard to remain alert, he falls into sleep and begins to snore!

This performance, in the play version as well as in the movie, tries to give a believable reason for Dogberry's inability to inform Leonato in time. In the film, Branagh has agreed with his actors to present Dogberry and Verges as "charismatically, indomitably mad." This element of danger also allows the public to remain in anticipation over the outcome of the Hero plot.

In *Much Ado About Nothing*, the characters use words in order to deceive, lie, and hurt, or, like Dogberry, do not know how to use them at all. In the programme for the 1988 Renaissance Theatre production, Russell Jackson provides this insight: "The watchmen are the least accomplished users of words in Messina. In love and hatred, finding out the truth seems to proceed by indirections, the arts of language seem to be at discount." Beatrice and Benedick master the art of witty dialogue but can admit they are in love only through *written* poems. When Leonato asks Claudio to repent on Hero's grave, he tells him to do so in a musical form: "sing it to her bones, sing it tonight." Music or singing seems to express the true feelings in the play. It is interesting to note that Branagh chooses to open his film with words drawn from a song and not from one of the play's famous epigrams.

The production of *Much Ado About Nothing* directed by Judi Dench contributed, without doubt, to the happy, relaxed, and sunny aspects of Branagh's film. In fact, in his screen adaptation, Branagh has attempted to preserve aspects of a live experience, to maintain the atmosphere of a theatre company. In a long scene filmed in one continuous shot, movie viewers have more freedom to look wherever they want and are less obliged to watch images chosen only by the director. They become more or less the masters of what they see. The long travelling shots in *Much Ado About Nothing*—the opening picnic and the final dance, for example—fundamentally work as substitutes to theatricality, producing the feeling of actually "being there" at the same time as the actors.

But, as much as Branagh has been inspired by Judi Dench's 1988 direction, he of course has not relied only on this theatre production to make his movie. We shall see later how Branagh made *Much Ado About Nothing* his own, in terms of textual, thematic, and cinematic aspects.

Notes

1. An interview for "Movie Show," broadcast on Paris-Première, at the release of *Dead Again* in 1991.
2. Kenneth Branagh. *Henry V: A Screen Adaptation*. London: Chatto & Windus, 1989, p. 15.
3. Quoted in Peter Whitebrook, "Branagh's bugbear." *Plays & Players* 378 (1985).
4. Quoted in Baz Bamigboye, "Once more unto the breach." *Daily Mail*, 18 Nov 1988.
5. Patrick Doyle. Liner notes to *Hamlet,* Renaissance Theatre in association with BBC Radio. Random Century Audiobooks, RC 100 (1992).
6. An interview with the author, Apr 10 1997.
7. An interview with the author, Apr 10 1997.
8. Kenneth Branagh. Liner notes to *Hamlet: Original Motion Picture Soundtrack*. Sony Classical, SK 62857.
9. An interview with the author, Apr 10 1997.
10. An interview with Charlie Rose, May 1993.
11. Russell Jackson. "How do you coach film actors to speak Shakespeare's lines." *Sunday Times*, 29 Aug 1993.
12. Quoted in Peter Sinden, "Do the Bard man!", *Film Review*, Mar 1997.
13. An interview with the author in Stratford-upon-Avon, 10 Mar 1997.

14. Quoted in Richard Corliss, "Branagh the Conqueror."
15. Quoted in Elizabeth Snead, "For Kate Winslet, the past provides the perfect roles." *USA Today*, 12 Apr 1996.
16. An interview with Charlie Rose, May 1993.
17. An interview with Charlie Rose, May 1993.
18. On the internet: www.Hamlet-movie.com (Warner Bros. Online).
19. An interview with Charlie Rose, May 1993.
20. Quoted in Ian Shuttleworth, *Ken & Em*, p. 158.
21. Kenneth Branagh. *Much Ado About Nothing: Screenplay, Introduction and Notes on the Making of the Film*. London: Chatto & Windus, 1993, p. xvi.
22. Kenneth Branagh. *In the Bleak Midwinter: The Screenplay*. London: Nick Hern Books, 1995, p. 45.
23. Kenneth Branagh. *Much Ado About Nothing: Screenplay, Introduction and Notes on the Making of the Film*, p. xi.
24. Kenneth Branagh. *Much Ado About Nothing: Screenplay, Introduction and Notes on the Making of the Film*, p. xiii.
25. Quoted in Clive Hirschhorn, "The Man Who Shot Shakespeare." *Applause*, Feb 1997.
26. Michael Skovmand (Ed.). Introduction. *Screen Shakespeare*. Cambridge: Cambridge University Press, 1994, p. 9–11.
27. Kenneth Branagh. *Henry V: A Screen Adaptation*, p. 10.
28. Kenneth Branagh. *Much Ado About Nothing: Screenplay, Introduction and Notes on the Making of the Film*, p. xiii.
29. Patrick Doyle. Liner notes to *Henry V: Original Soundtrack Recording*. EMI, CDC 7 49919 2.
30. Quoted in Bruno Talouarn, "Interview avec Patrick Doyle." *Main Title*, Jun 93.
31. Quoted in Christian Lauliac, "Interview: Patrick Doyle." *Ciné Scores*, Jan 1996. (My translation from the French.)
32. An interview on "Le Journal du Cinéma," broadcast on Canal+ (in French), Jan 1993.
33. Kenneth Branagh. "*Henry V.*" In *Players of Shakespeare 2*, edited by Russell Jackson & Robert Smallwood. Cambridge: Cambridge University Press, 1988, p. 102.
34. Kenneth Branagh. "*Henry V.*" In *Players of Shakespeare 2*, p. 101.
35. Irving Wardle. Review of *Henry V*, Royal Shakespeare Company, London. *London Times*, 30 Mar 1984.
36. Kenneth Branagh. "*Henry V.*" In *Players of Shakespeare 2*, p. 103.
37. Kenneth Branagh. *Beginning*, p. 138.
38. Susanne Fabricius. "The face of honour: On Kenneth Branagh's Screen Adaptation of *Henry V*." In *Screen Shakespeare*, edited by Michael Skovmand. Cambridge: Cambridge University Press, 1994, p. 97.
39. Kenneth Branagh. "*Henry V.*" In *Players of Shakespeare 2*, pp. 97–100.
40. Kenneth Branagh. "*Henry V.*" In *Players of Shakespeare 2*, p. 97.
41. Michael Manheim. "The English history play on screen." In *Shakespeare and the Moving Image*, edited by Anthony Davies and Stanley Wells. Cambridge: Cambridge University Press, 1994, pp. 129–130.
42. James Loehlin. *Shakespeare in Performance: Henry V.* Manchester: Manchester University Press, 1996, p. 89.

43. Kenneth Branagh. Henry V: *A Screen Adaptation*, p. 82.
44. Peter Donaldson. "Taking on Shakespeare: Kenneth Branagh's *Henry V*." *Shakespeare Quaterly*, Spring 1991.
45. Peter Donaldson. "Taking on Shakespeare: Kenneth Branagh's *Henry V*."
46. Michael Manheim. "The English history play on screen," p. 128.
47. Martin Hoyle. Review of *Much Ado About Nothing*, Renaissance Theatre Company, London. *Financial Times*, 5 May 1988.
48. Giles Gordon. Review of *Much Ado About Nothing*, Renaissance Theatre Company, London. *Plays & Players*, Oct 1988.
49. Kenneth Branagh. *Beginning*, p. 207.
50. Kenneth Branagh. *Much Ado About Nothing: Screenplay, Introduction and Notes on the Making of the Film*, p. ix.
51. Judi Dench. "A life in the theatre." In *Shakespeare: An Illustrated Stage History*, edited by Russell Jackson. Ohio: Ohio University Press, 1996.
52. Giles Gordon. *Plays & Players*, Oct 1988.
53. Michael Ratcliffe. "Love ever green." *Observer*, 8 May 1988.
54. Richard Alleva. "Beatrice Forever." *Commonweal*, 18 Jun 1993.
55. Quoted in Thierry Klifa, "Beaucoup de bruit pour rien." *Studio*, May 1993. (My translation from the French.)
56. Martin Hoyle. *Financial Times*, 5 May 1988.
57. Nicholas de Jongh. "A raw kind of loving." *Guardian*, 27 Aug 1988.
58. Kenneth Branagh. *Much Ado About Nothing: Screenplay, Introduction and Notes on the Making of the Film*, p. xiv.
59. Val Sampson. Review of *Much Ado About Nothing*, Renaissance Theatre Company, London. *Today*, 6 May 1988.
60. Vincent Canby. "A House Party of Beatrice, Benedick and Friends." *New York Times*, 7 May 1993.
61. Nicholas de Jongh. "A raw kind of loving."
62. Quoted in Jeff Dawson, "Healthy, Wealthy and Wise?" *Empire*, Sep 1993.
63. Paul Taylor. Review of *Much Ado About Nothing*, Renaissance Theatre Company, London. *Indépendant*, 5 May 1988.
64. Kenneth Branagh. *Much Ado About Nothing: Screenplay, Introduction and Notes on the Making of the Film*, p. 72.
65. Kenneth Branagh. *Much Ado About Nothing: Screenplay, Introduction and Notes on the Making of the Film*, p. 43.
66. Nicholas de Jongh. "A raw kind of loving."
67. Kenneth Branagh. *Much Ado About Nothing: Screenplay, Introduction and Notes on the Making of the Film*, p. 46.
68. Michael Billington. "Sweet and simple." *Guardian*, 5 May 1988.
69. Nicholas de Jongh. "A raw kind of loving."
70. Kenneth Branagh. *Much Ado About Nothing: Screenplay, Introduction and Notes on the Making of the Film*, p. xiii.

Chapter Three
Hamlet: A Long Way

For Branagh, *Hamlet* has always been an obsession. It was through this play that he discovered Shakespeare and decided to be an actor. Hamlet is also a role he wanted to tackle very early in his career, and which he played five times in sixteen years. Each time, Branagh gained an additional dimension to his interpretation and his 1996 film must be seen as the accomplished result of all his experiences. For him, "Hamlet is probably Shakespeare's most exposed, most naked creation"[1] and therefore an actor can only respond to the part in a very personal way.

Branagh has always played Hamlet as a man of action feigning madness. Yet his performance has been different each time he played him. It could even change from night to night in the course of a given production. During the 1993 RSC *Hamlet*, Colin Ellwood, Assistant Director of the RSC, said: "Kenneth Branagh's performance is a case in point. It changes more than any leading interpretation of a large classical part that I have ever seen, but it always makes sense of a journey."[2]

1980: The Lively Comedian

In 1980, during his last year at RADA, Branagh asked Principal Hugh Cruttwell if he could play the part of Hamlet in the final term's production. Branagh had been reading several actors' autobiography, including *A Life in the Theatre* by Tyrone Guthrie. Guthrie's advice to young actors is to play the major leading roles very early in their careers so they will have more opportunities to grasp these parts correctly later in their careers. We can read in *Beginning*:

> I wanted one day to be a great Hamlet. . . . A lifetime already
> seemed a short span to get anywhere near the heart of great act-

ing. I wanted to play Hamlet as many times as possible, so that each time I played it I would get better in the role, and would get closer to the truth of the character.[3]

RADA's 1980 *Hamlet* was directed by Malcom McKay and according to Branagh the production was "pacy, real and exciting. . . . All the voice teachers thought that I was the quickest Hamlet ever. . . . Too quick, they said." Hugh Cruttwell, pointing out the difference between humour and comedy, thought Branagh had produced, instead of a black desperate humour, a mere comedy to convey the Prince's "antic disposition." There was no melancholy at all, just a "lively irritability."[4]

Yet, for director Malcom McKay, "although technically the Jacobi production [of 1988] was more accomplished, I thought his RADA show was better because he was less confident and more vulnerable."[5] This vulnerability indeed disappeared in the three Hamlets which Branagh played in 1988, 1992 and 1993; but surprisingly, it comes back in his 1996 film as if Branagh had come full circle, finding again the extreme sensibility of his beginnings.

1984: The Other Side of the Mirror

In 1984, Branagh played Laertes in a RSC production featuring Roger Rees as Hamlet and directed by Ron Daniels. At the same time, Branagh was playing *Henry V* directed by Adrian Noble. His Laertes was so powerful and angry, he pushed Claudius so hard to plot a revenge for his father's death, that it almost diminished the king's calculating side.

With its design, this 1984 production clearly influenced the vision of the glittering, lavish and snowy *Hamlet* of Branagh's 1996 film. It was the only production of *Hamlet* in which Branagh acted where the story occurred in winter and Fortinbras came to Denmark in a snowy landscape. The interiors of Elsinore were, like in the film, glittering and royal: huge stairs, gigantic hall, a crystal chandelier. The richness of it was emphasized by several passages of parade music which sounded like Patrick Doyle's big Fanfare at the wedding of Gertrude and Claudius (Act I, scene ii) in the 1996 film.

Some gestures of Roger Rees's Hamlet reappear in Branagh's 1996 Hamlet, even though those gestures were never used by Branagh in any other stage production. When leaving Claudius before going to England (Act IV, scene iii), Roger Rees kissed Claudius on the mouth in exactly the same way Branagh does in the film. Rees's Hamlet also called Polonius to join him on the Mousetrap stage for the line "And what did you enact?" (Act III, scene ii), which Branagh repeats in his 1996 film.

Branagh's experience playing Laertes may at first seem unimportant in his "Hamletian" career, but in fact, it gave Branagh the opportunity to see the play from a different perspective, to move to the other side of the mirror. Some years later, Branagh went back to the RSC, this time to play the leading role. He told Samuel Crowl that the 1984 production had been very instructive to his evolving approach to Hamlet. In the introduction to his screenplay, Branagh explains: "I was able to observe much more clearly what is said about [Hamlet] by others. . . . Here was a chance to view the whole play, but from within. I was made aware of the double family tragedy."[6] It is also revealing that in 1996 Branagh casts Nicholas Farrel as Horatio, the character Farrel played in that 1984 production.

1988: The Dangerous Rebel

In 1988, as part of Renaissance Theatre's second season, Derek Jacobi directed Branagh in *Hamlet*. Branagh was giving his first professional Hamlet at the age of twenty-seven.

For Branagh, "it was not a relaxed experience. There was the pressure of being directed by a great Hamlet [Derek Jacobi]."[7] Nonetheless, unlike the "directors with concepts" with whom Branagh had worked in the past, Derek Jacobi gave practical advice for tackling the play and the roles. Branagh offers this perception: "Between actors a sort of shorthand develops. I would know what Derek meant before he finished a note. Instead of explaining an effect, he would talk about the means of getting it."[8]

The production lasted approximately three hours, which means the text was slightly cut. It was set just before the First World War. The style for the costumes and props was Edwardian, as in the later 1993 RSC production and in Branagh's 1996 film. The production had almost a melodramatic rhythm. Hamlet appeared as a frantic, headstrong, thoughtless avenger.

Branagh played Hamlet as a young unintellectual rebel reacting with emotional instincts, a dangerous terrorist running loose in Elsinore, full of energy but a bit shallow. He grabbed Polonius violently when Polonius interrupted the First Player with "This is too long" (Act II, scene ii), and during the closet scene (Act III, scene iv), only the ghost's apparition prevented him from raping or stabbing Gertrude. For Michael Billington, "Mr. Branagh is palpably dangerous (you feel he really could drink hot blood)"[9] and for Harry Eyres, "When he says, in the fourth act, 'from this time forth / My thoughts be bloody or be nothing worth,' his thoughts have been bloody from the beginning."[10] Branagh's Hamlet shouted more than delivered his lines and did so in an even rhythm without any reflective pauses. He showed "a reckless, energetic, feverish neurotic interpretation."[11]

The production was indeed seen by several critics as a genuine thriller. Michael Ratcliffe thought it was "more suggestive of great gangster pictures than traditional Shakespeare"[12] and, according to Maureen Paton, "Branagh . . . looks and behaves more like James Cagney as a young hothead full of nervous intensity."[13] In fact, Branagh had only just finished the first season of Renaissance in which, in his own play *Public Enemy*, he had played a young man in Belfast obsessed by Cagney.

Branagh's Hamlet distrusted anything and anybody. He kept looking for spies behind curtains. That attitude anticipated the 1996 film in which hidden doors behind endless mirrors stress the reigning paranoia of the palace. All through the movie, Hamlet escapes from the huge hall to his own private room whenever the matter for discussion becomes too important, as when Horatio comes to tell him about his father's apparition (Act I, scene ii). Yet, even the intimate space of his room is not safe enough. When Hamlet tries to escape Claudius's soldiers after killing Polonius, he takes refuge in his room after a long chase through the corridors (Act IV scene ii). For a few seconds, he thinks he is safe . . . until a gun is pointed at his temple.

Derek Jacobi had made a radical choice in his direction and his vision of the play was all but romantic.

In the first court scene (Act I, scene ii), Claudius delivered his first speech as if it had been prepared by Polonius, his Prime Minister. Polonius, who was played as a shrewd calculating man, prompted Claudius when he faltered. It was obvious that Claudius was doing a public performance and did not mean a single word of what he was saying.

The ghost was not physical. His presence was suggested by spectral footlights and stereo sounds. The order to kill Claudius thus became an internal rather than an external injunction. During the ghost's speech, Hamlet was distorted with pain, re-enacting his father's murder through his twisting body.

Hamlet read "What a piece of work is a man" in a book; and his line "And yet to me what is this quintessence of dust?" was then said to contradict what he had read.

He addressed "To be or not to be" directly to Ophelia and pointed to her thighs while delivering "the pangs of disprized love." For Derek Jacobi, transforming the famous soliloquy (Act III, scene i) into a direct speech to the young woman allowed Hamlet's vulnerability to be revealed more fully, as well as Ophelia's dilemma.[14] Hamlet is showing his secret intentions to her, he is pouring out his soul, yet she betrays him nevertheless, but not without having given several hesitating glances to the hidden Claudius and Polonius.

At the end of the monologue, "soft you now" was said as a whisper to Ophelia to remind her they should not talk so loudly: they could be heard. At the end of the nunnery scene, which was tremendously violent and tough, Hamlet rushed backstage and impulsively pulled aside the arras to find Polonius and Claudius spying on them indeed.

The role of Ophelia was made more significant in Jacobi's production. Jacobi chose to locate the intermission after Ophelia's "O, what a noble mind is here o'erthrown!" speech (Act III, scene i), and to keep her on stage as often as possible as an observer of the court's disintegration, including during the closet scene.

In his 1996 film, Branagh also takes a small licence with the text to make Ophelia's part larger. She is brought before Claudius by Polonius and Gertrude to read herself some of Hamlet's letter to her (Act II, scene ii); in the original text Polonius reads the letter. Branagh even inserts a non-Shakespearean cue for her: when Hamlet escapes from Rosencrantz and Guildenstern after he has killed Polonius ("The king is a thing . . . Of Nothing. Bring me to him" [Act IV scene ii]), Ophelia runs towards him screaming "My Lord!" reminding the audience even more vividly that Hamlet has just killed a father as well as a Prime Minister. Ophelia is also seen in several other added moments in the film: including love scenes with Hamlet in flashbacks, and a scene where she desperately tries to catch a glimpse of her father's corpse as it is taken away. This image of Ophelia clutching the palace gates and uttering a long primal howl gives the audience a logical explanation for her fall into madness.

During the Mousetrap scene (Act III, scene ii), in the 1988 production Hamlet helped Lucianus pour the poison into the Player King's ear. This action will be taken further in the 1993 RSC production and in the 1996 film, where Branagh takes the poison from Lucianus' hands and pours it *alone* into the Player King's ear. At the end of the play within the play, Claudius and Hamlet physically fought each other. Hamlet grabbed a lamp and projected its light onto Claudius's face as he will do again in 1993 and 1996 with a theatre spotlight.

The most extreme choice in Jaobi's direction occurred at the end of the production. Fortinbras's order "Go bid the soldiers shoot" became an order for the soldiers to kill the servants. Fortinbras was a ruthless warrior, a cruel invader, and this stern performance had a great influence on the 1996 movie in which, while he does not go so far as to shoot the servants, Fortinbras comes to the palace as an enemy, operating a putsch silently and efficiently to conquer the throne of Denmark.

1992: The Young Poet

The BBC radio production of 1992 stands out as the first time Branagh tackled the full-length version of *Hamlet*, a conflation of the Second Quarto and the First Folio. The production was very pacy and lasted only three and a half hours, quite fast for a presentation of the complete text. In his notes from the accompanying booklet, Branagh says:

> Presenting the play uncut has allowed the characters to reveal even more, and we discover extra details about them which are usually lost on stage. The political situation becomes clearer, and Hamlet is revealed as a knowledgeable man of the theatre in his discussion of the boy actors. . . . The restored lines are not mere padding, but reinforce the idea that the play is about a national as well as a domestic tragedy.[15]

This first encounter with the complete version made Branagh certain that were he ever to play the part again it would be with the uncut text. He would indeed do so a few months later on the stage of the Barbican Centre for the RSC.

Three actors from this radio production played the same parts again in the 1996 film: Kenneth Branagh (Hamlet), Derek Jacobi (Claudius) and Richard Briers (Polonius). It is interesting to see how Jacobi and Briers analyzed their parts in 1992 and then again four years later.

In 1992, Derek Jacobi said about Claudius:

> He's often played as a physically large, almost Falstaffian figure but I prefer to see him as a suave diplomat, even something of a

playboy, who genuinely loves Gertrude and who wants everybody to have a good time.[16]

This interpretation will be reinforced in the film where Claudius is presented as a slightly decadent man enjoying the pleasures of life. On Hamlet's speech "The King doth wake tonight and takes his rouse" (Act I, scene iv), a travelling shot shows Claudius drinking in the corridors before entering his room with the queen. Yet, the audience feels this is a man who became evil because of passion, a man who genuinely suffers from his guilt and seeks comfort in his wife. After Gertrude tells him about Polonius's death at Hamlet's hand, he delivers the line "My soul is full of discord and dismay" (Act IV, scene i) in deep discouragement while embracing Gertrude.

In fact, Claudius is charismatic and inspires respect and sympathy from the audience. In his first court scene, Branagh describes him in his script as "a man of genuine compassion." Even the flashbacks allow us to see how much Claudius was attracted by Gertrude *before* the murder of Hamlet's father. Then at the end of the play, when he shouts through the hall "Gertrude, do not drink!" his voice resounds with the same pathos as Lear's. Until Polonius's death, Claudius is pleasant and courteous to Hamlet, but after the murder of his Prime Minister he is obliged to act sternly. In 1996, Derek Jacobi commented:

> Claudius is a winner, a well-intentioned polished statesman who is both wiser and more effective than the ruler he has supplanted. . . . His opening speech is a miracle of diplomacy, one of the great thank-you addresses of all time.[17]

To show a seemingly unworried and affable Claudius allows for a greater shock, a greater contrast, when he openly begins to hate Hamlet.

For Richard Briers in 1992, Polonius "is not a fool—he's cunning and has the spy's practiced slyness. . . . He is a politician and he has the politician's rhinoceros hide which helps him bear all Hamlet's insults."[18] This approach is again pursued in the film where the hypocritical and calculating side of Ophelia's father is emphasized.

In the radio production, Branagh delivered the soliloquies in a very intimate and poetic voice. This was a marked break from his 1988 frantic Hamlet. Radio, like film, eliminates the need for actors to project the voice to the back rows. It allows a more intellectual presentation of Hamlet while keeping up the energy. For example, the closet scene drained Branagh and would finish him off completely when he played it on stage. For the film, he took four days to shoot it, bringing more gravity and a wider variety of emotions to the scene.

Some passages, such as "To be or not to be," took explicit advantage of the radio medium. Co-director Glyn Dearman confessed: "I recorded Ken, without him knowing, when he was just shuffling through that speech, trying it out, and it gave it that sense of newness, of discovery."[19] Branagh agreed with Dearman to use that recording for the first part of the speech, as it brought a naturalness of tone to the lines, the sense of a man experiencing his own thoughts, in the very process of putting words on his feelings. But Branagh may have taken this transformation too far as his new Hamlet was too mild and ethereal. He had lost his aggressiveness and his bitter mockery.

All the same, the 1992 BBC Radio production was a fine rehearsal for Branagh's 1996 film and a decisive step in Branagh's approach to Hamlet. It represents his first use of the complete text, which he would not give up again. Moreover, the radio medium allowed him to discover the character's poetic dimension which had been lacking in his performance until then.

1993: The Cynical Prince

In 1992, Adrian Noble asked Branagh if he would be interested in taking up Hamlet for the RSC. Branagh accepted and was to give his finest Hamlet on stage.

Noble had decided very early on to produce a complete version of the play, a first for the Royal Shakespeare Company. No word would be cut and the text would be a conflation of the Second Quarto and the First Folio (New Cambridge edition). The complete version was chosen partly to give all the characters their due importance, but also because Branagh thought the part of Hamlet would be less exhausting to play. Some of the restored scenes would provide him time to rest and find a second breath:

> The advantage of doing the complete text is that I'm a much less hectic Hamlet than the last time I played it. When you cut the play, you cut the scene between Reynaldo and Polonius and the Rosencrantz and Guildenstern discussion about the boy actors, which effectively contracts the part of Hamlet and brings the big scenes banging up against each other. [With the complete text], when you come on for the graveyard scene you've had forty min-

utes to sit quietly and prepare for it. I find those forty of the most delicious minutes I've spent in the theatre.[20]

The uncut text also allows the Fortinbras story to develop into a real diplomatic and military plot. Adrian Noble's production gave equal importance to both the political and domestic dimensions of the play making the ending all the more emotional and lyrical. It is no surprise then that Branagh wanted his film version to use the complete text again to reach the same emotional peak.

The production which reunited Kenneth Branagh, Adrian Noble as director, and Bob Crowley as designer eight years after *Henry V*, was post-modern, nostalgic, *and* traditional. It strove for realism in the performances, motivations, and psychologies of the characters, but with striking non-naturalistic and symbolic images in the staging and design. The production was set just before the First World War which allowed Adrian Noble to colour it with allusions to Ibsen and Bergman: "I have always been interested in Scandinavian art and culture, which have a strange mixture of rich, domestic warmth and remote, cold starkness."[21]

The 1996 film is again set between 1850 and 1900 and its design is also influenced by Scandinavian neoclassical style. Yet, if the film insists upon the glamour and luxury of this world, the 1993 stage production was more sober, choosing to present a Kafkaesque, bureaucratic world. Polonius was running the affairs of the state from a cold and ascetic office and looked for Rosencrantz and Guldenstern's files in piles of paper and tall shelves.

On several occasions, during a set change, a huge grey curtain came through the proscenium to suggest, according to H. R. Coursen, "the occurrences of fate."[22] Throughout the 1993 production, the Edwardian set and staging highlighted themes of the play, and reflected the progressive decay of the play's world. The Edwardian period was a transition between an old regime full of glamour to a mechanized diplomatic world and could effectively reflect the change occurring in Denmark with Claudius's coronation.

The first court scene (Act I, scene ii) was charming. Under a white curtain, dressed in bright, clear colours, Claudius (John Shrapnel) and Gertrude (Jane Lapotaire) smiled and drank champagne, the atmosphere reminiscent of a private celebration after a wedding. Then for Laertes's departure (Act I, scene ii) came Ophelia's well-organized room, with its bed, wardrobe, and piano. Designer Bob Crowley was inspired by Bergman's *Fanny and Alexander* for the room's light green colour and for the Scandinavian style of the furniture. This aqua colour was a symbolic echo of the phrase "green girl" as Polonius calls her, and anticipated Ophelia's aquatic death.

Yet by the end of the play, the stage had lost its integrity, all realistic structures had been dismantled, and the design was all fragments and visual allusions. For Ophelia's mad scenes (Act IV, scene v), the furniture was covered with a large grey canvas which gave the impression of a lunar landscape. Then for her last exit, wearing her father's bloody shirt as well as his shoes, much too big for her, Ophelia went off dragging the canvas behind her producing the airy, silky, and unreal effect of a parachute opening. A desolated landscape was revealed with Ophelia's piano in the middle of the stage, tables and chairs upside down, and pinkish crowns of dried flowers blown apart on the floor.

This overwhelming image reflected Ophelia's mental state and remained on view until the end of the play. Society was shaken. Its images of harmony had exploded. At the opening of the play at the edge of the stage near the audience, a small cemetery was represented with small crosses and crowns of dried flowers. By the end of the play it was as if the small cemetery now stretched over the whole stage. Ophelia began to play the piano, which her father had forbidden her after the nunnery scene. Fallen into madness, Ophelia could at last express herself through music.

From the Mousetrap scene to Hamlet's departure for England (Act III, scene ii to Act IV, scene iii), a bold design directly emphasized theatricality. The aim was to reflect back to the audience their own gaze, and to bring both the spectators and the characters to a metatheatrical awareness, according to Antony Dawson.[23]

Act III, scene ii opened showing the audience what was happening backstage as the Players prepared for their performance of the Mousetrap. Some were practicing their verses, others were dressing or applying their make-up in front of modern mirrors framed by light bulbs. The audience was thus able to share the preparations of the professional actors. Behind them a bright red curtain was closed from which Hamlet entered to give his advice.

When the play within the play was about to start, a sudden lighting change made the curtain transparent, revealing behind it an amazing red theatre: a vast curved auditorium with rows and rows of chairs on several levels.

The royal family and friends sat in the front row and were therefore both on a stage and in an auditorium at the same time. The spectators were faced with their looks and reactions and the real theatre reflected itself in the fake one. This, of course, made for endless virtual mirrors.

The 1996 film extends this device, with an extraordinary use of reaction shots during the Mousetrap scene and even reaction shots to reactions as the camera cuts from character to character. The medium of film really suits the text in this scene and conveys well all its back and forth gazes. For Branagh, "it felt like a very strong scene to treat cinematically and we went in determined to cover it with endless numbers of angles. In editing, we could construct it and we've spent probably more time on that scene than any other in the picture."[24] The passionate, dangerous, and intense red colour is also used in the 1996 movie not only for the auditorium but also for the Mousetrap stage which is covered with scarlet and purple material.

In the stage production, the design of the theatre within the theatre remained on view all through the dramatic scenes which followed (Act III, scene iii to Act IV, scene iii). According to Antony Dawson, Claudius's confession, Hamlet's decision to postpone his revenge, his murder of Polonius, his hysterical meeting with his mother, his reaction to the ghost's return, his capture, and his departure to England were thus turned into meta-theatrical events,[25] theatrical events which reflect on theatricality itself. During those scenes, the fake auditorium was still more or less visible. When it was not, as in the closet scene, the backstage props remained in view to remind the audience how thin the frontier between reality and acting is: the players' make-up table became Gertrude's dressing-table and the Mousetrap couch was used as a bed.

This meta-theatricality can be found again in the 1996 film in short but enlightening, almost meta-cinematic, moments. For example, after Polonius's death, a pursued Hamlet is joined by Rosencrantz and Guildenstern ("O here they come" Act IV, scene ii). Instead of frankly running away from them, he strangely imitates a man in the act of escape. It is as if he becomes external to his own being, laughing at himself and the oddity of the situation. When the chase begins in earnest ("Hide fox, and all after"), Hamlet is chased through the palace. He runs through room after room, effortlessly opening false doors. And the camera follows him in profile, in a fast travelling shot, as if the walls of the castle have been removed purposely for the "artificial eye" to follow the action in just such a manner. In fact, we are made suddenly aware that none of the walls in the castle are real and all the approved ways of moving from room to room are false, merely an appearance. This scene reminds us that the castle is actually a set— as the camera travels outside the illusionary "fourth wall" of each of the rooms, as the walls become insubstantial and obviously "constructed" for the purpose of film making.

It is always interesting to analyze how the meta-theatrical aspects of Shakespeare's plays are adapted to cinema. In *Henry V*, meta-theatricality appears in the character of the Chorus who reminds us we are watching a play and often prevents us from entering the fictional world of the play and identifying with the hero too closely. We saw that, in Branagh's screen adaptation, although the Chorus has been kept, he is no longer a producer of ironic distance.

In Branagh's *Hamlet*, the meta-theatrical aspects of Shakespeare's play appear mainly in the play within the play and in the soliloquies, in which the actor addresses the public almost directly. We have already noted that Branagh used extensive editing to adapt the play within the play to the screen. But the scene inevitably loses its meta-theatrical aspects, because the medium through which the scene is being presented is no longer theatre, but cinema. We lose the redoubling of a theatre public watching a theatre play before them on stage. But what about the soliloquies? How does Branagh adapt them to film?

In the 1993 stage production, Branagh insisted on the meta-theatrical aspects of the soliloquies. He asked the questions of the "What a rogue and peasant slave" monologue (Act II, scene ii) directly to the audience: "Am I a coward?" "Who calls me villain?" And, above all, he insisted on the sentence: "I have heard that guilty creatures sitting at a play," while explicitly pointing to the spectators.

Yet, in the cinema, this presentation of a soliloquy clashes with the traditional filmic ideology which aims at hiding the act of enunciation. For a long time, in order to bring realism and naturalness to his or her performance, movie conventions have forbidden the actor to look at the camera, to forget the camera's artificial eye and hide the mechanism of artistic creation. In the cinema, the actor is there to captivate the public, not to call him out.

Yet, Branagh's choice in filming the soliloquies—in contrast to other Shakespearean directors such as Richard Loncraine, Orson Welles, Franco Zeffirelli, and Trevor Nunn—has been not to cut them, either visually or verbally. He presents them in one single and continuous shot and treats the monologues as energetic flows, as inner journeys, with the camera often following the character in slow and fluid moves. All the soliloquies in Branagh's *Hamlet* have been shot in one single take. He states:

> We tried with most of the soliloquies to let them play in one take, in one sustained shot. I thought it would be easier for the audience to understand if the actor, from line to line, was, like in the theatre, following one thought into the other. I was concerned that cutting also cuts the sense of it as well. I often find that it's through having a run at it rather than doing it in bits that you can really maintain the overall sense of what Hamlet is saying.[26]

In his treatment of the soliloquies, Branagh thus remains closer to the theatre than anywhere else in his movies. His monologues do not show any reaction shots; moreover, he does not illustrate the words visually as he does with flashbacks and intercut images at some other points in his films. If anything, the soliloquies feature the relative simplicity of visual correlatives, such as the small model theatre at the end of the "What a rogue" soliloquy which illustrates Hamlet's plan to catch the conscience of the king in a play. In Branagh's treatment of the soliloquies, the vocal remains as important as the visual. The monologues become a series of physical as well as emotional journeys, a series of events through which Hamlet goes talking to himself and listening to his own voice.

Branagh's straightforward presentation of Hamlet stems directly from his own sense of Shakespeare. This is how Branagh interprets the play and the character on stage *and* on film. The transfer of Shakesepeare's plays to the screen has not influenced Branagh's understanding of the plays. His desire to present an uncluttered and not overly complicated Shakespeare does not depend on the medium in which he works. This is not to say that Branagh removes all ambiguity from the play: he makes Shakespearen movies without complicacies, not without complexities.

One of the greatest qualities of the 1993 stage production was its clarity and simplicity. Adrian Noble's direction was straightforward: Hamlet was really in love with Ophelia; his madness was feigned (according to Anny Crunelle-Vanrigh, "Branagh's [Hamlet] has lost his nerve, trust and confidence, certainly not his wits"[27]); Gertrude was innocent of her husband's murder and there was no doubt about the ghost's honesty. The 1996 film takes up this clear and simple vision.

Terrence Rafferty said about the movie: "Branagh's approach to Hamlet is audaciously straightforward: in each scene, his aim is to make literal, material sense of the play's complex action and of the characters' often confused motivation."[28]

When the house lights faded for the beginning of the play, from a trapdoor a ghost dressed all in white came up out of the small cemetery at the edge of the stage that would be Ophelia's final burial ground. Presenting his back to the audience, he went backstage and disappeared into a foggy twirling light. Only then did the soldiers who open the play appear on stage.

Asked about the problem of whether the ghost is a "spirit of health or goblin damned," RSC Assistant Director Colin Ellwood answered in 1993: "Deciding whether [the Ghost] comes from heaven or hell was not a priority in this production, because much more than Old Hamlet's spirit, he is young Hamlet's father. This is where we wanted to lay the emphasis."[29] The ghost in the 1993 production thus had a very human appearance. The 1996 film takes up this choice of a physical entity and emphasizes it with extreme and sensual close-ups on the ghost's mouth and piercing blue eyes.

On stage, the relationship between father and son was conveyed through the image of the hand, a recurrent motif in the movie work of Kenneth Branagh. In 1993, the ghost's hand pierced through the earth while Hamlet was exhorting Barnardo, Marcellus, and Horatio not to reveal anything about the spirit's apparition. As he was shouting "Swear!" to his friends, Hamlet held the gloved hand of his father. In the 1996 film, the ghost's hand was equally stressed. Shot in close up, it fades away just after "Adieu, adieu, Hamlet, remember me!" while Hamlet tries vainly to grab it. Although it is found in both the play and the film, this motif evokes a different feeling each time. In the movie, it is as if the relationship between father and son is aborted.

The end of the play reached an emotional climax. As Guy Woolfenden's beautiful music rose, four soldiers carried Hamlet's body in a crucified position—a position he will take up again in the 1996 film. A door opened at the back of the stage from which Hamlet's father in a magical mist appeared with his arms held out to welcome his son into heaven. Some critics found this ending too sentimental and melodramatic. Yet, the effect was striking and its emotional power stamped itself onto the young audience. The 1993 stage production thus began and ended with this fatherly image of the ghost. In 1996, the movie also begins and ends with the vision of Old Hamlet's war-like statue.

In the 1993 production, according to Adrian Noble the three main sets—Ophelia's aqua room, the glittering red of the theatre, and the final mortuary decay—marked the three symphonic movements of the play's progress to this emotional conclusion. The domestic crisis reached its peak in the nunnery scene. The professional players arrived and the image of the theatre dominated the middle movement. And all the characters were confronted with death in the final cemetery atmosphere. Let us now reexamine Adrian Noble's theatre production and see what choices in interpretation and direction have found their way to Branagh's 1996 film.

An atmosphere of domesticity first appeared in the private party Gertrude and Claudius gave after their wedding (Act I, scene ii). A Christmas tree on the left of the stage added to the family feeling. Then Laertes' departure (Act I, scene iii) was performed in Ophelia's private room with its piano and unmade bed. The domestic and secluded aspects of the room were enhanced by childish atmospheric music. Laertes entered and woke his sister. During their discussion, Ophelia got out of bed and washed herself with a sponge which she gleefully threw at her brother when he began to talk about Hamlet's intentions. Here was a happy playful family.

The nunnery scene (Act III, scene i) was also played within the domestic comfort of Ophelia's room. Polonius and Claudius, transgressing the privacy of the young girl, hid themselves in her wardrobe. This theme of transgression appears again in the 1996 film. When the palace guards are searching for Hamlet after his murder of Polonius, they break into Ophelia's room and even search her bed.

In the stage production, Ophelia took her "remembrances" from a small suitcase she kept on top of her wardrobe. These were love letters written by Hamlet to her. The beginning of the scene was very tender. Hamlet sincerely wanted to protect Ophelia but gradually came to understand that she was being manipulated and was only acting a role. After the line "Where's your father?" Hamlet became furious and scattered apart all her letters. Ophelia dropped to the floor to collect them up again. The scene ended with a terrible physical fight. Hamlet threw Ophelia to the ground and was at the point of assaulting her before he stood up again and spat in her face to humiliate her.

Adrian Noble explained his views on the nunnery scene. He chose to treat it straightforwardly without emphasizing the double meaning of "nunnery," which could also mean "brothel" during Elizabethan times:

> They do indeed love each other. In simple terms, she is his girl-friend. Instead of overcomplicating Hamlet's words with repressed anger or cunning double-entendre, we treated them straightfor-wardly: when he says those things, he means them. In effect, he is saying to Ophelia quite tenderly, "Leave this society; don't get married to anybody. Go to a nunnery." It's terribly moving if you play it literally. . . . In the second half of the scene, however, ex-traordinary sexual feelings come out because she has betrayed him.[30]

In the 1996 film, the scene begins as tenderly as in the 1993 play. Hamlet takes Ophelia in his arms and kisses her. Yet, as soon as Ophelia gives him back his letters, showing herself cold and reserved, Hamlet scatters the letters with a violent hand slap, as he did on stage. Then "This was sometime a paradox, but now the time gives it proof" is delivered in such a deep, sad and distressed manner that you can really feel the pain of a broken heart. Hamlet seems even more vulnerable than Ophelia.

In his script, we can see that Branagh was inspired by Adrian Noble's direction. Regarding Hamlet's advice to Ophelia, "Get thee to a nun-nery":

> *He can warn someone he loves to beware of CLAUDIUS,*
> *POLONIUS, and even him, a man unworthy of her love. He wants*
> *her to be safe. To escape.*[31]

As in the play, Hamlet's anger is ignited in the film by Ophelia's treason when she tells him Polonius is at home and not in the act of spying. He grabs her and drags her violently around the great hall, opening every mirrored door expecting to find the hidden Claudius and Polonius. Then he thrusts her against a two-way mirror behind which Polonius can do nothing but witness the scene and his daugh-ter's pain.

In the 1993 production, the ghost's apparition during the closet scene (Act III, scene iv) captured again this feeling of domesticity and was one of the most moving scenes in the whole play. In a white suit, the ghost quietly came towards Gertrude and Hamlet. He sat with them on the couch, reminding us of an earlier family tableau with Polonius, Ophelia, and Laertes. The ghost held his hand near Gertrude's face, almost touching her as she said "Yet all there is I see" and then took his son by the hand. Gertrude held Hamlet's other hand and desperately tried to bring him back to reality. The couple was physically reunited through their child. The audience could feel Hamlet's yearning to make the happy days live again.

Colin Ellwood explained Adrian Noble's motivations for creating such a tableau:

> Adrian Noble wanted to get a sense of the domestic in the play, of two families who were torn apart by the events. At one point he toyed with the idea of having children in the play—a child Hamlet, a child Ophelia, and a child Laertes playing together— a flashback in some way, in order to get a sense of something blown apart. We didn't pursue that idea, but had the family groups instead. Adrian Noble wanted to have each family together at some point. The only way to achieve this for the Hamlet family was in the closet scene, so that we had a sort of tableau there, with mother, father, and son together. This is one of the reasons why we decided against a ghost who was a product of stage technology. Hamlet's relationship to the ghost is a relationship between a father and a son, so there has to be something very solid about the ghost.[32]

In his 1996 movie, Branagh takes up this same idea of a family tableau and broken harmony. In his script, we can read:

HAMLET
On him, on him. Look you how pale he glares.

And he does. We see all three close. The complete family, now all unable to reach each other and all heartbroken by the frustration of the attempt.[33]

With the medium of film, Branagh can take Adrian Noble's idea even further. He inserts flashbacks, images of the family before Old Hamlet's murder. During the ghost's speech, he shows us the family playing happily together at curling; and later during the skull speech (Act V, scene i), he brings Yorick the jester to life at a remembered dinner party.

Beyond the tensions of the disintegrating domestic harmony, the 1993 stage production also featured moments of physical and emotional explosions that are left more or less unchanged in the movie version.

In the 1993 stage production, between the theatre audience and the court audience of the play, the Players performed the Mousetrap with expressive ballet gestures around a green couch. When the player portraying Lucianus, "nephew to the king," entered to poison the Player King, Hamlet invaded the acting space, threw the Player Queen into Lucianus' arms, took the poison from Lucianus and poured it into the Player King's ear himself. The past thus met the future, and Old Hamlet's murder and young Hamlet's plan to kill Claudius were combined in one single action. According to Colin Ellwood, "we also wanted to get a sense of the horror of somebody from the audience leaping onto the stage and starting to take over a part or to change the play."[34] In the 1996 film, Hamlet also leaps on the stage in order to unmask Claudius.

In 1993, the moving and symbolic meeting between Gertrude and her dead husband in the closet scene changed Gertrude's behaviour significantly. Until then, there had been a believable sexual tension between her and Claudius. They even stole a kiss when Polonius went off to fetch the ambassadors in Act II, scene ii. But when Claudius entered after the closet scene, she purposely avoided him. She eventually declined, fell into alcoholism, and died in the middle of the stage, alone. The 1996 film deviates from the 1993 production only in delaying this change in Gertrude's attitude until after her account of Ophelia's death (Act IV, scene vii). Claudius seems to be angry against her because she has upset Laertes again ("How much I had to do to calm his rage" is said as a strong and deep accusation). Then he asks her to follow him and Laertes ("Let's follow, Gertrude. . . . Therefore, let's follow") but Gertrude remains in the room, now the master of her own actions.

In 1993, when Hamlet was arrested after Polonius's death, Claudius punched him powerfully in the stomach as an answer to Hamlet's line "If your messenger find him not there, / seek him in the other place yourself." In his 1996 film, Branagh changes the punch to a slap on the second "Where's Polonius?" This change improves the pace of the scene because, on stage, the punch in the stomach required Branagh to find his breath again before being able to continue.

On stage, Laertes' return to Denmark (Act IV, scene v) was intense and rough. Laertes suddenly drew his gun and held it as close as he could to Claudius. In the 1996 film version, the gun is replaced with a sword, but the action is as swift and frightening: Laertes is holding his weapon one inch from Claudius's neck.

In 1993, the mad scenes were filled with sexual allusions. While Ophelia was singing "Young men will do it if they come to it," she repeatedly put her hand to her lap, as an imitation of the sexual act. This action is taken up by the film in the same song on the line "Before you tumble me, you promised me to wed." Ophelia lies on the ground re-enacting orgasm. Flashbacks showing Hamlet and Ophelia in bed together are inserted to remind the audience of their former intimacy.

For Branagh, this 1993 Hamlet was the most successful performance in his career. According to David Andrews: "Branagh's greatest skill . . . is to convince us totally, absolutely, that he is Hamlet without making a big fuss about it. He simply is."[35] And for Charles Spencer, "[Branagh] gives the finest performance of his career . . . [He] lets you into his character's mind with a complete absence of guile . . . and at almost every turn you feel you know exactly what he is thinking . . . and feeling. As a result many of the play's difficulties seem to dissolve."[36] With this 1993 Hamlet, Branagh wished indeed to convey the story and the verses as simply and clearly as possible. "Clarity" and "naturalness" were in fact the most frequent words under the critics' pen. Branagh told Samuel Crowl:

> With no other play did I know the lines as well, so I didn't have to invest new energy in trying to learn them. I had the chance to scour all the familiar passages carefully to find new subtleties in them so that they didn't come across as overfamiliar. That was helpful because I wanted to make sure that I understood everything I was saying—completely. . . . With this [Hamlet], I have enjoyed every single performance of it.[37]

That was, perhaps, one of the reasons for Robert Brustein's comment: "It is a tribute to this intelligent, well-fashioned production that it can be honestly described with a cliché: you think you're seeing the play for the very first time."[38]

In 1993, Branagh's Hamlet was a man of action: noble, mature, sincere and courteous, seeking authenticity. Horatio (Rob Edwards) was his true humble friend, uneasy when facing the court pomp. It was obvious that he had rented his suit to attend the "Mousetrap." This Hamlet held friendship and gratitude at a high rate. When Marcellus proclaimed his respect to the prince, Hamlet quickly followed with a very deep "Your loves! As mine to you." His love for the players and their art was also made clear: "You are welcome" was a real exclamation of joy.

According to Samuel Crowl, "[Branagh] was the first Hamlet in a generation to lend credibility to Fortinbras' judgement that 'had he been put on / [He] would have proved most royal.'"[39] This opinion was echoed by John Peter: "The indignant young troublemaker he played for the Renaissance Theatre Company . . . has now changed into a brooding, self-possessed prince, courtly and serious . . . under which you sense the glint of an agile, alert intelligence."[40]

In his 1996 film, Branagh brings back this portrayal of a noble, respectful, and courteous Hamlet. The 1996 Hamlet, as in the 1993 stage production, shows his love for the theatre. The news about the players' arrival enlivens him and gives him joy. In December 1996, during a seminar in Washington celebrating the film's release, Branagh commented: "Those kind of remarks like 'Nay, come, let's go together' show that Hamlet is solicitous and sensitive to other people's feelings. Princely of spirit is how I like to think of him."[41] And in his script, Branagh explains his way of delivering the cue "I shall in all my best obey you, madam":

> We see HAMLET's crushed body language. The sense of a head bowed. Nevertheless he is a Prince and this is clear in the manner of his reply.[42]

For Branagh, Hamlet is not indecisive. He is the same man of action in both 1993 and 1996, certain about what he has to do. At the film's release, Branagh said: "The reason he doesn't kill Claudius early on is that he simply never gets the right opportunity to do so."[43] In the film, when Hamlet returns to his private room after the First Player's speech and begins "Now I am alone" (Act II, scene ii), the regular ticking of a clock can be heard, reminding him and the audience that time is relentlessly flying away. We witness the frustration of a man who knows he must act but cannot do it because he cannot find the proper occasion. In Claudius's confession scene just after Hamlet's line "And now I'll do't, and so he goes to heaven, / And so am I revenged," in the film we see Hamlet stab Claudius in the ear, blood splashing all over. But the camera suddenly comes back to reality: Claudius is still alive praying. In the 1993 stage production, Hamlet took out his sword and left it beside Claudius after the "Now might I do it" speech. Claudius discovered it at the end of his confession, both frightened and amazed. For Russell Jackson: "[Branagh's Hamlet] understood the power of his emotional terrorism and his ability to shake Claudius."[44] The movie medium in 1996 thus allows the performance of 1993 to be extended.

In 1993 on stage, during the closet scene, Hamlet's violent assault against Gertrude was not driven by Oedipal feelings at all. Hamlet was consciously acting in the name of his father whose interests could only be defended by his son. In his 1996 movie, Branagh repeats this non-Oedipal interpretation: Hamlet is clearly his father's avenger, not his mother's frustrated lover.

His ironic and cynical side came out very often in the 1993 stage production. All the puns were deliberately stressed. For example, he looked at Polonius's thighs while talking about the "most weak hams" and delivered "I am too much in the sun" emphasizing each word. He made deliberately clear that "sun" could also mean "son," implying "You treat me too much like your son."

Hamlet's first appearance set the tone for the performance. Dressed in an Edwardian black suit, with a band around his arm, he was in obvious mourning. His hair was combed very seriously and his attitude was formal and rigid. This contrasted highly with Claudius's happiness and white clothing. The new king was smoking a cigar and looked like a "mafia godfather en route to the casino"[45] while Gertrude was drinking a glass of champagne. Hamlet stood with his back to the audience—a point of view he will regularly feature in the movie—and did not move until his first cue, "A little more than kin and less than kind." It is interesting to note that Branagh went to rehearsals in a suit to grasp the character's formalism in these first scenes.

The 1996 film also reflects this performance. Hamlet does not even appear on screen until this first cue. "A little more than kin and less than kind" is delivered in voice-over, as an unspoken thought, while a travelling shot from the far throne to the right edge of the hall reveals Hamlet's stiff and stern figure.

This rigid attitude faded away in the course of the 1993 production. As early as the battlements scene (Act I, scene iv), before the ghost's apparition, Horatio and Marcellus had to hold Hamlet back by force. But the prince's fury was too strong and he took Marcellus's pole-axe and threatened them with it. This move can be found again in the 1996 film. Hamlet's energy seems amplified at this moment. Then he runs through the woods looking for his father. All his formal and strict behaviour has dropped off.

On stage, when Rosencrantz and Guildenstern arrived, "[Hamlet's] body turned to rubber, clearly an expression of [his] antic, mocking, mimicking disposition,"[46] according to Samuel Crowl. This behaviour became more and more intense until finally Claudius used a strait-jacket during the capture scene to get Hamlet's body under control again. This prop also appears in the film where it is used to bridle poor Ophelia, driven into madness.

Moreover, in 1993 Hamlet used the strait-jacket to simulate madness even before it was forced upon him. It was Branagh's own idea:

> I wanted to be clear that this Hamlet puts on his antic disposition, which is why we used the straitjacket in the fishmonger scene; it's a prop that goes with his double-talk, and it made— waving the straitjacket's flapping arms as I walked backwards away from Polonius—a visual image for the bloody difficult line you struggle with, "you, sir, should be as old as I am if, like a crab, you could go backward."[47]

The strait-jacket not only brought a comic aspect to the play but it also confirmed that Hamlet's madness was totally *feigned*.

In 1993, Branagh put a lot of humour into his Hamlet and improvised the comic scenes each night. Anny Crunelle-Vanrigh comments:

> A lot of experimentation went into the comedy scenes, as shown by the many changes noticed from one performance to the next, and unmistakably a great deal of improvisation too, the brinkmanship of which seems to have contributed to the freshness and vitality of this production.[48]

Hamlet (Branagh) made fun of Polonius every time he saw him. He even imitated his nasal accent in his repetition of "My Lord, I have news to tell you." He laughed at Claudius and took the intonation of a spoiled child singing a song for his delivery of the line "Mother and father are man and wife, man and wife is one flesh." He also produced a parody of the pompous Osric delivering the "verity of extolment" speech in one single breath at great speed, something he repeated in the 1996 film.

These moments of humour allowed the audience to breathe and smile after some powerful and tragical scenes. For Anny Crunelle-Vanrigh:

Along with moments of violence, distress, and spiritual illumination, there is invigorating humour and jocularity in this production, and in Hamlet the smarting *joie de vivre* that only true pessimists can have. From black comedy to satire to farce, every kind of humour is a commentary that helps dramatize the stages of Hamlet's journey.[49]

With its transfer from London to Stratford-upon-Avon, the production gained in intensity and pace. The first performances lasted four and a half hours. At the end of the run, they lasted only three hours and forty minutes. From December 1992 to April 1993, the performances were quite different each night. The nunnery and closet scenes were improvised each night, as were other moments in the play, including as the arrival of Rosencrantz and Guildenstern ("Is it your own inclining?"), the "Would you play upon this pipe?" scene, and the "Where is Polonius?" scene.

In an interview just before the last performances at Stratford, Branagh gave a revealing answer to a question by Samuel Crowl who had seen the production three times, in January, February, and March, and had noticed the differences:

> Crowl: I hope you are still trying to ram that photograph of Claudius up [Gertrude's] dress in the closet scene.
>
> Branagh: [Big laugh] It comes and goes; it just depends on the moment each night.[50]

Branagh said that the different treatment of the text each night was mostly due to Joanne Pearce (Ophelia), "a very powerful actress who wants to make sure that nothing is taken for granted."[51] This desire to be visually explicit and bold probably stems from his taste for Hollywood movies, with their grand spectacular effects.

Knowing that Branagh is used to being visually inspired by a theatre production in which he acted or directed, Samuel Crowl gave him this piece of advice during an interview on the 1993 stage *Hamlet*:

> Crowl: If you are already thinking about a possible film to flow from this production, I think Bergman's style and landscape fit the play very well. Trains chugging along against a cold, white, bitter landscape.
>
> Branagh: Yes.

It is interesting to see that eventually Branagh followed this idea. In the film, when Rosencrantz and Guildenstern come to see Hamlet, they are actually perched on a small black train ("a primitive miniature steam train—a toy of the new king"[52]) which is running along a snowy desolated landscape.

The success of the 1993 play was immediate, especially with younger audience members. The box office broke a new record for the Royal Shakespeare Company. All the advance tickets for the Barbican Centre run in London were quickly sold out; and the queue to buy the remaining tickets started on some days at 4:30 a.m. It is interesting to note that fifty-two percent of the spectators had never read or seen the play of *Hamlet* before.

When the play transferred to Stratford-upon-Avon, one journalist asked Branagh whether he would shoot *Hamlet*. At this time, Branagh was still sceptical. He doubted he could raise the money for such a film and did not know if the world needed another film version of *Hamlet*. Without a doubt, the success of these performances helped convince him there was a great appetite for a complete and well-paced version of the play. In 1994, he began talking about filming *Hamlet* without cutting any of Shakespeare's words.

In his 1996 movie, the comedic aspects present in the 1993 production are softened, as a film does not need to work as hard to hold the audience's attention. The comedy has become a black humour, a bitterness that reveals the mental wounds of a very sensitive and vulnerable Hamlet. It is not surprising then to hear Branagh compare what in all likelihood will be his last performance of Hamlet with his very first performance: "I first played [Hamlet] when I was twenty at the Royal Academy of Dramatic Art and, I think that *in feel*, actually, [the film] is closer to that than any of the other productions I've been in."[53]

The way he greets his friends Rosencrantz and Guildenstern is typical: "Were you not sent for? Is it your own inclining? Is it a free visitation?" were delivered as curious questions in the 1992 radio production, as mocking questions in the 1993 RSC theatre production and sorrowful ones in the 1996 film. In asking these questions, Branagh's 1996 Hamlet is genuinely afraid he might be hurt or disappointed again.

In the scene following the Mousetrap, "S'blood, do you think I am easier to be played on than a pipe" has not really changed over the years. He has always been shouting it furiously, in order to produce a contrast with the suave beginning of this speech. Yet, the delivery of the small cue "Leave me, friends" has developed interestingly from indifference (1992 radio programme), to amusement (1993 stage production), and finally to aggressive irony (1996 film). In his script for the movie, Branagh even writes "friends" between quotation marks.

Compared with his previous stage performances, Branagh's Hamlet of the 1996 film is more restrained and avoids easy sentimentality: Branagh neither jumps down into Ophelia's grave, as he previously did, nor does he weep with her in his arms. Hugh Cruttwell, who coached his performance in the film, saw to this bare way of acting. For example he wanted Branagh to deliver "Alexander died, Alexander was buried . . ." mechanically and unemotionally because, unlike Yorick, Alexander does not belong to Hamlet's personal story. At the end of the film Branagh is less sentimental before dying. He stands for as long as possible before collapsing and does not let Horatio cradle him in a Pieta-like position. The emotion of their farewell has been moved to the earlier "The readiness is all" scene where Horatio holds Hamlet in his arms, falls to his knee, and tries to convince him to decline the duel. Hamlet drops only one tear on "Let be." Here, the two friends say farewell to each other with a dignity that is all the more moving. When the moment to die arrives, there are no desperate gestures. This time Hamlet does not have to wrest the poisoned cup out of his dear friend's hands: the power, the emotion of his words are enough.

Branagh has always wanted to play Hamlet as a man of action. According to Russell Jackson,[54] on the 1996 film set, they never talked about Hamlet's madness. It was always a given that it was feigned. And they never talked about the humour. For instance, from his scene with Polonius to the Hecuba speech, Hamlet is "on." And the issue was mainly to sustain the anger, the bitterness, the energy throughout those scenes.

Over the course of years and in various productions, Branagh has acquired the poetic and princely depth which he lacked early in his "Hamletian" career and has combined it with the anger, comedy, and cynicism that have always been more natural to him. He has been influenced by all the people who directed him in the theatre, especially Derek Jacobi and Adrian Noble. "Hamlet's internal life and my feeling how that might be conveyed is what has developed over the years from various productions," he said.[55] Considering the complexity of Hamlet's character, it is not surprising that Branagh looked to give a solid theatrical performance before tackling his screen adaptation and during the 1993 RSC stage production, his artistic vision came into focus. Branagh talks of this theatre experience in his introduction to the script: "I longed to allow audiences to join Fortinbras on the plain in Norway, to be transported, as Hamlet is in his mind's eye, back to Troy and see Priam and Hecuba."[56] Three years later, his movie will indeed transport the audience to both Norway and Troy. For Branagh, "[Hamlet] is wonderfully imperfect, it's a sort of perfectly drawn piece of imperfection." It is true to say that in his 1996 film Branagh gives us a Hamlet who is complexly human. He can be either heroic or cowardly, sensitive or cruel, funny or stern, brutal or tender.

Notes

1.   Quoted in Clive Hirschhorn, "The Man Who Shot Shakespeare."
2.   Quoted in Anny Crunelle-Vanrigh, "A conversation about *Hamlet*." *Cahiers Elisabéthains* 44 (Oct 1993).
3.   Kenneth Branagh. *Beginning*, p. 69.
4.   Kenneth Branagh. *Beginning*, p. 78.
5.   Quoted in Ian Shuttleworth, *Ken & Em*, p. 72.
6.   Kenneth Branagh. *Hamlet: Screenplay, Introduction and Film Diary*, p. vi.
7.   Quoted in Samuel Crowl, "Hamlet 'Most Royal': An Interview with Kenneth Branagh." *Shakespeare Bulletin*, Fall 1994.
8.   Quoted in Ian Shuttleworth, *Ken & Em*, p. 150.
9.   Michael Billington. "Hamlet without a quandary." *Guardian*, 27 May 1988.
10. Harry Eyres. "Ophelia's night." *London Times*, 9 Sep 1988.
11. Michael Billington. "Hamlet without a quandary."
12. Michael Ratcliffe. Review of *Hamlet*, Renaissance Theatre Company, London. *Observer*, 29 May 1988.
13. Maureen Paton. Review of *Hamlet*, Renaissance Theatre Company, London. *Daily Express*, 17 May 1988.
14. An interview in the video documentary *Discovering Hamlet*. Alexandria, Virginia: PBS Home Video, 1998. A4078-WEBHV.
15. Kenneth Branagh. Liner notes to *Hamlet,* Renaissance Theatre in association with BBC Radio. Random Century Audiobooks, RC 100 (1992).
16. Derek Jacobi. Liner notes to *Hamlet,* Renaissance Theatre in association with BBC Radio. Random Century Audiobooks, RC 100 (1992).
17. An interview with Susan Stamberg at the "Smithsonian's Stellar Shakespeare Weekend," 21 Dec 1996. Folger Library of Washington, DC.
18. Richard Briers. Liner notes to *Hamlet,* Renaissance Theatre in association with BBC Radio. Random Century Audiobooks, RC 100 (1992).
19. Quoted in John Whitley, "Mrs Dale and the Prince of Denmark." *London Times*, 23 Apr 1992.
20. Quoted in Terry Grimley, "Ken slows down for fourth Dane." *Birmingham Post*, 18 Mar 1993.

21. Quoted in Paul Nelsen, "Noble Thoughts on Mighty Experiences: An Interview with Adrian Noble." *Shakespeare Bulletin*, Summer 1993.

22. H. R. Coursen. Review of *Hamlet*, Royal Shakespeare Company, London. *Shakespeare Bulletin*, Spring 1993.

23. Antony Dawson. *Shakespeare in Performance:* Hamlet. Manchester: Manchester University Press, 1995, p. 15.

24. On the internet: www.bbc.co.uk/education/archive/hamlet/ (BBC Education)

25. Antony Dawson. *Shakespeare in Performance:* Hamlet, p. 16.

26. Leaflet accompanying the BBC2 documentary To *Cut or Not to Cut* on Branagh's *Hamlet.* Broadcast on "Learning Zone," Feb 1997.

27. Anny Crunelle-Vanrigh. "A detailed account of *Hamlet*." *Cahiers Elisabéthains* 44 (Oct 1993).

28. Terrence Rafferty. "Solid Flesh." *New Yorker*, 13 Jan 1997.

29. Quoted in Anny Crunelle-Vanrigh, "A conversation about Hamlet."

30. Quoted in Paul Nelsen, "Noble Thoughts on Mighty Experiences: An Interview with Adrian Noble."

31. Kenneth Branagh. *Hamlet: Screenplay, Introduction and Film Diary*, p. 80.

32. Quoted in Anny Crunelle-Vanrigh, "A conversation about Hamlet."

33. Kenneth Branagh. *Hamlet: Screenplay, Introduction and Film Diary*, p. 109.

34. Quoted in Anny Crunelle-Vanrigh, "A conversation about Hamlet."

35. David Andrews. Review of *Hamlet,* Royal Shakespeare Company, London. *Plays & Players*, Feb 1993.

36. Charles Spencer. "A Hamlet of hidden mysteries." *Daily Telegraph*, 21 Dec 1992.

37. Quoted in Samuel Crowl, "Hamlet 'Most Royal': An Interview with Kenneth Branagh."

38. Robert Brustein. "Architectural barriers." *New Republic*, 29 Mar 1993.

39. Samuel Crowl. "Hamlet 'Most Royal': An Interview with Kenneth Branagh."

40. John Peter. "What a piece of work." *Sunday Times*, 27 Dec 1992.

41. An interview with Susanne Stamberg at the "Smithsonian's Stellar Shakespeare Weekend," 21 Dec 1996. Folger Library of Washington, DC.

42. Kenneth Branagh. *Hamlet: Screenplay, Introduction and Film Diary*, p. 16.

43. Quoted in Clive Hirschhorn, "The Man Who Shot Shakespeare."

44. Russell Jackson. "Shakespeare at Stratford-upon-Avon 1993-94." *Shakespeare Quarterly*, Fall 1994.

45. Benedict Nightingale. "Princely noble in lunacy." *London Times*, 21 Dec 1992.

46. Samuel Crowl. "Hamlet 'Most Royal': An Interview with Kenneth Branagh."

47. Quoted in Samuel Crowl, "Hamlet 'Most Royal': An Interview with Kenneth Branagh."

48. Anny Crunelle-Vanrigh. "A detailed account of *Hamlet*."

49. Anny Crunelle-Vanrigh. "A detailed account of *Hamlet*."

50. Samuel Crowl. "Hamlet 'Most Royal': An Interview with Kenneth Branagh."

51. An interview with the author, 19 Apr 1993.

52. Kenneth Branagh. *Hamlet: Screenplay, Introduction and Film Diary*, p. 59.

53. On the internet: www.bbc.co.uk/education/hamlet (BBC Education).

54. An interview with the author in Stratford-upon-Avon, 10 Mar 1997.

55. An interview on the set of *Hamlet* for "Kaleidoscope," BBC Radio 4, 6 Feb 1997.

56. Kenneth Branagh. *Hamlet: Screenplay, Introduction and Film Diary*, p. vii.

> *"What means your lordship?"*
> —Hamlet, III.i

Chapter Four
From Shakespeare's Text to Branagh's Script

This chapter will focus on Branagh's *scripts*, what Branagh added or removed from Shakespeare's texts, how he made his adaptations accessible through line cutting and line reassignment, how he introduces a subtext through interpolated sequences and flashbacks to parallel or background stories.

Henry V: A Cruel and Earnest King

Branagh's *Henry V*, like Olivier's movie fifty years before, tries to make Henry V a hero of his time.

Branagh's intention was twofold: he wanted to defy nationalist and chauvinist interpretations of the play by insisting on the horror of war *and* to make a popular film that would attract a large audience. On the one hand, he wanted to make a "political thriller, a warts-and-all study of leadership, a complex debate about war and the pity of war, an uncompromising analysis of the English class system and of the gulf between male and female attitudes to this type of savage conflict";[1] and on the other hand, he wanted to make "a popular film that [would] both satisfy the Shakespearean scholar and the punter who likes *Crocodile Dundee*."[2] Branagh, in fact, has succeeded in making both. *Henry V* has been a great popular success worldwide without falling into populism.

To achieve this, Branagh has simplified the content of the play. The textual cuts keep the film well-paced and within the commercial length of two hours. Branagh first cut the most difficult aspects of the Pistol–Fluellen antagonism which culminates in the leek scene (Act IV, scene i). For him, putting this scene on screen would not make a modern audience laugh. He also removed redundant passages that slowed the action without adding anything to those aspects of the play he wanted to stress. Branagh thus eliminates the "conjure up Love" discussion between Henry and Burgundy at the end of Act V. Lines containing too many obscure Elizabethan phrases or rhetorical meanings have also been eliminated, "with only the most delicious-sounding phrases escaping sacrifice on the altar of instant understanding."[3] Russell Jackson even invented some verses to replace whole parts of speeches. For example, Henry's long speech to Lord Scroop in the traitors scene (Act II, scene ii) extending from "Treason and murder ever kept together" to "Such and so finely bolted didst thou seem"—which includes the famous "Why, so didst thou" sequence—has been replaced by the single line imagined by Russell Jackson "So constant and unspotted didst thou seem."[4]

One of the main elements of Branagh's textual adaptation is his introduction of three flashbacks, a bold way of clarifying the text and informing the plot.

The first flashback occurs at the mention by Mistress Quickly of Falstaff's illness (Act II, scene i). It presents Falstaff as a figure inspiring fear and respect, reminiscent of a Rembrandt self-portrait. According to Branagh:

> It was important for an audience that might have no previous knowledge of the *Henry IV* plays to have an idea of the background to *Henry V*, and I wanted to achieve the greatest possible impact from Mistress Quickly's speech reporting the death of Falstaff, a character that the audience would not otherwise have encountered.[5]

This first flashback is composed of scenes from the two *Henry IV* plays and recreates the good old days when Falstaff entertained his companions. Falstaff's close and free-wheeling relationship with the young Prince Hal is made clear, as well as his sudden banishment when Henry V ascended the throne.

From Act II, scene iv, of *Henry IV, part 1*, the response to Falstaff's plea "old Jack Falstaff, banish not him," Prince Hal's "I do, I will," is delivered in voice-over by the king. As if he could hear the sentence, Falstaff whispers: "But . . . we have heard the chimes at midnight, Master Harry. Jesus, the days that we have seen."—a line from *Henry IV, part 2* (Act III, scene ii) addressed to Master Shallow in Shakespeare's text. Still in voice-over, Henry gravely and slowly responds with "I know thee not, old man" from *Henry IV, part 2* (Act V, scene v).

Peter Donaldson noticed that, like many scholars, Branagh sees a motherly figure in Falstaff. Branagh includes in this flashback Falstaff's line from *Hanry IV, part 1* (Act III, scene iii) complaining about his skin hanging like "an old lady's loose gown" and in his stage directions, to describe Pistol in the process of recalling Falstaff, Branagh uses the words "caught in the flood of remembrance," a phrase drawn from D. H. Lawrence's poem *Piano*. As we read in Branagh's screenplay:

> *Caught in the flood of remembrance, [Pistol] turns his head towards the fireplace and his expression changes as we hear, as if in a dream:*

> FALSTAFF *(Voice-over)*
> Ay, and of a cheerful look, a pleasing eye
> and a most noble carriage.[6]

D. H. Lawrence's complete sentence, "The glamour / Of childish days is upon me, my manhood is cast / Down in the flood of remembrance, I weep like a child for the past," describes the narrator as unable to love a woman because he remembers the wonderful moments he spent with his mother when he was a child. To recall Falstaff thus is to recall an inhibiting motherly figure.

In fact, it is not surprising that Branagh, consciously or unconsciously, quotes from D. H. Lawrence, because Lawrence has had a great influence on Branagh's artistic and creative development. In 1985, Branagh played the part of young Lawrence in a television film entitled *Coming Through*. In the introduction to *Public Enemy*, Branagh declares his admiration for Lawrence:

> Researching the role [of Lawrence] I re-read a marvellous volume of Lawrence's letters covering the years between his sixteenth and twenty-seventh birthdays, and the insight it gave me into the working of Lawrence's genius encouraged me to try and develop an idea which had absorbed me for some time. I began writing the first draft of *Public Enemy*.[7]

The work of D. H. Lawrence inspired Branagh to express himself artistically in a passionate and intensely romantic way.

The second flashback in *Henry V* occurs just before Bardolph's hanging. We are again transported into the king's past, this time to a drinking bout. With lines from *Henry IV, part 1* (Act I, scene ii) spoken by Falstaff in the original text, Bardolph begs young Hal never to hang a thief when he is king. Henry is filmed apart, looking at the drinkers as if he is anticipating Bardolph's eventual execution. When he delivers his answer "No, thou shalt," the whole assembly is frozen. Bardolph's reaction is filmed in close up. The arms of his friends are around his neck as a strange foreshadow of the upcoming strangling, then the camera indeed cuts to Bardolph's face about to be hanged. For Chris Fitter, "[this] flashback's effect is to prioritize Henry's consciousness over that of Bardolph, simultaneously marginalizing Bardolph while ennobling the king as a hero of pious discipline."[8]

The last flashback occurs at the end of the movie when Burgundy describes the horrors of war (Act V, scene ii). This sequence replays the mental story of King Henry V in a series of faces of all the dead people he has left behind him.

These three flashbacks help to humanize Henry V's character; by giving him memories to face they create a personal story for him. Even though we watch Henry reject his old friends, our sympathy for him is thus won. Moreover, the king's words in voice-over allow us to enter Henry's mind and thus identify more with his character. The treatment of the first flashback is a case in point. At first we feel we are entering the nostalgic memories of Pistol who is remembering Falstaff's death. Yet the speaker we hear in voice-over is not Pistol but Henry. The flashback transforms into Prince Hal's memory and prepares us to follow the story as *his* journey to maturity.

This journey to maturity is also emphasized by Branagh's enlarging the part of Montjoy the French Herald. By reassigning the lines of another French messenger and several French nobles Branagh creates a new Montjoy who becomes the only Frenchman—except maybe for the French King—who respects Henry. In the movie, it is Montjoy and not the noble Rambures who delivers the line "That island of England breeds very valiant creatures" (Act III, scene vii) on the eve of Agincourt. As Montjoy's respect for Henry increases through the course of the film, we recognize and measure the king's evolution.

It is in fact very difficult for the audience to blame Henry. For example, Branagh plays the scene of Bardolph's hanging with deep sadness; we cannot reproach the king for this event, especially after his brave speech to Montjoy: "Yet, God before, tell him we will come on" (Act III, scene vi) which follows immediately after. Moreover, Branagh chooses to end the scene with a touch of desperate humour that enhances our compassion for the king. Just after having told

Gloucester: "We are in God's hand, brother, not in theirs," thunder is heard. Henry looks up to the sky and the rain immediately pours down, like a punishment directly from God.

According to James Loehlin, "Throughout the film, Branagh manages to make negative statements about war reflect positively back upon Henry."[9] Branagh's Henry is always shown sharing the same hard conditions as his men: mud, exhaustion, sickness, long marches with heavy burdens . . . He really is a warrior of the working day, sharing his suffering with his soldiers, and in this he becomes a true modern hero. As Paul Rathburn adds, "[Branagh's] Henry is an icon of the heroism of the common man."[10] For Stuart Klawans, "[He is] more a comrade than a commander"[11] and for Peter Donaldson, "Branagh's Irish working-class identity shows through his stage English, royal persona at strategic moments, giving depth to the king's identification with the common soldiers."[12]

Even when soldier Williams makes the king's authority falter for a time on the eve of the battle, Branagh quickly restores it. Henry's speech in his defence (Act IV, scene i) is largely cut and ends on "Every subject's duty is the King's, but every subject's *soul* is his own," delivered in a prophetic tone. Branagh thus avoids the way this scene alters the audience's sympathy for the king. Moreover, Henry's desperate prayer "O God of battles" shows us that, unlike Laurence Olivier's, Branagh's Henry does not believe that God is necessarily on his side before the battle. Doubt is his motto, and this makes him closer in his sympathies to a modern audience.

For Curtis Breight,[13] Branagh was constantly looking for his internal Hamlet[14] and would have stamped every aspect of Hamlet's part on King Henry. In *Beginning*, Branagh describes his vision of Henry: "He is haunted . . . not just by his father and their troubled relationship, but also by the *ghost* of Richard II"[15] (my emphasis) and in his introduction to the screenplay: "I tried to realize the qualities of introspection, fear, doubt and anger which I believed the text indicated: an especially young Henry with more than a little of the Hamlet in him."[16] It is interesting to note that shooting for *Henry V* began right after the end of the Renaissance theatre run of *Hamlet*. Moreover, on the eve of the first day of *Henry V* filming, Branagh wrote in his diaries of the shooting Horatio's famous line after Hamlet's death: "Good night, sweet prince."[17]

According to Breight, Branagh forces an introspective interpretation on the least reflexive king in all of Shakespeare. Branagh con-

verted the least meditative king into a "complex psychological por-
trait . . . which included guilt, doubt, and self-questioning."[18] For
Breight, "Branagh tries to capture the 'unsettled inner man,' but there
is no inner man to capture. This is no Hamlet but Fortinbras, a man
willing to fight for nothing."[19] According to Breight, the difficulty of
playing Henry V as Hamlet obliged Branagh to seek some advice. In
1984, when Branagh was still a young actor researching the role of
Henry for the Royal Shakespeare Company, his desire to talk to some-
one who had experienced royalty was so great that he managed,
through a variety of contacts and meetings, to be introduced to Charles,
the Prince of Wales, at Kensington Palace. Prince Charles told him
that only religion could help a king find comfort in isolation and loneliness, and this helped convince Branagh to play Henry V not only as
a ruthless killer but above all as a Christian king.

The treason scene is a case in point. When Lord Cambridge says:
"Never was monarch better feared or loved / Than is your majesty"
(Act II, scene ii) Shakespeare alludes directly to Machiavelli's *The Prince*:
"It is far better to be feared than loved if you cannot be both,"[20] pointing to the Machiavellian side of the king. According to Machiavelli, a
prince should endeavour to appear as a man full of compassion, as
well as a religious and earnest man. In this light, Henry V is simply
applying Machiavellian rules to establish his authority: he forgives the
drunk man who laughed at him, he thanks God for helping him discover the conspiracy.

In Shakespeare's time, army captains were being accused of avoiding battles and then killing their men to receive their wages—indeed,
Falstaff does so in *Henry IV, part 1*. Shakespeare's treatment of the battle
of Agincourt was informing against these foul practices and his presentation of Henry V's heroism is not without irony. For Curtis Breight,
Shakespeare's Henry does not try to earn the sympathy of his men,
but instead mystifies war and avoids responsibility for the massive
meaningless slaughter. In this interpretation, Henry spends most of
his time shifting responsibility onto others instead of assuming it
plainly. He rejects it onto Canterbury and onto the Dauphin (Act I,
scene ii), onto the people of Harfleur (Act III, scene iii), onto his very
soldiers, and even onto God (Act IV, scene i).

Branagh has removed this irony from his cinematical treatment.
When Henry says: "We charge you, in the name of God, take heed"
and "May I with *right* and *conscience* make this claim?" (Act I, scene ii,
my emphasis), Branagh is cold and sincere, a ruthless killer as well as

a Christian king. Machiavellianism only appears in the portrayal of the clergymen who are the real manipulators in Branagh's movie. Perhaps in this unflattering characterization of the clergymen we can see Branagh's rejection of the institution of the Catholic Church. Branagh was hurt by the religious problems in Northern Ireland early in his life, and in *Beginning* he admits: "To this day, I dislike churches and organized religion, which make me feel physically ill," and later in an interview: "I associate [churches] with fire and brimstone. I find them oppressive places. They are the most joyless, soulless places."[21]

Branagh's adaptation of Act I, scenes i and ii, is interesting to study because it removes a major ambiguity from the play. In an essay precisely entitled "Textual Ambiguities and Cinematic Certainties in *Henry V*," William Shaw shows how the irony of those two scenes is generally removed when they are treated on stage or film and how Branagh's *Henry V* follows that rule.

These first two scenes in *Henry V* are meant to show evidence of the king's machiavellianism and his gift for manipulation. Act I, scene i, reveals that the clergy have offered the king a great sum of money to convince him to go to war and thus not enact a law against their financial self-interests. The action in scene ii then becomes a brilliant performance from the king, with the clergymen's complicity, to present the nobles with a legitimate reason for his campaign in France. Presented in full these scenes should show a negative image of the king. Yet, both the Olivier and Branagh films have found a way to avoid blotting Henry's alleged noble cause. Olivier succeeds through directorial choices and the actors' performance, and Branagh through textual cuts.

Laurence Olivier begins his *Henry V* on the stage of the Globe Theatre as a filmed play. This allows him to present the king as a theatrical show-off, always giving a performance and never revealing any interior journey. It also allows him to present the clergymen as ridiculous clowns. Olivier cut very few lines from both scenes and retained the reference to the financial offer made to the king and his almost certain acceptance. Yet political machiavellianism was completely suppressed by the comic treatment of the two scenes. How can an audience take seriously clergymen played as shallow clowns who forget their lines and drop their papers? In Olivier's film, the spectators in the Globe Theatre laugh and shout throughout the first two scenes, banishing all seriousness from the introduction. Under these conditions, no duplicity between the king and the clergy is perceived by the audience.

Branagh's film, however, leads us immediately into a world of tension and political stakes. Branagh chooses a serious tone, an atmosphere of political calculations, but manages to blot only the image of the clergymen, making them the nobles' accessories—and not the king's—to convince the young Henry to go to war. The first scene with the clergymen is a conversation in low voices and whispers in a dark room, Canterbury throws distrustful glances, looking for potential spies. The atmosphere is oppressive. The wild days of the king and his sudden transformation are mentioned but much of this is cut in order to emphasize the clergymen's plot to protect their self-interests. According to Branagh, that first scene was "vitally important for establishing . . . the tone of the whole first section of the film. A conspiratorial mood; an unfriendly palace and a dark world beyond."[22] To achieve this, Branagh keeps only twenty-one lines of the first scene, from a total of ninety-eight. We learn that the clergy have made an offer to the king but we do not know anything of the nature of that offer. In Act I, scene ii, Branagh removes the passage which includes Henry's "We would be resolv'd . . . of some things of weight that task our thoughts concerning us and France," eliminating all allusions to a preliminary talk between the king and the bishops about a financial offer.

Moreover, Branagh suggests a secret conspiracy between Canterbury and Exeter to force Henry into a war. After the first words in Act I, scene ii, "Where is my gracious lord of Canterbury?" the camera shows Exeter looking uncomfortably at Henry as if he is anxious and nervous about their plot. When Henry alludes to the possible consequences of war ("Take heed . . ."), Exeter throws an understanding look to Canterbury and then to the other nobles. At the end of the "Salic law" speech, Exeter addresses Canterbury with a nod towards the king, as if saying: "It's the right moment. Persuade him!" Then, the juxtaposition of Canterbury's words "unwind your bloody flag!" with Exeter's ". . . rouse yourself" magnifies this atmosphere of conspiracy. The camera creates a tableau in which each conspirator enters the frame one by one: manipulated Henry is in the foreground, Canterbury enters in the middle ground, then Exeter rises behind him, and Westmoreland comes in the very background.

Direction notes in Branagh's script confirm this hypothesis:

Canterbury pauses briefly beside Exeter, who throws him a threatening glance. It is time to play the only ace.

[. . .]

Uneasy laughter and nervous looks compound the conspiracy to convince the King at all costs.

[. . .]

Now Westmoreland less fierce and calculating than Exeter but just as intent.[23]

Moreover, during the treason scene in the next act, when Henry tells Scroop "That this thy fall hath left a kind of blot, / To mark the full-fraught man and best indued with some suspicion," Henry throws a threatening glance at the nobles. Exeter, Bedford, and Westmoreland suddenly feel uneasy and look guiltily at each other, wondering whether the king is aware of their conspiracy.

Thus, according to William Shaw, "the ambiguity that adds texture and atmosphere to the first two scenes of Branagh's production . . . is the invention of Branagh, not Shakespeare."[24] The conspiracy created by Branagh between Exeter and Canterbury protects Henry's morality. At worst, the viewers may perceive him as naive, but this may only but add to his humanity and fragility.

During the "ceremony" speech (Act IV, scene i), the king's human side is likewise emphasized. Alone at night on the eve of the battle, we indeed feel Henry's doubts and internal dilemmas. Branagh transforms a mere rhetorical defense against soldier Williams' speech in the previous scene into a deep and earnest meditation. Any irony is again removed. At this moment in the play, Henry craves to be like "the wretched slave / who with a body filled and vacant mind / gets him to rest crammed with distressful bread, / never sees horrid night" even though he has just talked with three hungry and sleepless soldiers. Branagh removes the irony with a visual device: at the very moment Henry delivers these lines, we see in the camera frame several soldiers, now asleep, in contrast with the king's painful and tormented watch.

Branagh retains at least one passage from each scene of the original play up to Act IV, scene i, but he cuts some of the subsequent scenes entirely, including some that reveal the king's machiavellianism. As we already saw in Chapter Two, Henry no longer orders the death of the French prisoners.

The glove scene with soldier Williams after the battle (Act IV, scene viii) is reduced to a mere visual moment in Branagh's script:

> [HENRY] *walks over to where WILLIAMS is standing and hands back the glove with which he had challenged him the night before. WILLIAMS takes the glove gratefully, then suddenly realizes that the hooded figure with whom he argued was none other than HENRY himself. Shaking his head in disbelief, he moves out with the others.*[25]

By cutting this text and replacing it with the visual image of a surprised and relieved Williams, Branagh suppresses allusions to the complicated Elizabethan martial law, which exacted death for the most minor offences and which Shakespeare was perhaps denouncing here.

The treatment of the low-lifers in Branagh's movie—Bardolph, Nym, and Pistol—has been perceived by critics in two opposite ways, showing that Branagh has not eliminated all ambiguity from his movie.

For Curtis Breight, the king's old friends seem strangely absent from the "band of brothers" invoked in the St. Crispin's speech: "Branagh's strategy involves making the 'low-lifers' lower than they really are, while simultaneously homogenizing other characters—king, nobility, captaincy, and commons—into fraternal warriors." For Breight, the low-lifers are presented as thieves and corpse robbers while the captains are not corrupted, fight heartily, forget their national and social differences in the blood and mud of the battle, and eventually come out as heroic brothers. Captain Fluellen and Henry are each filmed killing a French soldier in exactly the same way: both are afoot, not on horseback, and pull their sword out of the French soldier's body in slow motion. Branagh thus links Fluellen and Henry even before their moving post-battle embrace. Moreover, the encircling and killing of the Boy, a member of the low-lifers, becomes in the film the tragic impalement of York. The sympathy therefore moved from the low-lifers to the nobles. Finally, when all the soldiers and the captains gather around the king to hear the numbers of dead, a bitter and disillusioned Pistol is shot *aside* leaning on a tree.

For Patricia Salomon,[26] on the contrary, Branagh has included the low-lifers in the "band of brothers" more than in the original play. She speaks of a true *communitas* between the king and his men. It would have made his old friends too nice and too sympathetic, for example, if Branagh had suppressed the scene in which Pistol ill-treats the French soldier Le Fer (Act IV, scene iv) in addition to cutting allusions to their greed ("like horse-leeches, my boys, / To suck, to suck, the very blood to suck!" Pistol says in Act II, scene iii) and cowardice ("You are a counterfeit cowardly knave" is spoken to Pistol in the leek scene). Salomon notes that several robbers are seen on the battlefield during the Non nobis procession, which diminishes Nym and Pistol's previous criminal actions. The comic and foolish aspects of the low-lifers are also suppressed. The leek scene is cut because, according to Branagh, it is "resoundingly unfunny."[27] For Bernice Kliman,[28] this absence of comedy draws more sympathy to the characters of Bardolph, Nym, and Pistol.

Katharine, the French king's daughter, is offered to Henry at the beginning of the play to prevent war. Henry maintains that this is not enough, declines the offer, and sets in motion the invasion of France. Yet, at the end of the play, Henry declares that Katherine is his "capital demand." Although Branagh includes both moments in the film, he hides their irony in the Chorus' distracting, speedy, and chaotic speech under the explosions of the Harfleur siege. As we saw in Chapter Two, Derek Jacobi's Chorus never provides an ironical point of view and does not question the actions or qualities of the king. Instead, he is Henry's ally. This is achieved with the help of massive line cuts and reassignment. Branagh keeps the Prologue and Epilogue almost intact but the Chorus' four speeches at the opening of each act in the original play are split into shorter pieces to work as introductions to scenes throughout the play. For example, in the original text, the Chorus introduces Act II, scene ii, with a forty-two line speech on the Englishmen preparing for war, on the Frenchmen fearing an invasion, and on the nobles' conspiracy. Branagh eliminates the last verses and cuts the speech in two. He uses lines 1–11 to introduce the tavern scene in which Nym, Bardolph and Pistol prepare to leave for war and lines 12–35 to present the conspiracy. This textual change helps the audience in two ways: it gives historical information when and as it is needed, and creates a real narrator who guides us through the story.

Yet, Branagh's textual adaptation contains an irony which was not necessarily intended in the original play. Branagh situates the numbering of the dead (Act IV, scene viii) *after* instead of before, Pistol's desperate speech (Act V, scene i). As a result, we discover a Pistol who has lost his friends, who learns that his beloved wife is dead and that he will not, therefore, be greeted on his return to England. He recalls all the soldiers returned from the wars in our time (especially Vietnam) who, as Norman Rabkin says, "returned home to find their jobs gone, falling to a life of crime in a seamy and impoverished underworld that scarcely remembers the hopes that accompanied the beginning of the adventure." When the king reads the list of the dead, after we have heard Pistol's speech, relief at the few English casualties may strike us with irony. For each dead, indeed, how many survivors will be only shadows of themselves upon their return?

Shakespeare's *Henry V* has always been considered a play that can be read in two opposite ways, extremely patriotic or shrewdly machiavellian. Norman Rabkin stresses this duality: "[Its] power is precisely the fact that it points in two different directions, virtually daring us to choose one of the opposed interpretations it requires of us."[29] Whether Branagh has been right or wrong to emphasize the good aspects of the character of Henry V over the bad ones we cannot say, but simply that, in his adaptation of the Shakespearean text, Branagh has chosen to present an interpretation many critics have had before him, one that sees the king as more pious and sincere than callous and machiavellian.

Those two different visions of the king have been repeated by critics at the release of both Olivier and Branagh's films. Laurence Olivier's movie was seen by critics as either the story of a chivalrous, patriotic, and triumphant king or the story of a calculating leader, always in performance. Branagh's movie divided the critics even more: the film was perceived as pro-war (even fascist), as anti-war, and for a few as a piece of work able to capture both the king's machiavellianism and sincere patriotism.[30]

Despite the reactions of the critics, the notable aspect of Branagh's film is its fundamental deviation from the traditional patriotism–machiavellianism dichotomy. Branagh removes all the political and social ironies of the play and stresses instead the king's psychological state. His performance is not unreservedly patriotic: Henry genuinely doubts, fears unjustly usurping the French crown and sending his soldiers to their deaths. Nor is he machiavellian: Henry reveals his friends' treason within a small group of people not in a public display as a machiavellian prince would do. Branagh's Henry V is a young man learning to be king.

Even though he is presented as a ruthless killer—Branagh retains the traitors scene and Henry's threatening speech to the governor of

Harfleur—he always remains sincere. And in this way Branagh's Henry V really is contemporary. Nowadays an audience prefers a killer obliged to kill for a cause in which he genuinely believes rather than a calculating politician—the very symbol of twentieth-century evil. In fact, in the word association game with a journalist at Cannes in 1993, Branagh himself answered the word "evil" with "Nixon."[31]

Michael Manheim sums it up best when he writes:

> It is very much a Henry for our time because what once seemed to us like noble image and sentiment—the wartime utterances of a Winston Churchill or a Franklin Roosevelt, the charms of a John Kennedy . . . now seem to many like façades. Knowing that political leaders, to one extent or another, all have followed the principles of *The Prince* in order to succeed, machiavellianism as a theme of political drama no longer has the appeal it did at mid-century. What now strikes home more deeply than the story of the subtle leader making war is that of the sincere leader making war.[32]

Branagh's textual adaptation perfectly inserts itself in its time.

Much Ado About Nothing: The Purity of Rhythm

Much Ado About Nothing marks a second stage in Branagh's filmic development. The movie recalls the theatre less than does *Henry V* and goes joyfully beyond the boundaries of a light stage comedy.

If with *Henry V* Branagh had to convince us that a modern screen adaptation was both possible and relevant, with *Much Ado About Nothing* he must prove that Shakespeare is a successful screenwriter. In fact, Branagh begins his film with Shakespeare's words on screen. He commented:

> The idea of seeing the words and hearing them spoken right at the beginning of the film . . . allows the audience to "tune in" to the new language they are about to experience and to realize . . . that they will easily understand.[33]

The effect of Beatrice reciting the "Sigh No More, Lady" lyrics as they appear on the screen also provides a kind of overture. Not only does it help the audience "tune in" to the language, but it immediately gives clues to her character and her opinions about relationships between men and women, and it introduces both the Beatrice–Benedick plot line and a major thematic element of the story.

The textual cutting in *Much Ado About Nothing,* above all else, moves the plot forward more rapidly. For Branagh a comedy should never last beyond two hours because "there's a certain time people [can] laugh for."[34] The opening scene has thus been shortened to bring us as quickly as possible to the soldiers' arrival. With Benedick and Claudio's imminent appearance on horseback, Branagh felt it unnecessary to spend too much time describing them in the introductory scene. Throughout, Branagh's cuts spare no passage in which characters re-establish the situation, repeat what has happened so far, or what will soon occur.

For the Dogberry scenes, Branagh cut lines whose comedy is dated or out of sync with a modern sense of humour. In 1988, he played Touchstone in *As You Like It* and transformed himself into a loud and extravagant music hall comedian in order to convey the old gags to a modern audience. On the screen, Branagh did not want to risk retaining this kind of humour. He told journalist Charlie Rose at the film's release: "I played a few Shakespearean clowns, and there are lots of four-hundred-year-old gags that don't work, believe me. So, we trimmed."[35]

In his script, Branagh cut Don Pedro's lines after Hero's funeral (Act V, scene iii) to maintain a purely musical transition from Bathalsar singing a hymn to the dead Hero to Benedick trying vainly to sing one of his poems (transposed in the film from Act V, scene ii). We can note once again that Benedick here tries to express his true feelings through singing instead of talking. Ellen Edgerton cogently said: "Is it any wonder that, in Branagh's conception, Friar Francis (the voice of reason) and the lowly Watch (the alert agents of rescue) are all musicians?"[36] Friar Francis plays the guitar to accompany Bathasar's songs, while the Watchmen provide a chorus to the "Sigh No More" sequence in the garden. Branagh demonstrates the power of music to convey the truth. The diegetic music in *Much Ado About Nothing* helps the characters to confide their feelings and allows the truth to be revealed.

Some lines from Beatrice and Benedick's famous gulling scenes (Act II, scene iii, and Act III, scene i) were cut to transform the scenes into one long, continuous sequence in the same garden. Branagh wanted to remove the formalism and repetition at the end of the first scene and the beginning of the second one. According to him, "it helped the believability of the two characters' falling for each other so swiftly."[37]

Moreover, the easiness of the transition takes some pressure off the women actors who, in the theatre, have the difficult task of following the men's funnier gulling scene.

It is interesting to note that the scene in which the women gather in Hero's room the morning before the wedding ceremony (Act III, scene iv) was shot by Branagh and then removed from the final cut. Test audiences found the scene frustrating and thought it held the action back. The night events in which the audience actually *saw* Claudio fall into Don John's trap led to a tremendous impatience to see the results of this deception at the wedding. Russell Jackson feels it is a shame this scene was cut because it is one of the few where the *women* can be seen as a group and it would have counterbalanced the many scenes where the men are filmed together.

Scenes have also been moved or transposed to better fit the logic and rhythm of a movie. For example, to draw more dramatic intensity out of the night scenes on the eve of the wedding, the scene in which Don John and Borachio are setting up their conspiracy (Act II, scene iii) has been moved to *after* the gulling of Benedick and Beatrice. This helps evenly distribute Don John's appearances through the movie but·also gathers together all the conspiracy events in one "fatal" night. Likewise, the Watchmen scene (Act III, scene iii) has been split and the first part of moved up so that Dogberry's comic character first appears earlier in the story. Don John's stratagem works: Claudio is convinced he sees Hero being unfaithful. Then the script returns to the second part of the Watchmen scene in which the guards put Borachio and Conrad under arrest. Thanks to this textual change, the night events occur with a true film logic.

Branagh's decision to put on screen the scene in which Claudio witnesses Hero's unfaithfulness was also motivated by the logic of film:

> There are certain levels of coincidence that occur in a theatrical production that a film logic doesn't quite buy. For instance, this duping of Claudio normally occurs offstage. . . . Whereas in the film, I think the audience could legitimately say: "eh, why don't we go and see that? Why aren't we being told?" So, we put that on screen and I think it also helped to understand if not forgive Claudio's very violent reaction to it.[38]

In Branagh's script, we read:

Exterior / INNER COURTYARD / WELL / Night
DON JOHN, DON PEDRO, and CLAUDIO's point of view. In
silhouette, we can see BORACHIO and MARGARET making love.
CLAUDIO lets out a cry and makes to run at them but is held by
DON PEDRO and DON JOHN. All three are shaking.

DON JOHN *(Intense, emotional)*
The lady is disloyal!
If you love her, then, tomorrow wed her. But it
would better fit your honour to change your
mind.

Close on CLAUDIO. Tears in angry eyes. DISSOLVE.[39]

This scene, created by Branagh, makes Claudio more likable in the audience's eyes. Branagh films the scene from Claudio's point of view, in a low angle shot, showing the audience how easy it is to confuse Margaret with Hero. Don John's lines from Act III, scene ii, which occurs before the balcony incident, are imported into this new scene. With this transposition, along with the ocular proof, the statement "The lady is disloyal" is all the more convincing. Claudio's tears are then shot in close-ups, which develops our sympathy even further. Branagh also cuts a whole section of Act V, scene i, when Benedick challenges Claudio which gave the impression indeed that Claudio was too insensitive to Hero's death.

In fact, almost all the critics have perceived the character of Claudio in Branagh's movie as Samuel Crowl does: "an insecure boy whose face is flushed by confusion and embarrassment as quickly as it is colored by the blush of romance."[40] This approach to the character appears as early as the opening scene. Claudio's question to Don Pedro: "Hath Leonato any son, my lord?" which can imply Claudio is more interested in Leonato's inheritance than his daughter, has not been cut in the film, but it is delivered in a conversational tone of honest inquiry, without any hidden pecuniary thoughts. As Russell Jackson made clear in the programme for the 1988 Renaissance production of *Much Ado About Nothing:* "[During Elizabethan times], his enquiry whether Hero can expect to inherit was unlikely to be taken in itself as a sign that he is a shallow or unfeeling young man." Branagh has insisted on this feeling of an ordinary question asked without guile.

With his screen adaptation, through camera choices, Branagh has also made all the small characters such as the Friar, the Watchmen and Leonato's household live, in both a realistic and evocative landscape. Friar Francis is seen several times playing the guitar in the fields and gardens. The Watchmen also sing during the Balthasar's "Sigh No More" sequence and all Leonato's household becomes agitated in every dramatic moment: the soldiers' arrival, Hero's rejection at the altar, and the final dance.

Considered for adaptation, Branagh thinks Shakespeare's comedies are open to radical and subjective views even more than the historical plays which have a stricter narrative frame. In fact, the very titles themselves—*Twelfth Night, or What You Will* and *As You Like It*—invite directors to be bold. But *Much Ado About Nothing*'s textual adaptations raise less issues than *Henry V* and result in few changes of meaning and interpretation. Branagh's cuts make for a well-paced movie and the textual transpositions for a true film logic. Except perhaps for Claudio whose ambiguity has been flattened in favour of a more sympathetic character, the movie follows more or less a traditional approach to performing the play. *Much Ado About Nothing*, even more than *Henry V*, is a film whose gaiety, *joie de vivre,* and naturalness, has allowed an extremely large and diversified public to discover Shakespeare. Moreover, as a model Hollywood romance featuring Hollywood stars, it is one of the most profitable Shakespearean screen adaptations in the past decade and is known as the film which contributed most to Shakespeare's current revival.

Hamlet: The Monument

With his adaptation of *Hamlet*, the main question is not the cuts or simplifications, but rather Branagh's decision to preserve every line and word. Why the complete text of the play when even stage productions are often shorter, amended versions?

Branagh's two previous experiences with the uncut version in 1992 and 1993 convinced him that a film using the full text would be easier to watch. Some scenes would work as natural pauses and allow the audience to assimilate what had happened so far. It avoids having the big scenes bang up against each other and swamp the audience under a flood of energy and information. Branagh also appreciated the perfect construction of the play. For him, "Everything connects in this piece. Everything."[41]

The full text helps us understand both the domestic and political elements of the play. The film clearly shows Elsinore preparing for war when Horatio explains the political situation to Marcellus and Barnardo at the beginning of the story. As Branagh says, "Claudius has more than a Hamlet problem, there's [a] Fortinbras problem."[42] This "Fortinbras problem" will reveal itself to be huge indeed, as the Norwegian prince eventually takes possession of the castle by force. His soldiers break into the hall through the windows just after the duel between Hamlet and Laertes. Here the political meets the domestic. Fortinbras's military coup also makes for a finale that preserves the emotional peak of the sword fight until the very end.

In Laurence Olivier's 1948 film adaptation, the parts of Fortinbras, Rosencrantz, and Guildenstern were completely cut. In 1990, Zeffirelli restored the two friends in his *Hamlet* starring Mel Gibson; they had become too famous since the success of Tom Stoppard's play *Rosencrantz and Guildenstern are Dead* to leave out. These two characters help explain Hamlet's suffering, showing him betrayed by his close friends. Yet, Zeffirelli followed Olivier in his suppression of Fortinbras' character, thus removing one of Hamlet's foils. Like Hamlet, Fortinbras has an uncle on the throne and has just lost his father, but Fortinbras can wage a war for a mere "straw," while Hamlet weighs the death of a single man. Seeing himself reflected in Fortinbras before leaving for England may be what gives Hamlet the courage to return to Elsinore to face his destiny.

The Hamlets of Mel Gibson and Kenneth Branagh are both clearly distinct from Olivier's. In 1948, nobody would have accepted a whining Hamlet, while in the nineties, Gibson and Branagh let the flood of their emotions comes out. Moreover, if Olivier's movie features a chaste and Oedipal Hamlet, the two Hamlets of the nineties openly display their sexuality. Gibson assails Gertrude in an almost sexual way and Branagh inserts flashbacks of Hamlet and Ophelia in tender lovemaking.

Branagh's vision for his 1996 movie is founded on a simple premise:

> It's nongothic, nongloomy. The film is bright and full of—wherever it can be—hope. I do not feel these are people who are melancholic. These are vibrant people, alive people. People in crisis, certainly, but who are not self-indulgent. I'd say that we are less tolerant of self-indulgence now.[43]

When Mollie's character in *In the Bleak Midwinter* learns about her brother's intent to produce *Hamlet*, she fears that he will face a wall of misunderstanding:

Great. Hello kids. Do stop watching *Mighty Morphin' Power Rangers* and come and watch a four-hundred-year-old play about a depressed aristocrat. I mean it's something you can really relate to.[44]

Branagh's version directly answers this criticism and shows how much Hamlet's doubts are still relevant and close to us.

As in *Henry V*, Branagh inserts flashbacks to stamp events and characters more firmly onto the audience's mind. Yet unlike *Henry V*, he adds images to illustrate words, sentences, or whole bits of speeches, providing a more varied visual texture and clarity to the text. Sometimes, a flashback raises further questions: is it a flashback bringing us back to a real past, a remembered past, or is it merely an illustration of what a character is saying? Who sees these images: the one who delivers the words or the one who hears them?

Branagh's use of illustrations and flashbacks is clearly different from Olivier's, which show those offstage events reported by characters. Branagh doesn't show us the distracted Hamlet coming into Ophelia's room and then going out still looking at her (reported by her in Act II scene i), or the pirates' attack at sea (reported in Hamlet's letter, Act IV, scene vi), or Ophelia romantically floating along the river before drowning (reported by Gertrude, Act IV, scene vii), although we see one image of her, already dead, still underwater.

In Branagh's *Hamlet*, the flashbacks are there to make explicit a situation (for example, the intimate relationship between Hamlet and Ophelia) or to accustom the audience to characters who are only evoked in words or rarely present in the original play. From the outset of the film, images of Fortinbras illustrate Horatio's speech and the report of Claudius's messengers. When the Prince of Norway eventually takes possession of the Danish throne at the end of the play, he is already a familiar character. In the same way, we also see Hamlet's father, Yorick the jester, and the King of Norway.

Branagh included Claudius's murder of Old Hamlet, in a sequence of interpolated flashbacks, with close-ups on the infected ear and on the king's painful spasms, for several reasons. First, it relieves the pressure on the actor playing Hamlet to react to the ghost's words through his long speech. Branagh has always found it difficult to play this scene (Act I, scene v) and thinks it is easy for an actor to fall into exaggerated acting. Moreover, presenting the murder on screen helps enormously to convey the urgency of Hamlet's mission and the importance of the issue he must face. It also allows for visual texture in a rather long scene which, for Branagh, "seemed to cry out for some kind of illustration."[45]

Some critics have complained that this way of filming destroys all the suspense in the story: it reveals the ghost's honesty and Claudius's guilt too soon. Yet, according to Branagh, the flashback is not necessarily real but only illustrates the ghost's words: "although we present it in screen terms, Hamlet has only the ghost's word for it."[46] A case in point of the ambiguity created by such illustrations. But whatever the nature of those images, they create sympathy for the ghost of Hamlet's father and take us back to the 1993 theatre production in which the spectre's honesty was not at issue.

The interpolated images clarify the characters' words as well as their actions. When the spectre reveals his horrible secret to his son, a flashback shows us a moment from the past when the king, his wife, Claudius, and Hamlet are playing curling in Elsinore's corridors. Claudius has already begun to seduce the Queen. A shot of a hand hastily unlacing a corset illustrates the "shameful lust" described by the ghost.

During the First Player's speech (Act II, scene ii), Branagh inserts a sequence in which, among the ruins of Troy, we watch Hecuba discover Pyrrhus killing her husband Priam and howl in pain. With that scene, Branagh wanted to transport the audience in the same way that Hamlet is transported by the mere power of speech, transported to a time when actions were more heroic and full of destiny. He thus shows us the immense power of imagination, in fact, the same power which Hamlet hopes, when Claudius is confronted with the play, will "catch the conscience of the King."

One of the strongest choices in Branagh's direction was to present a sexual relationship between Ophelia and Hamlet. Branagh justifies it as a natural reaction to the death at the heart of the play:

> When Hamlet came back [from Wittenberg], he was in the midst of grief which does extraordinary things to people. There's often a huge urge to celebrate the life force. People become involved in physical relationships in a surprising way in the wake of these traumatic losses.[47]

As Gertrude would have found in Claudius a man who understands her, loves her, and allows her to remain Queen, Hamlet would have found the same comfort in Ophelia's arms.

Branagh has also pursued the idea that this was Ophelia's first physical relationship, charged with all kinds of expectations and feelings. Polonius's order forbidding her to see Hamlet thus becomes even more cruel and painful. Moreover, the potential happiness in the love between Ophelia and Hamlet makes for a greater tragedy when Ophelia eventually goes mad. For Branagh, the intimacy of the relationship also explains Ophelia's madness: her beloved father is murdered by the man with whom she made love for the first time. It also lends more believability to Hamlet's feelings when he shouts at the funeral: "I loved Ophelia. Forty thousand brothers / Could not, with all their quantity of love, / Make up my sum" (Act V, scene i) even after we watched his ruthless rejection of her during the nunnery scene.

Ophelia's madness is treated in the film in accord with the nineteenth century's very cruel methods: confinement, straitjackets, cold showers . . . Ophelia chooses, if not suicide, at least escape in reaction to her hardships. After Horatio receives Hamlet's letter, he glances into the cell where Ophelia is being given a forced shower, but he does not notice what the camera reveals only to us: from her mouth, Ophelia takes out a small key she has stolen in order to escape and end her sufferings.

Branagh has again moved some scenes and lines to different places in order to achieve the rhythm of a movie.

When the ghost appears to Horatio, Marcellus, and Hamlet, Hamlet's speech beginning "Angels and ministers of grace defend us!" (Act I, scene iv) is moved, which brings together Horatio's two cues: "Look, my lord, it comes. . . . It beckons you to go away with it." The "Angels and ministers" speech is moved down to the next scene just before "Whither wilt thou lead me? Speak. I'll go no further," and spoken while a distressed Hamlet is running through the woods. The speech is illustrated with images from Old Hamlet's funeral. Images from the father's burial slip though the son's bewildered run and create a more disturbing and supernatural feeling. This transposition speeds up the pace and allows a rather long speech to be animated by brisk action.

At the end of the "pipe" scene, after Hamlet dismisses Polonius (Act III, scene ii), the scene cuts directly to Claudius's delivering of "I like him not, nor stands it safe with us / To let his madness range" (Act III, scene iii), this enhances the feverish, thriller elements of the story. Then, when Claudius moves into the chapel to begin his confession, the camera comes back to Hamlet for "'Tis now the very witching time of night."

Several small cues not in Shakespeare's original text have been added by Branagh.

Polonius calls "Ophelia!" after his long report to Claudius and Gertrude on Hamlet's supposed madness (Act II, scene ii). This creates a transition to the next lines where Ophelia—and not Polonius, as in the original play—reads Hamlet's letter to her.

"My Lord!" which Ophelia shouts at Hamlet after he has killed Polonius reminds the audience of the familial tragedy that Hamlet has just brought about.

The advice "Stay!" which Hamlet whispers to Horatio before leaving for England, explains why Horatio does not follow his dear friend into exile even though, at the end of the story, he wants to follow him into death. In the same way that Hamlet forbids Horatio to drink the poisoned cup, he gives him notice to stay at court.

"Attack!" shouted by one of Elsinore's guards when he catches sight of Fortinbras' charging army, increases the thriller element again. The scream is quickly interrupted by a smack from an assailing soldier.

With his 1996 film, Branagh has given a cinematographic rhythm to *Hamlet* in spite of its length. He illustrates the characters' words as often as possible, clarifying meanings and circumstances, and avoiding fixed, monotonous images. Some critics have accused Branagh of not trusting the text enough, and allowing the words themselves to create images in the audience's minds. It is true that in *Henry V* the threatening speech to the governor of Harfleur needs no illustrations for the audience to feel they have seen the rapes and assaults described. Yet, *Hamlet* is a text of unmatched density and richness; certainly its speeches are longer than in *Henry V*. Not expecting his audience to have read or seen the play before, Branagh has attempted to enhance their experience of Shakespeare's poetry. The illustrations work as landmarks throughout the story, give a context to the words, and participate in creating an original and accessible vision of the play.

Notes

1. Kenneth Branagh. *Henry V: A Screen Adaptation*, p [??].
2. Press kit for the release of the film *Henry V*.
3. Kenneth Branagh. *Henry V: A Screen Adaptation*, p. 11.
4. An interview with the author in Stratford-upon-Avon, 10 Mar 1997. Russell Jackson told me this verse was unconsciously created from a line in *A Midsummer Night's Dream* (Act 1, scene i, line 110): "Upon this spotted and inconstant man."
5. Kenneth Branagh. *Henry V: A Screen Adaptation*, p. 12.

6. Kenneth Branagh. *Henry V: A Screen Adaptation*, p. 32–33.
7. Kenneth Branagh. *Public Enemy*. London and Boston: Faber and Faber, 1988, p. vii.
8. Chris Fitter. "A Tale of Two Branaghs: Henry V, Ideology and the Mekong Agincourt." *Shakespeare Left and Right*, edited by Ivo Kamps. London: Routledge, 1991.
9. James Loehlin. *Shakespeare in Performance:* Henry V.
10. Paul Rathburn. "Branagh's Iconoclasm: Warriors for the Working Day." *Shakespeare on Film Newsletter*, Apr 1991.
11. Stuart Klawans. "Films." *Nation*, 11 Dec 1989.
12. Peter Donaldson. "Taking on Shakespeare: Kenneth Branagh's *Henry V*."
13. Curtis Breight. "Branagh and the Prince, or a 'royal fellowship of death,'" *Critical Quarterly* 33.4 (1991).
14. Branagh's autobiography ends with the words "The readiness is all."
15. Kenneth Branagh. *Beginning*, p. 137.
16. Kenneth Branagh. *Henry V: A Screen Adaptation*, p. 9–10.
17. Kenneth Branagh. *Beginning*, p. 222.
18. Kenneth Branagh. *Beginning*, p. 143.
19. Curtis Breight, "Branagh and the Prince, or a 'royal fellowship of death'."
20. Curtis Breight, "Branagh and the Prince, or a 'royal fellowship of death'."
21. Quoted in Ginny Dougary, "Oh, what a roguish and peasant slave." *Times Saturday Review*, 21 Nov 1992.
22. Kenneth Branagh. *Beginning*, p. 223.
23. Kenneth Branagh. *Henry V: A Screen Adaptation*, p. 23.
24. William Shaw. "Textual Ambiguities and Cinematic Certainties in *Henry V*." *Film Literature Quarterly*, no. 2, 1994.
25. Kenneth Branagh. *Henry V: A Screen Adaptation*, p. 113.
26. Patricia Salomon. "The Sentimentalizing of Communitas in Kenneth Branagh's *Henry V*." *Shakespeare Bulletin*, Winter 1995.
27. Kenneth Branagh. Introduction. *Henry V: A Screen Adaptation*.
28. Bernice Kliman. "Branagh's Henry: Allusion and Illusion." *Shakespeare on Film Newsletter*, Dec 1989.
29. Norman Rabkin. *Shakespeare and the Problem of Meaning*. Chicago: Chicago University Press, 1981.
30. For this last interpretation, see Sara Munsn Deats, "Rabbits and ducks." *Literature Film Quarterly* 20.1 (Oct 1992).
31. An interview on "Le Journal du Cinéma," broadcast on Canal+ (in French) by Isabelle Giordanno in May 1993.
32. Michael Manheim. "The English history play on screen," p. 130.
33. Kenneth Branagh. *Much Ado About Nothing: Screenplay, Introduction and Notes on the Making of the Film*, p. xiv.
34. An interview with Charlie Rose, May 1993.
35. An interview with Charlie Rose, May 1993.
36. Ellen Edgerton. "'Your answer, Sir, Is Cinematical': Kenneth Branagh's *Much Ado About Nothing*." *Shakespeare Bulletin*, Winter 1994.
37. Kenneth Branagh. *Much Ado About Nothing: Screenplay, Introduction and Notes on the Making of the Film*, p. xv.
38. An interview with Charlie Rose, May 1993.

39. Kenneth Branagh. *Much Ado About Nothing: Screenplay, Introduction and Notes on the Making of the Film*, p. 56.

40. Samuel Crowl. "*Much Ado About Nothing*." *Shakespeare Bulletin*, Summer 1993.

41. Quoted in David Patrick Stearns, "He unveils epic visions of *Hamlet*." *USA Today*, 7 Jan 1997.

42. An interview with Susanne Stamberg at the "Smithsonian's Stellar Shakespeare Weekend," 21 Dec 1996.

43. Al Weisel, "Idol Chatter: Kenneth Branagh." *Premiere*, Dec 1996.

44. Kenneth Branagh. *In the Bleak Midwinter*, p. 23.

45. An interview with Susanne Stamberg at the "Smithsonian's Stellar Shakespeare Weekend," 21 Dec 1996.

46. An interview with Susanne Stamberg at the "Smithsonian's Stellar Shakespeare Weekend," 21 Dec 1996.

47. An interview with Susanne Stamberg at the "Smithsonian's Stellar Shakespeare Weekend," 21 Dec 1996.

Chapter Five
Images, Action and Movement:
The Cinematic Adaptation

In an interview with Samuel Crowl during the 1993 stage production of *Hamlet* Branagh tells of an improvisation one night with Joanne Pearce (Ophelia):

> We had a good moment there last night, actually. A bit of a break-through in terms of clarity of storytelling. As I was delivering the lines about the power of beauty to transform honesty from what it was to a bawd, I picked up one of the letters and then used it as a concrete object to underscore "I did love you once."[1]

Given a statement like this, which shows Branagh striving to make every single line a visual, literal reality, it is no surprise he is inclined to transform Shakespeare's plays into films. Even the plays he has directed on stage have been filled with visual and realistic effects. He had, for example, real water pouring down during the storm scenes in his 1990 Renaissance production of *King Lear*.

In fact, the medium of film is used by Branagh to extend what the stage cannot. Notably, the flashback in *Henry V* in which Henry remembers his former friend Bardolph before ordering his execution, expands the moment on the RSC stage in 1984 when Henry stood still for a silent minute, looking at Bardolph before he was garotted by Exeter. What, on stage, was a moment of silence in which the audience could only guess the sadness of the king, becomes, thanks to the medium of film, access to the king's memories and helps us understand the effort the execution demands of Henry. In *Hamlet*, film again permits Branagh to explore both the most intimate aspects of the play—Ophelia and Hamlet's relationship—as well as the most epic ones—the marching of Fortinbras' army and the attack of the palace.

This chapter will examine Branagh's cinematography, his choice of lighting and colours, camera angles and editing, and how they are deployed to illustrate with images and bring meaning to his Shakespearean movies.

Henry V: Mud and Blood

When a film adaptation of *Henry V* is considered, a question quickly arises: since film allows for absolute realism, is the Prologue, in which the Chorus apologizes for the inability of Shakespeare's bare stage to adequately represent the fields of France, the charge of horses and the Battle of Agincourt, needed? In his 1944 film, Laurence Olivier justified the presence of the Chorus by beginning his movie on the bare stage of the Globe Theatre, as if we were attending a play in Shakespeare's time.

But what about Branagh's film, which starts in a deserted film studio? Branagh's Chorus is justified, I suggest, given the structure and form of his movie. *Henry V* is, indeed, far from a movie with great technical effects. The setting of the Harfleur siege is just one well-lighted and smoky wall. The French army's charging at Agincourt is filmed with medium shots so that we see in the frame no more than four or five French nobles looking down at the "poor condemned English" from the top of a hill. This low-angle shot alone suggests the feeling of an overpowering French army. The Saint Crispin speech is literally addressed to a "band of brothers," to some "happy few," as the English army is also filmed in close-up. Even the battle of Agincourt needed a minimum of extras: the camera is always following small groups of fighters. In fact, only the *"Non nobis"* sequence, when Henry walks through the battlefield after the battle, shows us the entire setting. Bernice Kliman noticed this aspect of the movie:

> Whenever the film shows us a room setting, it keeps so tight a rein on the camera that we rarely see the whole. A bit of wall or ceiling, a prop or two, warm lighting and we imagine the rest. . . . Even when the film moves to location settings, the camera denies us broad vistas, maintaining almost always the image in near long shot at most, and more often depending on close-ups and medium close-ups. The film has no establishing shots for its settings, that is, high angle-shots that reveal the whole world.[2]

The lack of wide, panoramic, establishing shots is, of course, partly due to practical reasons. *Henry V* was Branagh's first movie as a director, and the budget of four million pounds, as well as the shooting time, seven weeks, were limited for a historical feature film. In Branagh's *Henry V*, the Chorus does not apologize for the bare stage as he did in Olivier's *Henry V*, but for the poor technical means the movie could afford. Nonetheless, these restrictions do not hamper the effectiveness of the film, or inhibit our sense of the scale and grandeur of the drama, nor our ability to fully imagine the scenes. In fact, even though most of *Henry V* is composed of close or medium shots, some people—even film critics used to analyzing images—felt they had seen something grand. The tight shots on the soldiers' faces are so suggestive that Nicolas Saada, in *Les Cahiers du Cinéma*, writes of "these array of technical means, extras, setting, and sound effects producing a spectacular show."[3] It is almost as if the advice the Chorus gives us at the beginning—"on your imaginary forces work"—has successfully influenced many who saw the movie! From close shots, they have imagined epic and grand shots.

While Lawrence Olivier's *Henry V* was very colourful—inspired by medieval miniatures—luminous, impetuous, and displayed across a panoramic space, Branagh's *Henry V* limits itself to a palette of primary colours and a succession of medium and close shots. The camera, above all, films the actors and captures their facial expressions: the tears of Mistress Quickly; the dirty faces of Bardolph, Pistol, and Nym; the gravity of the French King; the pride and arrogance of the Dauphin.

All the actors have taken advantage of these close shots to give rich, powerful, and accessible performances. This method of filming also helps Branagh perform Henry as a "Hamletian"; through close-ups, voice-overs, and flashbacks, Branagh is able to demonstrate the introspection of the king.

Branagh knew that the music was going to be essential to the film's success. The music had to be "classically rich in tone but instantly accessible."[4] Branagh did not want authentic medieval sounds: "I encouraged [Patrick Doyle] to be as bold as possible. The film was taking what I believed to be legitimate historical licence with costumes, sets, and military details. I wanted the musical approach to be equally uninhibited . . . And always, always encouraged size: the epic approach, thunderous, full-blooded, heroic size."[5]

When the first words appear on the screen, written in red on a black background, Doyle's first musical phrases are distant, ghostlike flutes. Patrick Doyle originally composed this music for an overture scene that was cut from in the movie. Branagh had wanted to open the film with a pan across the French coast, continuing on the English coasts, and ending on the meditative face of King Henry, thinking in voice-over the "hollow crown" soliloquy from *Richard II*.

The bare and simple music was inspired by the image of this lonely king facing the sea and throughout the movie it helps the audience perceive the king's doubts and feel his loneliness. James Loehlin comments that "the 'Upon the King' speech . . . is backed up by music which makes Henry's isolation heroic and Hamlet-like."[6] In composing this musical theme, Doyle explains he was thinking of Jesus alone in the garden of Gethsemane:

> What I thought of Henry V is that he is in constant deliberation. He has tough decisions to make. I saw him like Jesus in the Garden of Gethsemane. The King knows he has been betrayed and he has this continuous turmoil to keep him awake. Those recurrent thoughts was what maybe made me think of a recurrent motif. The relentless worrying.[7]

Like Jesus, Henry has been betrayed indeed by his closest friends. Like Jesus, he prays all night long to be able to face tomorrow's suffering. The machiavellian king is far away; here rather, is a heroic and martyred king.

Henry V plays itself out between two monumental doors. The Chorus delivers the Prologue ironically, in a deserted movie studio where we can spot props used later in the film. Then, the Chorus opens wide the huge wooden door that separates the present from the past, reality from fiction. He does so with an almost diabolical vehemence which contrasts with the kindness of his words: "Your humble patience pray, / Gently to hear, kindly to judge, our play!" At the end of the movie, Derek Jacobi's Chorus closes the door again this time quietly in order to finish the film with dignity and solemnity.

The first entrance of the king makes use of this recurrent door motif. A majestic shadowy figure wearing a long cape enters through an impressive doorway, almost gliding towards the camera while the music soars. A succession of candlelit close-ups show the courtiers' reactions and demonstrates that the king's is a constantly observed, public life. Only when the music stops does the camera reveal to the audience the king's face. Filmed in a medium shot on his throne, he takes off his cape. He looks very pale and extremely young. The juxtaposition of this harmless figure with the Wagnerian god of the previous shot is striking. Here Branagh's approach is opposite to Olivier's, in which the king first appeared as a nervous actor clearing his throat before growing to a god of the stage in his emphatic delivery of the play's first lines. Branagh instead shows the power of the king's position before reminding us immediately of his human and fragile condition.

This door motif punctuates Branagh's entire movie, marking transitions between scenes and indicating changes in power. The door of Princess Katherine's room, as well, marks a frontier in the political battle. In her secluded pastel-coloured room, the princess seems protected from the war. Yet, at the end of her English lesson, she opens the door to the corridor at the very moment her stern-faced father walks by. The reaction shots stress the difference between the princess's eager anticipation and the constraints endured by her father. The English tongue has already penetrated the French castle, anticipating the victory of Henry.

The threatening ultimatum speech to the governor of Harfleur is filmed in a low-angle shot and in close-up. Henry's isolation, together with his brutal images and harsh words, somehow intensifies his possible destructive power. When Henry shouts: "Your naked infants spitten upon pikes," the camera fixes his tormented face, covered with dirt, mud, and ashes. During the speech, shots on the king are interrupted by long travelling shots of the English soldiers. They do not look like the "blind and bloody soldiers" to which Henry refers, but they seem to become aware of their own destructive power. The dramatic force of the scene is intense and overwhelming.

This method of interrupting the king's speech with shots of his soldiers also appears during the "Once more unto the breach" speech, which contains six reaction shots followed by a succession of quicker shots right at the end of the speech, and during the St. Crispin's speech, which has three reaction shots followed by another series of shots of enthusiastic soldiers at the end. Those reactions to the King's words are filmed in medium and close angle. As Bernice Kliman points out: "this film is less about action than about responding to action."[8] Because the soldiers' faces reflect such an unreserved approval of the king's words, the audience is also persuaded to follow Henry. During "Once more unto the breach," Pistol is indeed so moved that he brings his hand to his throat; and Williams, hearing "And you, good yeomen," draws out his sword heartily.

The treatment of Bardolph's hanging includes brief shots of the condemned man inserted between longer shots on the king, emphasizing again the king's and his men's humanity.

The film's focus on the personal qualities of Henry and his men reaches its peak in the battle of Agincourt. Unlike Olivier who uses the entire space of the screen in a long chivalric travelling shot under a bright sun, Branagh makes us experience the onset of the battle through breathtaking close-ups on the English soldiers' faces. The eyes are bulging, the mouths are open, their expressions turning from anguish to desperate terror. The camera goes from the nobles to the common men, with no class distinctions, from Erpingham to Harry, from the Boy to the soldiers, and then accelerating to York, Bates, Exeter, and Fluellen while the noise of the galloping horse hooves soars. The French charge is suggested only by the heavy noise of their horses.

Then, Branagh's camera plunges immediately into the scrimmage to follow the fate of each fighter. The battle is not an anonymous struggle. Almost every shot features a recognizable character. We see Bates drown a Frenchman in a pool of mud. We spot Pistol and Nym robbing corpses. We follow the young and brave York, who asked to lead the charge, as he is encircled and slaughtered, spewing and regurgitating blood. As for Exeter, he knocks down French soldiers like an blacksmith pounding his anvil.

As Branagh said in a *Film Comment* interview:

> [Agincourt] wasn't a great Arthurian adventure at all. . . . I wanted to convey that terror. It was worth doing this piece now, to suggest not an obscure medieval battle but a timeless conflict—because clearly we haven't seen enough wars to stop us from fighting.[9]

Branagh wanted so much to present the ugly and brutal side of the battle that he interrupted the shooting whenever the sun pierced the clouds. The fight is a muddy and bloody chaos but thanks to the easily recognizable characters presents the humanity and pathos of soldiers caught up in brave and desperate struggles. Moreover, slow motion and solemn, harrowing music are used to bring a kind of beauty to the battle. As the real noises of battle are replaced by music and choked, distant noises—we hear only the piercing neigh of horses and the dull sound of bodies crashing in the mud—the horror becomes magnificent.

Peter Donaldson sees in this plunge into the midst of the muddy battle a ritual submersion from which the king emerges not only victorious but also in communion with his men, a communion he has sought from the very beginning of the film. According to Donaldson, "It is as if, having rejected Falstaff and other 'low' companions, he cannot form a new, more honorable community until he has returned voluntarily to baseness, to dirt."[10] When, after the battle, Branagh's camera fades from a Henry covered in mud and blood to a Henry superbly dressed with combed hair and clean face, the transformation seems miraculous and reminds us of his change from the shallow youth referred to by the clergymen earlier in the movie.

At the beginning of the boys' slaughter, a long howl of pain is heard over all the battlefield. The camera follows in slow motion the king's desperate run towards the boys; the slow motion stresses the futility of his action and the inevitability of the slaughter. When Gower and Fluellen arrive on the killing field, the camera returns to normal speed and the music suddenly cuts out, conveying the shock of discovery. Branagh then uses a technique proper to documentary, going from one child's corpse to another in a continuous shot as if by the hand-held camera of a journalist sent to cover the war. This technique is used earlier in the film, as well. During the retreat at Harfleur, just before the "Once more unto the breach" speech, the soldiers, running to escape the horrors at the walls of Harfleur, are filmed with their backs toward the audience, as if followed by a reporter. This film technique very effectively adds realism to the action. The war correspondent is evoked again when we join the Chorus just before the battle of Agincourt. He walks rapidly towards us along a palisade of wooden stakes earnestly describing the enormous event about to take place.

The most famous scene in the whole film, the *"Non nobis"* sequence, is a slow four-minute travelling shot crossing the battlefield littered with dead and dying bodies. James Loehlin pays homage to its evocative power: "it is a bold sequence, the most memorable in the film, and it illustrates the degree to which visual interpretation outweighs text: there is not a word of Shakespeare in it."[11] This scene after the battle is crucial for marking the king's moral rising above the atrocities of war, to cleanse him of his sins. Branagh's cinematographic challenge is to go from the horrors of war to the romantic comedy of the final scenes.

The sequence begins with the *a capella* song of soldier Court, answering the king's order "Let there be sung *Non nobis* and *Te Deum*." The king takes the body of Falstaff's Boy on his back and begins to work his way through the ruins of the battlefield. As the camera follows him, we recognize in the background other characters in the film and their individual fates. Pistol is cradling the corpse of his friend Nym in his arms; the English nobles take York's body away; Henry briefly pauses, looks at the dead Constable and talks to the Dauphin; a crowd of French mothers and widows rushes towards Henry but is repulsed by Montjoy. Eventually, Henry reaches a cart piled high with dead bodies. He delicately lays the Boy's corpse down, kisses his forehead and stands up again, looking at the surrounding field. In his script, Branagh describes this moment:

> We cut close on his bloodstained face, the dreadful price they have all had to pay for this so-called victory clearly etched into his whole being. His head drops as if in shame.[12]

Yet, many critics have perceived these images as triumphant. For Peter Donaldson, "[this moment] may be understood as the film's most conservative moment, a glorification of war, or, with equal validity, as the film's crowning irony, . . . for the 'glory' the hymn speaks of as belonging properly to God . . . consists of shedding blood."[13] This ambiguity is due above all to Patrick Doyle's music which evokes mixed feelings of patriotism and shame, of pain and happiness.

Asked by Pierre Berthomieu about the debate over the *"Non nobis"*—funeral elegy or patriotic and chauvinist anthem—Patrick Doyle answered:

> I can see the critics. The music may appear as warlike or manipulating. It doesn't glorify war. . . . It expresses harmony. And above all, at this moment, it expresses the collective consequence of the battle.[14]

The *"Non nobis"* theme appears as early as the beginning of the film, underscoring passages anticipating or recalling the war's casualties. It is outlined first during the credits then taken up again when the king threatens Montjoy and invokes for the first time the victims of war: "For many a thousand widows / Shall this his mock mock out of their dear husbands." The music begins the battle with martial drums and then transforms to an elegy on the *"Non nobis"* theme, as if weeping for York's death, weeping for Englishmen as well as Frenchmen, for nobles as well as common soldiers. Thus, even before the famous travelling shot after the battle, the *"Non nobis"* theme reveals itself to be an anthem to the dead, and in the film's last flashback, in which the faces of the dead haunt the screen during the peace negotiations, the *"Non nobis"* can be heard one last time.

During the travelling shot, Doyle takes up the theme on a grand scale and makes it even more lyrical to convey the king's redemption. After the king's order "Let there be sung *Non nobis* and *Te Deum*," the *"Non nobis"* begins as an *a cappella* solo sung by soldier Court still in shock after the battle. Court is joined by another singer, then by another and another . . . until the singing becomes a magnificent chorus, backed by an orchestra. The music swells in step with the expanding focus of the travelling shot and Doyle's music draws the film away from the pains and mud of the battle. At the end of the sequence, as we fade to the courting scene, the battlefield is in view no more. Only Henry remains, a lonely and forgiven hero.

Much Ado About Nothing: Sunny Shakespeare

The opening image of *Much Ado About Nothing* pans from Leonato's painting of his villa, amid a beautiful Tuscan landscape, to the actual villa and landscape, the models of his painting. The tone is set: Branagh will make art come to life, as he makes Shakespeare live again from the written pages.

The film was not shot in the original setting of the play, Messina, Sicily. Branagh wanted a less dry, more luxuriant setting, and chose Tuscany. The superb landscape and the divine Italian house with its patios and gardens transport us to a privileged world, "a kind of Shakespearean movieland" according to Ellen Edgerton.[15] This magic setting, apart from our world, both in time and space, assists our escape from reality and brings us into a fairy-tale world. It is interesting to note that Don John "the villain" does not belong to this enchanting world. For most of the movie he is filmed in underground cellars by ominous firelight, suggestive of Hell.

It is sometimes difficult to believe in the disguise and hide-and-seek games of Shakespearean comedies except in the theatre, but in Branagh's *Much Ado About Nothing*, all disbelief disappears. Branagh has created a version which is not confined to one specific time but evokes an imaginary world that could have existed anytime between 1700 and 1900, distant enough for the characters to speak in elaborate and metaphorical language and diffuse enough to evoke a fairy-tale atmosphere. According to Branagh,

> When you adapt Shakespeare, I think that above all you try and feel what makes the essence of a text. And precisely in that play, sexuality is omnipresent. As this story occurs in Italy, I wanted to create almost a Latin atmosphere, with hot-blooded characters. I even told the actors to play as if they were in *The Godfather*. I wanted intense, intuitive reactions.[16]

As early as the credits, Branagh puts on screen his sensual vision of the play. The women are running in the fields. The soldiers are arriving on horseback in a rhythmic gallop, bouncing on their saddles in slow motion (almost as if anticipating their upcoming sexual bonding). We see close-up shots of the horses' breasts and nostrils, hooves hitting the ground, and an impatient expression on the men's faces. The camera work proclaims that Shakespeare's words will be as sensual and energetic.

Pierre Berthomieu comments on this masterly overture:

> Emblematic, the horsemen's flag invades the screen in the credits' first shot. Waved by the wind, the flag movement is put in slow motion. . . . Slow motion makes us wait for the horsemen as well as increases the importance of their arrival. [It] allows . . . to deny the fugacity of human emotion, to contemplate its expression. To put in slow motion is to induce an emotional time of increased participation and an effect of distanciation, of analysis, of a better understanding.[17]

Slow motion is an effect we frequently find in Branagh's film work. We can spot it, as we have seen, in the battle scenes of *Henry V*, in the apocalyptic finale of *Dead Again*, in *Mary Shelley's Frankenstein* when the creature leaps on his creator, and in *Hamlet* during the sword fight between Laertes and Hamlet. Slow motion above all brings *power* to a sequence. It produces a lyrical, dramatic, and passionate pause in the action. Slow motion reoccurs in *Much Ado About Nothing*, when, after the gulling scenes, the images of Benedick and Beatrice are superimposed on the screen, he splashing in the fountain, she swinging in the air. Here slow motion savours the emotions, allowing the audience to share them with the characters. Moreover, the superimposing of Beatrice and Benedick on screen acts as a marriage of souls, joining them in the happiness of their discovery of love, and anticipating their future wedding.

When they reach the villa the characters take their clothes off and bathe. The sequence is a well-paced and merry, alternating between shots of women and men getting prepared for the night's revels: naked bodies diving into pools as if into the Fountain of Youth, laughter, busy hands and feet . . . all is rhythm, sensuality and vitality. The film Overture recalls Branagh's mission: to take the dust out of Shakespeare. At the end of the Overture, the characters place themselves on a virtual chessboard, in a symmetrical V filmed in a high-angle shot. This arrangement foresees the strategic games of bluffing and counter-bluffing that will indeed occur in the film.

In *Much Ado About Nothing*, the camera angles and editing stress the comic aspects of the play. During the gulling scenes, the camera shows in close-up the funny reactions on Beatrice and Benedick's faces: astonishment, disbelief, pride, exasperation, relief . . . Benedick even turns his head suddenly towards the camera, looking directly at the audience, on Leonato's cue "My daughter is sometime afeard she will do a desperate outrage to herself." When Benedick spies Beatrice arriving to bid him come to dinner, his words "By this day, she's a fair lady" and "I do spy some marks of love in her" are not in tune with what we see on the screen: Beatrice walking quickly and unwillingly, at the last stage of exasperation,.

Yet, this technique also enhances the tragic side of the play, especially by way of close-up shots on faces: tears in Claudio's angry eyes as he catches sight of Margaret with Borachio at the window; the pain of rejected Hero; Beatrice's sorrow after the humiliation of her cousin.

For *Much Ado About Nothing*, the music was very important. With its mix of the epic and the pastorale, the huge and bold overture contains most of the movie's musical themes. The music is romantic and melodious but also impulsive and energetic. It perfectly fits the images of the galloping horsemen and the running women, and underlines both the feminine and masculine elements. For Doyle, the most complex scene to put to music was the wedding scene when Hero is rejected, because the emotions are constantly changing but the dialogue is uninterrupted: "Ken wanted the music to be present all through the scene. . . . It is a scene close to an opera: a person is accused and the characters react. I composed the music of that sequence after all the others, because I wanted to put all the other musical themes in place through the movie."[18]

It is Batlhasar's song "Sigh No More, Ladies," however, that contains the very lesson of the movie. As with the *"Non nobis"* theme in *Henry V*, the audience hears the song several times in the film. It is recited first by Beatrice with both an ironic and relaxed tone; then sung by Bathasar in the idyllic garden setting where it echoes Claudio's romanticism; and finally as the film is closing, it rings like a confirmation of the bonds between men and women. Branagh and composer Patrick Doyle recorded this final anthem on location because they wanted the joy and exuberance of the shooting to come through in the film.

For this movie, Branagh made good use of the steadicam, with which a cameraman can walk or run alongside the actors and produce the same smooth movement as a standard camera. It brings energy, dynamism, and fluidity to the action. The steadicam was used in only two shots in *Henry V* and does not appear in *Hamlet* because the 70 mm camera was too heavy.

The steadicam is ideally suited for many of the sequences in *Much Ado About Nothing*, such as the "Sigh No More, Ladies" scene. The song is sung by Balthasar in the middle of the film, and during this sequence the camera travels full circle in the garden, showing the daily life of the household as well as the beautiful Tuscan landscape, contemplating the harmony of man and nature. Yet, it is the last sequence, the "Strike up, pipers!" dance, which is most typical of Branagh's steadicam work. The camera pans from the chapel, joins in the happy farandole, follows the dancers through the gardens and patios, then rises on a crane for a last aerial shot. We attend this gigantic feast, this dance that celebrates life and happiness in the here-and-now. The cheerfulness, the dynamism of the camera work makes us feel the same exhilarating joy as the characters.

The movie's last shot is an ascent towards the beautiful blue sky, as if after all those loving adventures, those cunning interludes, those betrayals and reconciliations, the camera expresses the futility of all this compared to the beauty of the sky, taking us away from this enchanting Shakespearean world before a last fade to black.

Hamlet: **Between Snow and Mirrors**

If Branagh remains faithful to the original text of *Hamlet*, he treats it cinematically with action, lyricism, and glamour. The images of countless soldiers approaching the palace in a snowy landscape, or Hamlet delivering "How all occasions do inform against me" as a Henry V–like exhortation surrounded by ice and snow, lend an epic and heroic quality to the film.

Branagh's decision to perform Hamlet as a character not predisposed to melancholy, whose personality is vibrant, curious, and positive, has been translated to the film score. Three main themes divide the score: Ophelia's theme, a childish, descending melody which is nostalgic but not gloomy; the Claudius theme, whose tormented and dark soul we feel through a feverish canon played by a string quartet; and Hamlet's theme, around which the whole score is built. "For *Hamlet*, Branagh wanted a music that kept rising, the opposite of down, of depressing down-beat music. Because the production is all very glamourous. But behind the glamour, there is tragedy. So the music had to be heroic, with a degree of melancholy, with inevitability in it but not depressing inevitability. *Positive* inevitability. Like a man climbing a mountain *knowing* he is not going to get to the summit but he tries and tries . . ."[19] The bright and military aspect Branagh wanted to give the film is reflected in the music; neither Hamlet nor Ophelia belongs to Claudius's dark world.

The exteriors for the movie were shot at Bleinheim Palace, one of the most impressive castles in England, because Branagh wanted to place the action in premises where the destiny of nations could easily be decided, where a personal story could affect the fate of an entire country.

Branagh chose to shoot in a 70 mm format instead of the more usual 35 mm (which uses a negative four times larger), creating a film made up of a series of perfectly framed postcards. As a result Branagh has been able to capture infinite snowy landscapes with such detail that distant soldiers are not lost in the expanse and to film faces in extreme close-up, heightening each tiny emotional detail. Sometimes, in fact, the entire frame is filled with an ear or a mouth. The 70 mm format thus allows him to show both the domestic and epic sides of the story. Michael Wilmington describes it this way: "*Hamlet* suggests a fusion of Ingmar Bergman's chamber dramas with David Lean's romantic epics."[20]

The play is set between 1850 and 1900, much like *Much Ado About Nothing*. This brings the story of *Hamlet* closer to our time and culture, while keeping it distant enough for the characters to speak in heightened language. The setting of *Hamlet* could almost be the same as the 1968 movie *Mayerling*—which tells the tragic love story of Rodolph, son of the Austrian Empress Sissi. Branagh's *Hamlet* is indeed strongly reminiscent of the Habsburg or Romanov's era, a period when large, powerful royal families ruled Europe. The royal symbol appears in the movie as early as the transition between the first and second scenes. After Horatio and the two soldiers decide to inform Hamlet of the ghost's appearance, Branagh has the camera zoom in on the crest on the palace gates. Close up on the royal blazon, a crown, it anticipates the pomp of the court scene a few seconds later, and in fact, dissolves into the shape of the extravagant hall-crossing bridge which opens that scene. The transition between the first and second scene prepares us for what we are going to see, both aesthetically and symbolically.

According to designer Tim Harvey: "Ken wanted the sets to be as accessible as possible and to be far removed from the rugged medieval gloom one usually associates with this play."[21] Alexandra Byrne took advantage of the lavish sets and the indefinite period to create stylized and unreal costumes. She explains: "Ken wanted the costumes to be sexy . . . so I began to look at shapes and outlines. The women's costumes ended up quite near the 1880s because of the extreme body sculpting of those outfits."[22] The colours of the women's costumes changes in the course of the film and, as in the 1993 theatre production, mark the significant stages of the plot: red for the play, cream for the duel. The men's costumes, in a style more military than Branagh's previous theatre productions, were conceived to contrast with the black worn by Hamlet in the first part of the film: red for Claudius, cream for Laertes. After his return to Denmark, Hamlet wears white, cream, beige and brown, revealing a new fatalist and serene attitude towards both death and destiny.

Branagh also wanted the costumes to emphasize the hierarchical and military aspects of the play in order to convey the feeling of a state on alert, ready to face an invasion. In the first court scene, the colours of the various costumes identify distinct groups of courtiers and officers: some are dressed in red, others in white or yellow, showing their different ranks.

After all this glittering and lavish pomp, when Gertrude and Claudius exit the throne room, a shower of confetti descends on the court and shows, in dreamlike slow motion, the potential for happiness in the palace.

Under the glittering façade, however, there is corruption. The oversized hall is bright, sumptuous, but communicates with numerous smaller, darker rooms, through secret doors hidden behind mirrors. This creates a very real atmosphere of paranoia. One of these secret rooms will even become a padded cell for the mad Ophelia. The floor of the hall is composed of black and white squares, creating a huge chessboard, a kind of intimation of order in a world full of disorder. By contrast, when Hamlet joins the intimate circle of the players for "Speak the speech I pray you," we feel that he finds an interior peace there, a feeling of harmony. This impression is conveyed by the warm colours of the players' room, which contrasts with the immense military-style hall and its cold colours.

Inspired by the Mirror Gallery in Versailles, Branagh placed thirty huge mirrors on each side of the grand hall, hiding as many secret doors. Apart from the dangerous fragility and superstitious misfortune they represent, mirrors evoke a rich, opulent, narcissistic and vain world, one where people are constantly looking at their own appearance and for their deepest selves. In fact, they provide a visual echo of the characters in the play who keep secrets and reflect distorted images of themselves to others.

The idea of delivering the famous "To be, or not to be" soliloquy in front of a two-way mirror, with the camera fixed on Hamlet's reflection, occurred to Branagh very early. He wanted Hamlet to look into himself while Claudius observed from the other side of the mirror, making the soliloquy seem to present this alternative: I'll kill you or I'll kill myself. It also produces a fitting parallel with Claudius's confession scene in which he is unaware of Hamlet spying on him.

This choice to film "To be, or not to be" with Hamlet looking at himself can also be linked to an interpretation that sees Hamlet as a version of Narcissus. In his essay "Hamlet and the curious perspective," Professor Pierre Iselin says of Shakespeare's play that "[its] obsession with mirror effects reminds us of the mythological figure of Narcissus" and he quotes Granville-Barker who says of Hamlet: "It is his own disposition that prompts this image. He is always looking at himself in the glass of his own conscience."[23]

Like the mythological Narcissus who cannot respond to the love of the nymph Echo because he is absorbed by his reflection in the water, Hamlet cannot respond to the love of his own nymph Ophelia ("The fair Ophelia! *Nymph*, in thy orisons, be all my sins remembered" he says just after the "To be, or not to be" soliloquy)—because he is too much absorbed by his own self-reflection. In Branagh's movie, this self-reflection becomes literal, and Hamlet is the fascinated prisoner of his own image.

It is interesting to note that Branagh's first idea for shooting the "To be, or not to be" soliloquy used even more reflections:

> There's a shot in *Citizen Kane* where Orson Welles walks by a mirror, appears to walk by, and then a minute later, he does walk by in actual fact. . . . An infinite number of Orson Welleses are walking across the mirror. And I think that's what I wanted with the "To be, or not to be" soliloquy.[24]

Branagh eventually chose the simpler single reflection in order not to distract from what can be an already complicated speech for the audience. Yet, it is revealing of Branagh's awareness of the play's multiplicity of visual illusions. In *Citizen Kane*, the use of mirrors underscores the central question of the movie: who is the real John Foster Kane? And in *Hamlet*, as so many characters report on him in so many different ways, we are also led to wonder who is the real Hamlet.

Another interesting parallel with Orson Welles in *Citizen Kane* is that Branagh also worked on *Hamlet* as both a director and an actor. This in turn gave birth to endless visual as well as mental reflections, as Branagh recalls in an interview:

> In order to have a look at how the scene was going, which obviously I was in, I had to have a small video monitor in my hand. So I was doing "To be, or not to be," looking in the mirror, walking towards the mirror, and watching the same speech happen there. So reflected there, reflected back here, in the video monitor, and a certain kind of madness, quite frankly, going on inside my head.[25]

In a strange parallel with his experience making *Henry V*, in the making of *Hamlet*, Branagh finds himself in more or less the same position as the character he is portraying. Hamlet is indeed an actor, in that he simulates madness or disguises the meaning of his words: "In this my tongue and soul be hypocrites" Hamlet says before meeting his mother in her closet (Act III, scene ii). And he is also a director: he gives advice to the actors and sets up the staging of the "Mousetrap" to "catch the conscience" of Claudius.

The mirror image is also a metaphor of *Hamlet,* the play, in which so many characters reflect one another. Laertes is eventually in the same position as Hamlet: his father has been murdered and must be revenged; Fortinbras, like Hamlet, has lost a father and his uncle Old Norway is on the throne; and the main characters in the play all meet their doubles, reflections of their conscience, played on the stage by the "Mousetrap" actors.

Branagh's cinematographic editing highlights at crucial points the many different parallels present in *Hamlet.* Thus, during the Mouse-trap scene, on Lucianus's words "else no creature seeing," Branagh shows us Claudius being observed by Horatio through opera-glasses and reminds us that the murderer is wrong: he *is* being observed. If, in the action of Lucianus, the play melts together Claudius's murder of Old Hamlet and Hamlet's intention to kill Claudius, Branagh's cinematic treatment insists also on those reflections. Extensive use of reaction shots at strategic moments in this scene link Claudius, Hamlet, and Lucianus through visual images.

Finally, no one in *Hamlet* escapes reflection in the mirror of death. During the cemetery scene, Hamlet is thus put face to face with Yorick, and Branagh indeed films Hamlet as if he is mirrored by the skull, alternating shots successively from Hamlet's face to what remains of Yorick. Even Gertrude does not escape the mortuary mirror: Gertrude is musically linked to Ophelia through the film, underlining Branagh's decision to present Gertrude as innocent, and not an accessory to Claudius's murder of her former husband. After Gertrude's report of Ophelia's death, the image of her face dissolves into the image of the drowned Ophelia under the surface of the water, as if Gertrude is seeing the image of her own imminent death.

Branagh's film also illustrates a theme dear to Hamlet's character: Denmark as a prison (Hamlet bluntly calls it that while talking to Rosencrantz and Guildenstern). Branagh often films characters through bars, prisoners of Elsinore's closed world or of their own conscience.

Hamlet is thus filmed through the palace gates while the ghost appears to him. Claudius is seen through the lattice-work of the confessional after confessing his crime. After Laertes' departure, Ophelia is shot behind the chapel gate which Polonius closes on her himself, symbolic of his fatherly overprotection. Later, she is seen again through the gates of Elsinore, howling at of her father's dead body, prisoner of a world that has ravished her of her father and will soon confine her to a padded cell. Even Elsinore Palace is frequently featured through its own gates, the prison conquering the entire dramatic scene.

Branagh has filmed entire scenes in one single travelling shot from the great hall through the corridors and into the rooms. This gives the audience a feeling of labyrinthine anguish. Those long travelling shots through the corridors also help make the whole palace organization live, as did the steadicam in *Much Ado About Nothing*. Rosencrantz and Guildenstern's arrival is thus an occassion to present daily life in the palace: the beginning of the day for the king and queen, the transmission of daily news . . . Rosencrantz and Guildenstern are then led into a whirlwind of intense activity during two and a half minutes of continuous travelling. The rather cold and indifferent welcome Claudius gives Hamlet's two friends shows how much the palace lives in its own autarchy, protected from the exterior world and dangerously retreated from the Danish people.

The different rooms of the palace reflect the personalities of their occupants.

For Gertrude's room, Tim Harvey wanted to give the impression of a luxurious blue cocoon with curved furniture to evoke a gentler, feminine feeling and contrasting with Claudius's severe, red rectilinear room.

Hamlet's room shows the interest of its occupant for reading, geography, and theatre. Each prop is used to illustrate Hamlet's words or intentions all through the film, to help the audience apprehend the stakes at each turn of the plot. An entire wall is thus occupied by a bookcase from which Hamlet draws a book illustrated with dances of death after having learned about the ghost's appearance. When Hamlet decides to stage a play to confront Claudius face to face with his crime, he plays with a model of a miniature theatre. While delivering "The play's the thing / Wherein I'll catch the conscience of the King," he opens a trap-door in the miniature stage and the King figurine falls through. The model theatre is also used when Hamlet, returned from his trip at sea, recounts for Horatio his escape. On his words "they had begun the play," he touches the miniature theatre again, illustrating the "play" imagined by those who want his death. Then, when he mentions rewriting the letter to the king of England, Hamlet comes near a writing desk for the line "wrote it fair."

Throughout the movie, Branagh illustrates the words of Hamlet and the other characters to help the audience grasp the Elizabethan language. These illustrations may act either explicitly or subliminally but always participate in the film's accessibility. They are indeed explicit in that they do not contradict the characters' words. Branagh, as far as his cinematography is concerned, remains faithful to the text:

> You do have to make a kind of choice that takes it from the theatre into the film otherwise you go for a filmed play. You try and make sure that all the images that you come up with cinematically that do not exist in the play are a response to the text. . . . Every additional illustration, flashback or illustrative images, comes from the text.[26]

In the very opening scene, Branagh illustrates Barnardo's words "When yon same star that's westward from the pole" with a shot of the starlight sky; and Horatio's "But look, the morn . . . walks o'er the dew" with a shot of the rising sun. At the end of the movie, in Horatio's speech to Fortinbras, Branagh inserts shots of those lying dead which act as recapitulative illustrations:

> "of deaths put on by cunning and forced cause"
>   (*Laertes lying on the floor*)
> "purposes mistook fallen on th'inventors' head"
>   (*Claudius, dead, prisoner of the chandelier*)

During Claudius's confession, Hamlet decides to postpone his revenge and lists the occasions when it would be better to kill him. Branagh repeats images which have previously appeared in the film to stress each occasion.

> "When he is drunk asleep . . ."
>   (*Claudius staggering in the corridors*)
> ". . . or in his rage . . ."
>   (*Claudius quarrelling with Polonius*)
> "Or in th'incestuous pleasure of his bed, . . ."
>   (*Claudius in bed with Gertrude*)
> ". . . or about some act
> That has no relish of salvation in't . . ."
>   (*Claudius hiding behind a mirror before the nunnery scene*)

This last illustration, interestingly enough, anticipates the killing of Polonius in the next scene. It helps us understand Hamlet's impetuous murder of the man hidden behind the arras: this man is indeed "about some act / That has no relish of salvation in it" and risks going directly to hell if killed at that very moment.

After the intermission, a bold editing choice visually reminds the audience of the events which have occurred during the first part of the movie. By using Claudius's speech "When sorrows come they come not single spies, / But in battalions," imported from later in the text, as he did with Claudius's confession, Branagh illustrates each event with an image the audience has already seen:

"First, her father slain . . ."
    (*Hamlet stabbing Polonius*)
"Next your son gone . . ."
    (*Hamlet captured and exiled*)
". . . the people muddied,
thick and unwholesome in their thoughts and whispers
For good Polonius's death."
    (*A whispering courtier*)
". . . and we have done but greenly
In hugger-mugger to inter him;"
    (*Polonius's bloody corpse carried away by soldiers*)
". . . poor Ophelia
Divided from herself and her fair judgement . . ."
    (*Ophelia howling at the palace gates, trying to see her father's body for the last time*)
". . . her brother is in secret come from France, . . ."
    (*Laertes, seen during the wedding at the beginning of the film*)

This technique visually recapitulates the situation, and impresses the events on the viewer's memory, who may have never read Hamlet before and could easily be left behind by the turns in the plot.

In a less literal way, Branagh also inserts images not to illustrate the text but to provoke correlative feelings. For instance, when Hamlet is running through the woods after the ghost's call and is thinking the speech "Angels and ministers of grace defend us!" Branagh inserts the image of an explosion in the forest and eruptions of white smoke from the earth exactly on the word "burst" in the line "tell [me] why thy canonized bones . . . have burst their cerements." Here, the image does not illustrate a corpse or ghost escaping its coffin, but rather the impression of horror and alarm linked to this outburst.

This less literal visual juxtaposition is interesting to note during Fortinbras' charge on the palace. This scene does not exist in the original play and Branagh, keen on presenting Fortinbras as an attacking warrior, chooses to show us the charging soldiers during Hamlet's apology to Laertes before their duel. In that speech, Hamlet maintains that it was not him but his *madness* that was the cause of all his faults. Thus on each "madness" spoken by Hamlet, the audience sees instead of Hamlet a massive army running towards the palace, which is in fact another kind of human madness that runs through the play. With this full scale attack on a castle too preoccupied with a domestic crisis to defend itself, Branagh presents the absurdity and folly of war.

Earlier in the film, another juxtaposition of image and sound anticipates the violence of Fortinbras' final assault. When Ophelia howls at the palace gates, distraught to see her father's corpse, her scream continues under the succeeding shots. From the gates, the camera moves to a long shot on Elsinore; from Elsinore lost in an icy environment, to the snowy mist out of which appear Fortinbras and his captain. Ophelia's scream is held throughout this transition, until with the appearance of Fortinbras, it anticipates the very collapse of Elsinore.

Composer Patrick Doyle begins his work by identifying moments in the film powerful enough not to need music. It is interesting to locate some striking passages Branagh and Doyle chose not to back with music. In *Henry V*, during the tennis balls episode and Falstaff's death described by Mistress Quickly, and in *Much Ado About Nothing* for Beatrice's furious speech "O that I were a man!" the music is silent. In the movie *Hamlet*, Hamlet's first soliloquy "O that this too too solid flesh would melt" is delivered against a stark silence. Asked about this lack of music, Doyle answers:

> It was all to heighten the drama. Music can be very effective when it's been in for a while and then stops. Subliminally, the audience is aware of the silence or the difference in the atmosphere. So, it is used as a dramatic effect.[27]

Hamlet's speech "O that this too too solid flesh would melt" comes up right after the big fanfare marking Gertrude and Claudius's withdrawal. Doyle explains: "I wanted his voice to be ringing that hallway. I just felt that was far more important."[28] Hamlet's voice, in this sudden silence, is all the more overwhelming.

For "To be or not to be," the Hamlet theme is merely outlined. For composer Patrick Doyle, "Hamlet questions the source of existence, he comes back to the sources. The music tries to express this move [back] to primal, primitive forms: a bare rhythm, then the voice."[29] The music does not begin in earnest until the first occurrence of the word "death" in the soliloquy—"For in that sleep of *death*," eleven lines in. Doyle used percussions and horns, as well as voices, from masculine low voices to sopranos, to reflect the fundamental question asked by the character. The result is a feeling of mystery, cavernous fear, plunging abyss, echo, and discovery, a direct parallel between the word and the irrepressible fear linked to the idea of death.

In addition to illustrating the characters' words with objects, props, and other visual juxtapositions, Branagh but also uses specific camera positions, moves, and precisely constructed shots.

During the closet scene, Gertrude flings at an enraged Hamlet: "O Hamlet, speak no more! / Thou turn'st mine eyes into my very soul, / And there I see such black and grainèd spots / As will not leave their tinct." For this line, Branagh creates a two-part image. The right half of the screen is occupied by Gertrude sitting on her bed in the background. The other half is entirely filled by the black suit of Hamlet in the foreground, with his back turned to us. This produces an overwhelming visual parallel: exactly on Gertrude's words "black and grainèd spots," the audience sees one half of the screen in total blackness.

During the First Player's speech on Hecuba, when "And bowl the round nave down the hill of heaven, / As low as to the fiends!" is delivered, he films the First Player with a low-angle shot. When the latter is imitating the fall of the wheel, the breaking of its spokes, with a falling, sweeping hand gesture, the low-angle shot reinforces the visual evocation.

If the camera work illustrates the characters' words, it can also convey their perspective and the emotions they experience. This increases our identification with the characters.

During Laertes' departure scene, Ophelia and Laertes are walking in Elsinore's gardens. Branagh films Laertes' various advice to his sister with cuts indicating short ellipses in time, which convey the boring, repetitive nature of his lecture. Here we enter Ophelia's mind, weary of listening to the same thing again and again.

When Claudius, infuriated by Hamlet, eventually decides to send him to England and his death, he delivers "Do it, England" in both a furious and desperate voice. Driven to the wall by circumstance, Claudius is explicitly filmed with his back up gainst the door of his room. All through the movie, Branagh chooses, if not to have us sympathize with the king, at least to make us understand his dilemma and his own tragedy.

Yet, Branagh's cinematographic work above all allows the audience to live Hamlet's experience, to fully identify with him. Hamlet's character is indeed very often shot with his back turned towards us. The spectators therefore share his point of view, both visually and mentally. They even find themselves directly confronted with Yorick's skull, a *memento mori* of their own, for some very intense seconds.

When Hamlet kills Polonius the sequence lasts for only ten seconds but consists of more than fifteen alternating shots on Hamlet, Polonius, and Gertrude. That succession of images and reactions, those rapid cuts, drive us directly into Hamlet's overheated mind.

The duel at the end of the film begins with a long shot of the hall. This shot is filmed slantwise, producing a feeling of discomfort and recalls the treachery with the swords, the twisted uncertainty which Hamlet must face. Here again the audience is directly confronted with a character's fate.

At the beginning of the nunnery scene, Hamlet approaches Ophelia and kisses her tenderly. She interrupts the kiss and pushes him back slightly. The camera then shows Hamlet standing in the left side of the screen, and Ophelia in the right. In the centre, a long corridor opens up, appearing to separate the two lovers. The camera creates a gulf between the two characters and an atmosphere of misunderstanding and treason. When the rejected Ophelia weeps lying against the frame of a mirror-door, the half-open door is a symbol of exit, a way out to the protected and secluded place Hamlet wishes for her. Branagh's camera itself presents Ophelia with a choice, which makes her eventual death even more tragic. In the first of Ophelia's mad scenes, she is described by Claudius as "divided from herself and her fair judgement." Branagh films her sitting on the ground near a mirror; so the spectators really see a doubled Ophelia whose reflection symbolizes this division between herself and her reason. During the second mad scene, Branagh orchestrates another shot which this time reflects the choice Laertes must make. Laertes is filmed in the centre of the scree. To his right, Ophelia has returned to her padded cell, her face to the wall. To his left, Claudius invites Laertes to patience and soon to murder. The screen is divided and illustrates Laertes' dilemma: shall he listen to his heart and go comfort his sister; or listen to his honour and Claudius's plot for revenge?

In Branagh's *Hamlet*, if the characters double themselves in the mirrors, many visual images also reflect one another, answer to one another. They are often doubled and even tripled.

Branagh cuts from an extreme close-up on the ghost's mouth when he orders Hamlet to "Revenge his foul and most unnatural murder" to another extreme close-up on Hamlet's mouth when he answers "Murder?" The two images reflect each other and echo the doubling of the word "murder." They help to produce the impression of an intimacy close to suffocation. Branagh then includes three close-ups on the spectre's eyes, to which immediately echo three shots on Hamlet's eyes. The cinematic treatment takes us back to Hamlet's previous words: ". . . methinks I see my father . . . in my mind's eye."

Close-ups of Hamlet's eyes return at one other point in the movie: when Hamlet imagines in voice-over some better occasions to kill Claudius. The speech "Now might I do it pat" is textually full of references to the ghost. Branagh illustrates "A took my father grossly" by showing again the flashback in which Claudius murders his brother; and "'Tis heavy with him" by another shot on the white infernal smoke erupting from the earth. And close-ups on the eyes are included to recall the first meeting between Hamlet and his father's ghost. The repetition of shots reminds the spectators of the emotion present during that first encounter as well as the enormity and urgency of the decision that Hamlet faces.

Fortinbras also benefits from shots focused on his eyes, emphasizing his power and determination. On Valtemand's report to Claudius "But better looked into, he truly found / It was against your highness," Branagh shows in close-up Fortinbras' face looking fixedly in one direction, followed by an exterior shot of Elsinore. The intensity of the eyes' expression is amplified in the words "better looked into"; and Fortinbras' warlike intentions are clearly revealed by the shot of Elsinore castle. Just before the charge, Fortinbras sweeps his sword in front of his face shot in close-up, inspiring a feeling of force and quiet will. In the text, he is the ultimate man of action and movement. Most of his cues begin with "go": "Go Captain," "Go softly on," "Go bid the soldiers shoot." This impression of resolute enterprise is enhanced in the movie by the performance of Rufus Sewel. Apart from the scene in which Fortinbras is rebuked by his uncle—and is momentarily inferior—Sewel hardly blinks his eyes until he reaches his goal and has conquered the throne of Denmark. Only at the end of the film, on the exact moment when the crown is placed on his head, does he relax and let by his almost inhuman determination.

One of the most important pictorial decisions in the movie was to present the ghost coming out of a stone statue of Old Hamlet dressed as a warrior, gazing on Elsinore Castle from his pedestal. Branagh has been influenced here by *Don Giovanni's* Commandor or by Richard Eyre's stage production of *Hamlet* in the late 1980s at the London National Theatre. Designer John Gunter had indeed conceived a huge statue representing Old Hamlet whose fatherly shadow cast itself over the action of the play.

The grave statue of Old Hamlet gives birth to the last scene of Branagh's movie. In dreamlike slow motion, the statue is broken to pieces by Fortinbras' soldiers, the sounds of their hammers melting into the echoes of gunfire. The movie therefore ends in destruction, the definitive last word on both the political and domestic story. The final scene is itself a *memento mori*. After all these events, nothing is left. Death dismantles all.

Notes

1. Quoted in Samuel Crowl, "Hamlet 'Most Royal': An Interview with Kenneth Branagh."
2. Bernice Kliman. "Branagh's Henry: Allusion and Illusion."
3. Nicolas Saada. "Le théâtre apprivoisé."*Cahiers du Cinéma*, Jan 1991. (My translation from the French.)
4. Kenneth Branagh. Liner notes to *Henry V: Original Soundtrack Recording*. EMI, CDC 7 49919 2.
5. Kenneth Branagh. Liner notes to *Henry V: Original Soundtrack Recording*.
6. James Loehlin. *Shakespeare in Performance:* Henry V.
7. An interview with the author, Apr 10 1997.
8. Bernice Kliman. "Branagh's Henry: Allusion and Illusion."
9. Quoted in Graham Fuller, "Two kings." *Film Comment* 25 (1989).
10. Peter Donaldson. "Taking on Shakespeare: Kenneth Branagh's *Henry V.*"
11. James Loehlin. *Shakespeare in Performance:* Henry V.
12. Kenneth Branagh. *Henry V: A Screen Adaptation*, p. 114.
13. Peter Donaldson. "Taking on Shakespeare: Kenneth Branagh's *Henry V.*"
14. Quoted in Pierre Berthomieu, *Kenneth Branagh: Traînes de feu, rosées de sang*, p. 246. (My translation from the French.)
15. Ellen Edgerton. "Your Answer, Sir, Is Cinematical."
16. Kenneth Branagh. "Funny Shakespeare." *Studio*, Mar 1993. (My translation from the French.)

17. Pierre Berthomieu. *Kenneth Branagh: Traînes de feu, rosées de sang*, pp. 28–29. (My translation from the French.)
18. Quoted in Christian Lauliac, "Interview: Patrick Doyle." (My translation from the French.)
19. An interview with the author, Apr 10 1997.
20. Michael Wilmington. "A noble *Hamlet*." *Chicago Tribune*, 24 Jan 1997.
21. On the internet: www.hamlet-movie.com (Warner Bros. Online).
22. On the internet: www.hamlet-movie.com. (Warner Bros. Online).
23. Pierre Iselin (Ed.). "Hamlet and the 'curious perspective,' or the uncertainties of the gaze." *Hamlet: Essays*. Paris: Didier Eruditions—CNED, 1997, p. 45.
24. In a talk given at Yale University, 8 Nov 1997.
25. An interview with Susanne Stamberg at the "Smithsonian's Stellar Shakespeare Weekend," 21 Dec 1996.
26. In an interview given to the CBC Radio (Canada) at *Hamlet's* release.
27. An interview with the author, Apr 10 1997.
28. An interview with the author, Apr 10 1997.
29. Quoted in Pierre Berthomieu, *Kenneth Branagh: Traînes de feu, rosées de sang*, p. 242 (My translation from the French.)

"the abstract and brief chronicles of the time"
—Hamlet, II.ii

Chapter Six
Branagh's Cinematic Themes and Codes

In their essay "Recycled Film Codes and the Study of Shakespeare on Film," Lawrence Guntner and Peter Drexler ask why the cinemato-graphic adaptations by Laurence Olivier, Orson Welles, Akira Kurosawa, Grigori Kozintzev, Peter Brook, Roman Polanski, and Franco Zeffirelli have stamped themselves on our memory while the majority of the other 750 TV and movie adaptations have been forgotten. They conclude that the success of such adaptations consists in their ability to recycle filmic codes to which the spectators are used. Through the course of his career as a film director, Branagh has developed a per-sonal repertoire of images and techniques which he deploys in his Shakespearean and non-Shakespearean movies alike. And as we shall see later in this chapter, he successfully recycles filmic codes drawn from and easily associated with Hollywood's most popular genres: westerns, musicals, thrillers, war movies, gangster movies, and oth-ers.

From Shots to Meaning

Alex Thomson, the director of photography on *Hamlet*, confided to a journalist:

> John Huston once told me you shouldn't move the camera if you want people to listen. I told Ken that, but he said "What are we going to do? You can't have a static camera when you are shout-ing seven pages of dialogue. The audience's going to fall asleep if they aren't interested."[1]

The remark is telling. Branagh's interests are foremost the audi-ence's interests. With his camera moves, Branagh wants us to enter into the characters' mind as often as possible: zooming and close-up shots to feel the king's doubts in *Henry V;* frantic steadicam travellings to feel the feverish and sunny exaltation of *Much Ado About Nothing;* tracking shots and backward moves to experience the intricate and epic *Hamlet.*

Similar methods of arranging and filming characters in space can be found in all of Branagh's movies. The technique of encircling the actors with the camera in one continuous shot has been used by Branagh in all his movies: the hypnosis scenes in *Dead Again;* the friends' arrival in *Peter's Friends;* the final dance in *Much Ado About Nothing;* the birth of a child to Victor's mother in *Mary Shelley's Frankenstein;* Claudius, Gertrude, and Polonius advising Ophelia before the nunnery scene in *Hamlet.* This circular uncut filming creates the impression of being right there with the characters. We share the happy meeting in *Peter's Friends,* join the dancers in *Much Ado About Nothing,* and feel helpless and horrified at the bloody, deadly delivery in *Frankenstein.* We participate in the plot against Hamlet, and even identified with Ophelia's guilty feeling, on the brink of betraying her lover.

From film to film, Branagh has expanded his use of this circular movement. The length of these shots has increased until in *Hamlet* it gives a feeling of continuity in discontinuity. In one single encircling shot, the setting changes and the shot's tableau transforms itself: Hamlet, as the camera circles him, moves from the gigantic hall to a smaller room to advise the Mousetrap actors. There is no cut; the shot remains intact, and the cinematic treatment imitates the very nature of *Hamlet,* a play that glides insensibly from one subject to another while leading us to a predestined and universal ending.

The progressive, forward movement of the camera, zooming up to a character experiencing a loss—loss of a loved one, a parent, his or her soul—can be found in all of Branagh's films. The slow close-up on Mistress Quickly as she recalls Falstaff's death in *Henry V* parallells the same camera motion on Gertrude reporting Ophelia's death, Claudius vainly trying to confess himself, Ophelia weeping for the loss of Hamlet's love, and later, for her father's death.

Certain pictorial or symbolic motifs recur and punctuate Branagh's movies, many of which contribute to the success of the final vision of *Hamlet.*

Branagh loves the image of the triptych: a central figure is filmed facing the audience with two characters in profile on each side. This arrangement implies a conspiracy against the central character. The young King Henry V is presented thus in his first scene, flanked by two plotting clergymen—youth manipulated by experience, innocence by machiavellianism. In the first court scene, Hamlet also is featured face on, with Claudius on his right and Gertrude on his left, both in profile. They persuade him to stay in Denmark and he must obey. During the "What a piece of work is a man" speech, Hamlet is seen again from the front, this time flanked by Rosencrantz and Guildenstern as they try to draw information out of him.

Branagh has always included motifs of doors in his films. His very first entrance in a Shakespearean movie occurs when young King Henry enters the throne room through a huge shadowy door. The story of *Henry V* itself begins and ends with the opening and closing of a heavy wooden door by the Chorus. In *Dead Again*, the door motif is present in several lines about returning to the past: Frank Madson's "The door is open, my dear" marks the beginning of the hypnosis sessions, and Mike Church's "The door is closed" marks the end of the curse from the past. In *Peter's Friends*, the imposing doors of the manor are closed behind the arrived friends, as the doors of Leonato's villa are closed behind the soldiers returned from war at the beginning of *Much Ado About Nothing*. Branagh thus marks the transition to another world: in both *Peter's Friends* and *Much Ado About Nothing*, that of the reunited friends. In these last two examples, Branagh signals the literal confinement of a small group of people whose self-contained world is going to be followed by the camera. When Peter's group of friends knit together again at the end of the movie, Vera, the housekeeper, closes the door of the living room, inviting the spectators to retire, to abandon their quasi-voyeuristic position. The door is closed and, as in *Henry V* and *Dead Again*, the film ends.

This use of the door is extended in *Hamlet*. The interior of Elsinore features countless apparent as well as secret doors, like a space full of holes where everything opens and closes, a world of paranoia where everyone can observe and be observed, even through doors that are also two-way mirrors. At the end of the first court scene, Claudius and Gertrude, in a rain of confetti and with a big fanfare, withdraw through an immense door. The servants close the door behind them, the music stops, and Hamlet finds himself alone for his "O that this too too solid flesh would melt" soliloquy. Here again, the door marks a transition, a passage from the exuberance of the previous scene to the gravity of the current one. It amplifies the contrast between the merry crowd's agitation and Hamlet's morose loneliness. The proliferation of doors in *Hamlet*, hidden and otherwise, becomes in the frantic chase sequence, a comment on the false theatricality of life in the palace as Hamlet passes through a succession of rooms in one shot that makes the walls appear insubstantial. In Branagh's movies, doors are symbols of passage from one state to another, the transition of power, of progress, of realizing a new order—or in a world over-done with doors, the vanity of hoping to achieve any such state.

A recurrent element in Branagh's cinema is his use of masked faces, which break out suddenly in front of the camera, like terrifying or supernatural monsters. In *Dead Again*, the thriller Branagh directed in 1991, the character of Roman Strauss is invited to a Hollywood party where every one is disguised in Venetian Carnival costumes. When Roman discovers his wife talking outside to another man, he walks towards the camera and draws his mask down on his face. The entire frame is invaded by this threatening masked figure. In the masked ball scene of *Much Ado About Nothing*, Branagh shows us a whole series of close shots on masks turning suddenly towards the camera. The sensuality of the masks is emphasized in his new film adaptation of *Love's Labour's Lost*: the moment in which the men desguised themselves to meet the women becomes a torrid, masked dance number backed by Irving Berlin's "Let's Face the Music and Dance".

The same use of masks in *Much Ado About Nothing* and *Hamlet* often allows characters to reveal their feelings all the more by hiding them. Borachio enters Don John's cellar wearing a *commedia dell'arte* mask before recounting the rumours of an upcoming wedding. In *Hamlet*, the beginning of the Polonius-Hamlet meeting is thus described in Branagh's script:

POLONIUS
How does my good Lord Hamlet?

Boo! A great skull appears around the pillar. It is HAMLET wearing a grotesque commedia dell'arte *mask. He takes the mask off, and attempts a zany dismissal. Eyes bulging.*[2]

This image of the mask appears at the exact moment when Hamlet reveals his real feelings and his contempt towards Polonius under the very *mask* of madness.

Branagh frequently uses candles and torches to create an atmos-phere both warm and mysterious, as well as a cinematography of visual texture and vacillating light. King Henry V first enters through a door skirted by two large torches. The hypnosis sessions in *Dead Again* begin and end with a circular shot of a candle. The yuletide season of *Peter's Friends* is an occasion to feature many candles and an illuminated Christmas tree. The masked ball in *Much Ado About Nothing* transpires by torchlight, and the "Pardon Goddess of the Night" scene begins with a procession of torches. In one of the opening scenes of *Mary Shelley's Frankenstein*, Victor playfully passes his finger through a candle flame.

Hamlet uses this motif of candles or torches the most. In almost every scene the motif is there, from the opening shot where fire howls amidst the snow in front of Elsinore's gates to the candelabra of the grand hall which traps Claudius in the final scene.

There is, in fact, a fascination with snow and fire in Branagh's cinematic work. This fascination is most prominent in *Hamlet* and *Frankenstein* where the opposite elements compete with one another and vast icy exteriors contrast with the glowing indoor scenes. It is not surprising, then, that Branagh has chosen to set many of his screen and theatre productions at Christmas. Which other period better combines winter's snowy landscapes and festive candlelight? Christmas is a time of year when all feelings are exagerated, emotions are more intense in happiness as well as in despair, which fits Branagh's romantic cinematic temperament.

Twelfth Night, a play he directed for the stage in 1987, was set during Christmas, in a snowy setting. A Christmas tree served as a hiding-place for Toby Belch and Maria to observe the gulling of Malvolio. In *Peter's Friends*, we again find a Christmas tree which Branagh enjoys filming in a circular movement during Roger and Mary's song. Moreover, the action of *In the Bleak Midwinter* is set in the two weeks before Christmas and, all through the film, Joe Harper links Christmas with his moments of doubt and sadness: "I was thinking about the whole Christmas thing, the birth of Christ . . . and quite frankly I was depressed," and ". . . as the yuletide season takes us in its grip I ask myself what is the point in going on with this miserable tormented life?"[3] However, after the stage performance succeeds wonderfully, the joy reaches its peak and the actors exclaim together "Merry Christmas!" ending the film on a festive and cheerful note.

The recurrence of Christmas through his work suggests a strong interest in religious feeling (not to be confused with organized religion). Is it any wonder that in Branagh's performance young Henry V is a genuinely religious king? Or that a church is the place for the rehearsals and stage show in *In the Bleak Midwinter*? In fact, in actor's slang a theatre is often called "a church," and Joe Harper sees how apt the link is: "Churches close and theatres close every week because finally people don't want them."[4]

A chapel is the space where Benedick reveals his love to Beatrice in *Much Ado About Nothing*, where Victor begs Elizabeth not to leave him in *Mary Shelley's Frankenstein*, and where Ophelia confesses her relationship with Hamlet to her father, and Claudius confesses his sins in *Hamlet*—as if admitting a love or a sin is always a sign of penitence or prayer. The cross of Christ is apparent in all these chapels. In *Hamlet*, the image of a cross links the characters of Hamlet and Ophelia: Ophelia, fallen into madness, struggles in a cross-shaped cell; Hamlet, dead, is carried away by soldiers in the symbolic position of the crucified Saviour.

The image of a character alone in an immense room or lost in an infinite landscape is another repeated theme in Branagh's cinema and can be found in most of his films. Henry V appears in the framing of the door, advancing into a room whose great size overwhelms him. During the *"Non nobis"* procession, the camera loses the king amidst a vast muddy and bloody field full of piles of corpses. Again, in *Frankenstein*, when Victor goes to meet the creature in the sea of ice, he is filmed in close-up, sticking his ice-axe into the rock. Then, while the music soars, the camera moves backward, further and further, until he becomes a mere black dot lost in the immensity of mountains. This shot is taken up again in *Hamlet* during the "How all occasions do inform against me" speech: Hamlet delivers the soliloquy in front of a landscape of snowy mountains in which Fortinbras' army marches past. The camera progressively retreats until it reveals an infinite scenery of where man is lost in space and dissolves, as if Branagh has made one of Hamlet's wishes come true: "O that this too too solid flesh would melt."

It is not surprising that *In the Bleak Midwinter*, the film most revealing of Branagh's artistic approach, features this theme thoroughly. In the movie, designer Fadge presents her concept for the play: "You see, we must make the design all about space. People in space, things in space, women in space, men in space."[5] It is also revealing that Branagh has talked often of adapting Thomas Hardy's *Return of the Native* to the screen. The story takes place in the desolated moors of Egdon Heath, where scattered houses are situated several walking hours from one another, where each family is isolated, lost in the wilderness of rushes and peat.

Dancing regularly appears in Branagh's movies to express the happiness of the instant, a joy in the here-and-now. Even before filming a dancing and singing version of *Love's Labour's Lost*, Branagh inserted dancing moments in his movies. In *Dead Again*, Mike Church invites Grace to dance on the roof of his house. Grace suffers from a loss of memory, but she has no need of memory to dance. On the contrary, dancing is the anti-memory act; it removes the grip the past holds and takes no heed of the future. *Peter's Friends, Much Ado About Nothing,* and *In the Bleak Midwinter* all end with a dance that celebrates restored friendship, love, and success. Even in *Frankenstein*, dancing is present, where it takes a ghastly form when Victor waltzes with a reborn but monstrous Elizabeth. By dancing, Victor is trying to project himself into the past, to make the music and happiness of the ball live again. And here, Branagh inserts short flashbacks to previous scenes when Victor and Elizabeth enjoyed happier days. The dance becomes unwholesome and provokes our horror precisely because it does not reflect a celebration of the here-and-now, but a desperate attempt to make the past live again. The function of dancing is perverted and linked more to death than to life.

At first, it is astonishing that Branagh has not included any dance scenes in *Hamlet*. In fact, Branagh filmed a ball scene that we can see in part in the movie trailer. Trailers are edited before the final cut and it is common to spot in them scenes or shots that are not included in the final release. This swift and colourful ball was meant to occur just before the Mousetrap performance, while Hamlet and Horatio talked. In the end, Branagh decided not to include it because he felt it smoothed over the drama of the Mousetrap scene. Nonetheless, some passages in *Hamlet* directly evoke the style of a musical. The first court scene contains some elements proper to a musical: entry and withdrawal in fanfare, confetti, synchronized advancing of the courtiers, shots of the people reacting and applauding in the galleries, etc. According to *The Australian*, "When Derek Jacobi and Julie Christie as Claudius and Gertrude hold court in a spacious ballroom, rose petals rain from the ceiling. It's just like a Vincent Minelli MGM musical extravaganza: you expect them all to start dancing."[6] All this transforms the scene into a gigantic and virtuoso ballet.

In Branagh's movies, cinematic shots convey the characters' inner experiences and his recurrent motifs create a world of flesh and blood, of fire and ice, that brings a vital energy and sensual density to his Shakespearean adaptations.

The Recycling of Filmic and Cultural Codes

We live in a time when most artistic creations recycle achievements from the past, pay homage to them or make fun of them. Likewise, Kenneth Branagh's Shakespearean adaptations hold a mirror up to our own time. Branagh's movies speak to our sensibilities precisely because they allude to famous recent or old movies. Branagh acknowledged in 1993:

> When making both *Much Ado* and *Henry V*, I've been influenced by a number of movies. I seem to know a lot of war movies, a lot of battle movies. I remember bits of Orson Welles's film, *Chimes at Midnight* and Kurosawa's *Ran* as also being very influential. Everything, from *The Great Escape* through *The Longest Day*, *The Magnificent Seven* . . . you name it. A whole pile of stuff that I can't coherently reference. Ideas stolen from everywhere.[7]

In fact, for *Henry V*, his first movie, Branagh, gave composer Patrick Doyle Paul McCartney songs and A. C. Benson's "Land of Hope and Glory" as starting references; he wanted the *Henry V* score to be instantly accessible. For *The Australian*, "watching his *Hamlet* is like channel surfing late at night when the old movies are let out."[8]

By making use of popular references, Branagh allows the audience to connect with Shakespeare more easily. By featuring well-known formulas that evoke familiar emotions, he helps his viewers link Shakespeare's words to feelings in a more immediate way.

Laurence Olivier also chose to borrow from Hollywood genres. For his *Henry V* in 1944, during the Second World War, he borrowed from the western, a genre that fitted the patriotism he wanted to evoke. As in a western, his is a straightforward story with caricatured characters, polarized of good and evil, and horsemen rather than Branagh's infantrymen. Olivier used long panning shots and travelling shots to produce an impression of wide open spaces (like the plains of the Far West). The editing in alternating cuts of the two charging armies directly evokes the Indians and Cavalry of the western. Even the duel between Henry and the Dauphin recalls a final showdown between two cowboys.

Laurence Olivier's *Hamlet* uses elements from German expressionist *film noir* and its offshoot, the American detective story. According to Guntner and Drexler,

> The atmosphere in Olivier's Elsinore would remind his 1940s audience of the abandoned American inner city at night; Olivier's alienated Hamlet would evoke memories of Humphrey Bogart or Dick Powell as Philip Marlowe or Sam Spade, who also try to solve bizarre murder cases in a murky and threatening world in which the real and the unreal, good and evil, intersect.[9]

Some critics even saw the influence of Orson Welles' *Citizen Kane:*

> The prince stands on the top stairs, calling down to Ophelia as she kneels in the cold wide hall—"Nymph, in thy orisons be all my sins rememb'red"—just as Charles Foster Kane does, coming out of the darkness to hurl questions at Susan, who sits miserably with her jigsaw below.[10]

All the famous screen adaptations of *Hamlet* perfectly insert themselves in their times. Grigory Kozintsev's Russian version, in the middle of the sixties, follows a Marxist interpretation: Elsinore is overpopulated, and as a *clin d'oeil* to Stalinism, Denmark is a prison full of spies. Some years later, the adaptation of Tony Richardson suits the "hippy" years: Claudius and Gertrude, who are still quite young, deal with the public affairs from their nuptial bed like John Lennon and Yoko Ono. Zeffirelli's version, at the end of the eighties, confirms Mel Gibson's reputation as an action hero: *Hamlet* becomes another *Lethal Weapon.*

Branagh's Shakespearean adaptations fit our nostalgic, post-modern era in which most of artistic creations recycle achievements from the past, pay homage to them or make fun of them. *Henry V* uses codes from Vietnam movies: muddy ground, transcended pains, manly friendships. *Much Ado About Nothing* is shot in the musical mode with a jolly beginning and ending, and developed around recurrent musical themes. *Hamlet*, on the other hand, transforms itself into an epic thriller, even a horror film: bloody close-ups, heart-breaking screams, and speedy chases through the corridors of Elsinore.

This analysis is not meant to suggest that Branagh has been consciously or unconsciously influenced by the movies mentioned below. Rather, because these allusions have been perceived by movie critics, scholars, and spectators[11] they can only help an audience who has seen, for example, war classics such as *Platoon* at the cinema and *Doctor Zhivago* on late-night television to grasp these Shakespearean stories.

Yet, even though Branagh is influenced by these well-established filmic and cultural codes, his films are by no means parodies or homages. The final vision in all cases remains a truly personal one, whose clarity and boldness is introducing Shakespeare to a new, young audience at this end of our century.

Western and Adventure Movies

In its glorification of male bonding (Henry and Falstaff in the old days, Henry held by Exeter after the siege of Harfleur, Henry weeping in Fluellen's arms after the battle), Branagh's *Henry V* takes us directly back to John Wayne westerns, such as Howard Hawk's *Rio Bravo*, where this theme prevails. Moreover, during the Harfleur siege, Henry arrives on a rearing horse, according to Michael Pursell, just like a "Lone Ranger."[12]

In *Much Ado About Nothing*, the allusion is even more obvious. When the soldiers return from war on galloping horses in the opening scenes, their number (seven) as well as their arrangement (side by side in line) directly echo John Sturges' *The Magnificent Seven*.

As far as *Hamlet* is concerned, the ending recalls adventure movies of the 40s and 50s: Hamlet and Laertes fight like musketeers with swordplay and clever thrusts and parries, taking the lead in turns. When finally Hamlet throws his sword at Claudius like a javelin, grabs the chandelier rope and swings down through the hall to finish off his uncle, the film reproduces the great final moments of an Errol Flynn movie.

Sports

Henry V is full of sports references, especially football and rugby. All the ingredients are there: the players kissing the ground before the match, the scrimmage, the tackling of Montjoy, the mud, the scratched and bloody faces, the wet hair, the embraces and hugs after the match . . .

For Chris Fitter, "the tonality seems taken from a brutal British rugby match"[13] and the English press used sports metaphors at the movie's release:"Branagh has fielded the first XV" (I. Johnstone, *Sunday Times*, 8 October 1989), "This is how Englishmen play their foot-

ball, so it seems a perfectly natural style in which to wage their wars"
(A. Lane, *The Independent*, 30 September 1989), "The English take
Harfleur with the help of one horse and the first XI" (A. Bilson, *Sunday Correspondent*, 8 October 1989). Michael Pursell has even perceived Henry on the cart at the end of the *"Non nobis"* as a victorious
sportsman, bending his head to receive his medal while listening to
his national anthem.

It is interesting to note that Branagh marks the beginning of his
passion for theatricality at age twelve when he became the captain of
the football and rugby team, "I suspect for my innate sense of drama—
I loved shouting theatrically butch encouragement to 'my lads'."[14]

War Movies

In its use of mud, music, and slow-motions, Branagh's *Henry V* clearly
recycles the war movie genre. Orson Welles' *Chimes at Midnight* (with
its famous battle of Shrewsbury) and Kurosawa's bloody and misty
Ran are never very far off. Chris Fitter notices: "the structure . . . owes
much . . . to Vietnam movies of the 1980s, particularly its moral
ambiguity: war is hell but it heroizes."[15] Branagh's battle of Agincourt
indeed recalls Stanley Kubrick's *Full Metal Jacket* when the marines
stagger through the mud under a continuous rain, as well as Oliver
Stone's *Platoon,* in which Sergeant Elias is chased and eventually killed
by a Viet Cong in tragic slow-motion accompanied by harrowing
music.

One must not forget that Branagh's *Henry V* was shot in England at
a time when films expressing the horror and disillusion of war were
inevitably influenced by the war in the Falklands. Those movies principally focused on the destructive effects of the First World War on
returned soldiers. In 1986, Branagh played the part of a young First
World War soldier suffering from deep emotional trauma in the film
A Month in the Country, whose director of photography, Kenneth
McMillan, also worked on *Henry V*. When we watch the first scene of
A Month in the Country in which a dirty, exhausted soldier is crawling
in the muddy trenches, we cannot but think of the Battle of Agincourt
shot two years later. References to the First World War abound in
Branagh's *Henry V*: the British soldiers are shown in muddy trenches
during the siege of Harfleur and the geographical map on which we
follow the progress of Henry's army through France recalls the place
of names of famous battles between 1914 and 1918.

Henry V follows a contemporary movie pattern which has been described as "Ramboesque" by Curtis Breight: "[It is] almost as though all the Rambo films were collapsed into *Henry V*: Johnny Rambo human and vulnerable, then insulted and attacked, hence violent; Rambo on the offensive against all odds; Rambo betrayed by his own side; Rambo killing huge numbers of Russians and Vietnamese and sustaining few casualties."[16] Although this comparison can be read as criticism, it does demonstrate that Branagh has succeeded in recycling a code very familiar to a whole generation. As Pursell says, "With all these contemporary cultural references . . . Branagh is clearly concerned not to return us to an idealized past but to a visibly constructed present."[17]

Hamlet as well features a scene reminiscent of a classic war movie. After Ophelia's funeral, Branagh chooses to shoot Elsinore's gates in the morning mist. Francisco is keeping the watch alone. Later in the film, he will catch a glimpse of Fortinbras' massive army advancing on the palace. Branagh conveys here the same feeling as in Darryl Zanuck's *The Longest Day* when a German soldier enjoys his breakfast in a coastal bunker and then suddenly sees the D-Day fleet approaching.

Thrillers

Interviewed on the set of *Dead Again*, Branagh gave his opinion of the thriller genre: "It's a great genre, and it's the one more than any other American genre—more than westerns, more than sci-fi, more than action or light comedies—that I and God knows how many millions of people have really identified with."[18] It is no surprise that Branagh has recycled so many elements of the thriller in his Shakespearean adaptations.

Branagh admitted he wanted the Southampton treason scene in *Henry V* to be "Hitchcockian, fast-moving, tense and violent."[19] The scene occurs in a secluded place, in an atmosphere of claustrophobia. The scene starts with a shot of the doors being locked, as if we were about to attend a Mafia-style settlement. Kenneth Rothwell writes: "[Henry's] wrath and fearful assault on the hapless traitors are reminiscent of the post-prandial entertainment at a Hollywood version of a Mafia dinner party. He and Exeter take everything but a baseball bat to his erstwhile friends."[20] Rothwell obviously alludes to a scene from

Brian de Palma's *The Untouchables* in which Robert De Niro as Al Capone takes a baseball bat to the skull of a traitor.

In the treason scene in *Henry V*, the traitors are threatened with knives and thrust against the walls with a ruthlessness that takes us back to the gangster movies of the 1940s. Branagh, a dedicated fan of those films, in 1987 wrote the play *Public Enemy*, paying homage to the William Wellman movie in which James Cagney plays a dangerous gangster. In 1991, *Dead Again* was also a thriller with countless references to Welles and Hitchcock.

This forceful thrust of a character against the ground or a wall is often repeated in Branagh's movies. In *Henry V*, Lord Scroop is thrown down onto a table and Montjoy the herald is forced into the mud of the battlefield; in *Much Ado*, Benedick violently thrusts Claudio against the wall to challenge him. The tackling even happens in *Hamlet's* opening scene:

> BARNARDO O/S
> Who's there?
>
> *FRANCISCO whips around to his left, but not quickly enough.*
> *CRASH! A body, from right of frame, bundles him forcibly to the*
> *ground.*[21]

When Hamlet runs through the woods following the Ghost, he is suddenly thrust against a tree and violently grabbed at the throat by the spectre's hand, in exactly the same way the Creature attacks his creator several times in *Mary Shelley's Frankenstein*.

While he was promoting *Hamlet*, Branagh repeated over and over that he considered his film to be a thriller. In fact, this idea had been with him for a long time. Branagh's own film *In the Bleak Midwinter* reveals the thoughts of its director when Joe Harper says to his actor playing Barnardo:

> [You're playing it] a bit limp. . . . He has seen a ghost and he is probably expecting to see another one. Listen, Hamlet is a tremendous ghost story. I want to see that fear—I want to smell that fear.[22]

In an interview, Branagh echoed this idea by referring to a cinematographic landmark by Steven Spielberg:

> The first five, ten minutes ought to be suspensefully shocking. It should be reminiscent of *Jaws*. There's something out there. These

men on the battlements have been scared stiff. You've got to make that as personal, as real and as scary as possible.[23]

Another more direct echo is to the first scenes of *Mary Shelley's Frankenstein* where the sailors are scared by a howl that later reveals itself to be the creature's::

GRIGORI *(terse, low)*
There's something out there.

WALTON *(to himself)*
What's out there?[24]

Branagh's artistic journey, which includes the directing of two thrillers (*Dead Again* and *Frankenstein*) and the writing of a violent play (*Public Enemy*), has thus helped him bring to the beginning of *Hamlet* this sense of visceral, looming danger and supernatural fear. According to the daily paper *The Australian*, "it could just as likely be anything . . . from Lon Chaney Jr's *Wolf Man* and *the Creature From the Black Lagoon* to Hannibal the Cannibal. It's not just a thriller; it's all thrillers."[25]

Hamlet not only begins but continues in the thriller mode. When Hamlet is chased through the corridors after killing Polonius, he takes Rosencrantz hostage to protect himself from the guards exactly as a James Cagney character would to escape the police. Then, the great chase through room after room directly recalls American action movies and all their famous chase sequences. Hamlet finally finds his way to his private room and believes he is safe for a few seconds . . . until a gun suddenly enters the frame and is pressed to his temple. That same suspense can be found in Alan Parker's 1978 *Midnight Express*, in which Billy Hayes, chased through the streets of Istanbul, thinks he has escaped from his pursuer; close-up on his sweaty but relieved face, quickly replaced with a desperate look, the camera pans left and we discover a revolver against his ear. In a two-minute sequence, Branagh's direction reprises three classic moments from movie thrillers: the hostage, the chase, and the revolver *coup de théâtre*.

Even the actors' performance often recalls the thriller genre in Branagh's Shakespearean adaptations. Branagh's portrayal of Henry V evoked the performances of famous actors. Donald Hedrick saw in Henry a "Clint Eastwood king—isolated, just, and capable of necessary ruthlessness that is spontaneous rather than calculating"[26] and Frank Occhiogrosso talked of "Branagh's Brando-like monotone of his opening scene."[27] The meeting between Hamlet and the first gravedigger was rehearsed as if it was the confrontation between Robert De Niro and Al Pacino in the film *Heat* by Michael Mann. Both actors, Branagh and Billy Crystal, substituted a typical Mafia dialogue for their lines to help them to deliver the text in the most natural and modern way possible.

Science-Fiction, Fantasy, and Horror Movies

The line between thrillers and fantasy films is porous and Branagh's filmic allusions also cross this boundary.

The dark image of Henry V wearing a cape entering like a threatening and mysterious figure has been compared to Darth Vader from George Lucas's *Star Wars* and even to Batman. For Michael Pursell, Henry V is "the dark invader . . . a point supported as he moves into the court by the over-the-shoulder camera position that frames the back of his head and the faces of his courtiers in an obvious *Star Wars* trope."[28] He even sees in the armoured Exeter threatening the French king another Robocop or Terminator, "a killing machine praying for war." The robotic side of Exeter appears on several occasions in the film. The way he accuses the traitors ("I arrest thee of high treason . . .") is repetitive and unemotional and the music backing him is often heavy and ungraceful.

Some may argue it is more appropriate to say Branagh uses cultural antetypes or psychological archetypes rather than specific echoes of films. In this view, Exeter would not be derived from Robocop, but rather, both characters draw their source from an archetype of the dehumanized, mechanical warrior, with Robocop as an extremely literal expression and Exeter a subtler one. This however fails to acknowledge the impact the most famous movies have had on the public, and on Branagh himself. When a movie using an archetype becomes a hit, the movie image supplants the archetype and comes to stand for it in the popular imagination. In fact, Branagh often makes reference to famous movies when he describes actions or characters' thoughts in his screenplays. For example, the reference to Robocop appears in Branagh's own words in the screenplay of *Hamlet*. For the duel between Hamlet and Laertes, costume designer Alex Byrne made leather tunics which closely moulded the fighters' bodies as Branagh wanted them to give the impression of "two graduates of the Robocop academy."[29]

In *Hamlet*, another moment alludes to a famous sci-fi movie. Branagh goes from a close-up on Ophelia howling helplessly at the palace gates to a long shot of Elsinore in a snowy desolated landscape. Ophelia's scream is lost amidst an endless expanse of ice, producing a feeling of inevitability: nobody will ever come and help her. It is almost reminiscent of the slogan on the famous *Alien* poster: "In space no one can hear you scream," and echoes movies such as James Carpenter's *The Thing*, set in an arctic wasteland.

The recycling of horror codes is also frequent in *Hamlet*. When the Prince looks for the ghost in the woods, the earth is quaking, splitting and releasing an infernal smoke. The spectre speaks with a reverberating voice that a number of critics have compared again to Darth Vader, and the murder of Old Hamlet includes extreme close-ups on the ear into which the poison is poured: the skin blisters and blood bubbles out. The killing of Polonius later ends in a spreading pool of blood shot in close-up as if a bloody ocean were about to invade Elsinore. Hamlet slowly walks towards the bloody pool. The viewer begins to imagine Hamlet stamping his feet in the blood but, at the last moment, he turns around it. Branagh, like the best directors of thrillers, only evokes our sick fear and imagination which are indeed more powerful than action itself. The gore is present to the end of the movie: Osric is stabbed in the stomach and then shows his hand full of blood to report "this warlike volley."

Comedies, Romances, and Musicals

The recycling of codes from musicals, romances, and comedies can clearly be found in *Much Ado About Nothing*. According to Pierre Berthomieu, "The movement of love, the pure eroticism of the bodies, the kinetics of the groups: Branagh's prologue is truly a *musical*. . . . *Much Ado About Nothing* . . . sends us back . . . to Robert Wise's *The Sound of Music*."[30] Even the final dance through the patios refers to the scene of *The Sound of Music* in which the children and Maria dance in the gardens near the house.

Critics have also noticed explicit allusions to Stanley Donen's *Singin' in the Rain*. Benedick, believing in Beatrice's love, plunges into the fountain. Samuel Crowl speaks of "Branagh's Gene Kelly–like splashing in the fountain."[31] Gene Kelly's character, in love, sings "I'm ready for love" under a pouring rain. Benedick, just as ready, joins in.

Even *Hamlet* recycles codes from movie musicals. As we saw, *The Australian* described the first court scene in which music soars and confetti fall down as reminiscent of an MGM musical extravaganza. Some spectators have even linked the choreographic moves of the final duel with Robert Wise's *West Side Story.* Laertes and Hamlet land upstairs in the same synchronized position as the two rivals in the famous musical.

The bizarre riding of Dogberry and Verges suggests *Monty Python and the Holy Grail* in which the Knights of the Round Table go their way on invisible horses, imitating the noise of hooves with coconuts. For Steve Starger, "Keaton mugs and growls through stained teeth and bizarre business, including a Monty Python trot on an invisible horse,"[32] and for Adam Mars-Jones, "The pair of them ride imaginary horses, an idea seemingly pinched from *Monty Python and the Holy Grail.*"[33]

Branagh's acting in *Much Ado About Nothing* has borrowed from famous comic actors. When vainly struggling with the deck-chair, he obviously imitates Chaplin. Moreover, when Benedick is waiting for Beatrice to "bid [him] come in to dinner," Branagh deliberately refers to Billy Wilder's *Some Like It Hot.* We can read in his script:

> BENEDICK *has thrown what he thinks to be a gallant and sexy leg up on the edge of the fountain. He strikes a pose and a tone of voice that reminds one of Tony Curtis as Cary Grant in* Some Like It Hot. *It is a face frozen in a grin that is trying to convey sex, romance, intelligence, wit, and warmth, all at once. In short, he looks ridiculous.*[34]

Emma Thompson as Beatrice, on the other hand, has been compared to Katharine Hepburn. The tone of the movie is very reminiscent of Hollywood fast-paced comedies of the 40s and 50s, the Branagh–Thompson opposition, married to each other at the time, reminiscent of the famous duet of Spencer Tracy and Katharine Hepburn.

At the end of the movie, when Benedick and Beatrice are presented with the undelivered sonnets that were secretly stolen from each of them, Branagh and Thompson both throw a curious glance at each other's "piece of art." Through a simple dumb show, they critique each other's style and content. We can here think of Leo McCarey's 1957 romantic comedy *An Affair to Remember:* Cary Grant and Deborah Kerr use the same dumb show when they comment on photos taken of them on the cruise ship without their permission. A scene from *An Affair to Remember* also occurs in a chapel where the two heroes become aware of their mutual love.

This trend of importing romantic and musical codes reaches its peak in *Love's Labour's Lost*. The play is adapted as a classic Hollywood musical inspired by the Fred Astaire and Ginger Rogers movies. It includes famous numbers like *Shall We Dance, Cheek to Cheek, The Way You Look Tonight*, and even presents a synchronised swimming sequence which evokes the aquatic ballets of Esther Williams. The artificiality of the sets creates a fairy tale atmosphere recalling the look of musicals from the thirties to the fifties, and sometimes even destroying the filmic illusion when Don Armado kicks the moon out of the set during his number *I Get a Kick Out of You*.

Branagh sets the play at the eve of an imaginary World War, which gives him the opportunity to import motifs from famous film romances. When the men and women have to part, the "farewell" scene takes place at a deserted airport in the mist, a moment very reminiscent of the end of *Casablanca*. Then, although Shakespeare's play ends ambiguously, leaving the audience to wonder whether the boys will ever meet the girls again, Branagh adds a sequence showing us the different destinies of the characters during the war, and then reuniting boys and girls at the Liberation. Branagh thus chooses to suppress the ambiguity and ends the film in a restored, romantic harmony.

TV Serials and Cartoons

Branagh has always loved TV sagas as epitomized by *Dallas*. Just before the release of *Henry V*, Branagh explained: "What would make my eighteen-year-old sister see this? It's the first exposure to Shakespeare for a lot of kids [and] you have to remember they've been watching *Neighbours* the night before and want something that comes from the same world."[35]

This taste for TV sagas can be found in Branagh's use of flashbacks which work like a summary of the previous episodes. In *Henry V*, as in a TV serial, the flashbacks are there to remind the audience of the previous plays (*Richard II, Henry IV, parts 1 and 2*) and Branagh does not cut the Chorus's last lines which allude to the continuing story (the three plays of *Henry VI*).

In *Hamlet*, the establishing shots of Elsinore work like the exterior shots of the Southfork ranch in *Dallas*. Moreover, after the intermission, a bold flashback sums up what has happened in the first part: images we have seen earlier in the film underscore Claudius's speech "O Gertrude, Gertrude, / When sorrows come they come not single spies, / But in battalions."

As far as cartoons are concerned, some critics and spectators have even perceived echoes from Tex Avery's cartoon repertoire in Branagh's *Hamlet*: Hamlet ironically kissing Claudius on the mouth before leaving for England ("Farewell, dear mother") recalls a typical funny scene of Bugs Bunny kissing hunter Elmer Fudd.

The music Patrick Doyle composed for *Hamlet* also features some moments which strangely recall cartoons in the style of Tex Avery, the creator of Daffy Duck and Bugs Bunny. When Hamlet tells Horatio how much he esteems him and that there should be no reason to flatter a poor man, the music progressively rises in deep masculine and warm sounds until "Ay, in my heart of heart, / As I do thee," at which point the violins quiet to let us hear the sound of a little flute. The scene, at risk of becoming too sentimental, actually mocks its own excess of sentimentality, as in a Tex Avery cartoon where emotions are both stressed and laughed at by the score. It perfectly suits Hamlet's next sentence: "Something too much of this."

The same little flute appears again in the movie, this time diegetically, inside the story itself, with the arrival of the "recorders." When Hamlet, simulating madness, takes Guildenstern apart for a private conversation before the "pipe" scene ("To withdraw with you . . ."), he gets rid of Rosencrantz with a gesture both brusque and funny. Simultaneously, one of the "recorders" plays some descending notes recalling the background score of a cartoon gag.

Epics

For *Hamlet,* and even *Henry V*, Branagh admits he has been inspired by the great epic movies. These two movies gladly participate in the long tradition of Hollywood epic and spectacle. References to Victor Fleming's *Gone With the Wind* abound in both movies. The long march from Harfleur to Agincourt, under the rain and in the mud, is an obvious reminder of the Confederates' long defeated procession out of Savannah. The scene even features the same acts of solidarity among the soldiers: one of the exhausted English soldiers collapses and is helped up by another walker. In *Hamlet*, many spectators have also compared the "My thoughts be bloody" sequence to the scene in *Gone*

With the Wind when Scarlett swears "As God is my witness, I'll never be hungry again!" The camera moves backward until the heroic character is lost in an infinite space: Scarlett under the Tara tree; Hamlet in a snowy landscape where, in the distance, Fortinbras' army marches past.

The sheer length of *Hamlet,* the scope of its vision, reminds us of such epics as William Wyler's *Ben Hur* or Cecil B. De Mille's *The Ten Commandments.* The army charging on horses in the snowy plains of Russia in David Lean's *Doctor Zhivago* has inspired the charge of Fortinbras' soldiers on Elsinore in *Hamlet.* In *Henry V*, Branagh has referred to another David Lean movie, this time in his performance: he told the *Daily Mail* "Henry is like Hamlet, in that he questions what he's done, in a similar way to Alec Guinness at the end of *The Bridge on the River Kwai* when he says: 'What have I done, what have I done?'"[36]

The last elegiac march at the end of *Hamlet, "In Pace"* sung by Placido Domingo, takes up one last time this epic rhythm. As Hamlet is carried out of the palace by four soldiers, Patrick Doyle's music weaves together the Hamlet and Ophelia themes, allowing the two characters to meet in death and peace with a moving dignity. This grand elegy underlines the pathos of Hamlet's fate but also evokes a kind of release for the character. The words for *"In Pace"* were taken from of the Book of Wisdom and slightly adapted by Russell Jackson:

> Diligite justitiam, o judices terrae
> Justorum animae in manu Dei sunt, et non
> tanget illos tormentum mortis.
> Visi sunt oculis insapientium mori, et
> aestimata est afflictio exitus
> illorum—illi autem sunt
> in pace.
>
> Tyrannus impius non habet spem, et si
> quidem longae vitae erit, in nihilum
> computabitur.
> Princeps autem justus,
> ille in pace est.[37]

For Branagh, "In the end, you don't feel Hamlet is melancholy or suicidal. You feel he's reached some sort of peace."[38] And Hamlet has indeed been looking for that peace all through the movie.

By inserting his adaptations into our contemporary culture, Branagh brings Shakespeare closer to the young people and what they are used to watching everyday at movie theatres or on television. This recycling of filmic and cultural codes helps to make Shakespeare as simple, natural, and understandable as possible. There were Olivier, Welles, Kurosawa, Kozintzev, Brook, Polanski, and Zeffirelli. No doubt Kenneth Branagh has already joined them among Shakespeare's spiritual sons in modern times.

Notes

1. Quoted in Bob Fisher, "Tragedy of Epic Proportions." *American Cinematographer*, Jan 1997.
2. Kenneth Branagh. *Hamlet: Screenplay, Introduction and Film Diary*, p. 56.
3. Kenneth Branagh. *In the Bleak Midwinter*, pp. 1 & 53.
4. Kenneth Branagh. *In the Bleak Midwinter*, p. 53.
5. Kenneth Branagh. *In the Bleak Midwinter*, p. 17.
6. "To See or Not to See—That is the Question as the Post-Modern Version of *Hamlet* comes to Town." *Australian*, 21 May 1997.
7. Quoted in John Naughton, "The Return of The Magnificent Eight?" *Premiere*, Sep 1993.
8. "To See or Not to See—That is the Question as the Post-Modern Version of *Hamlet* comes to Town." *Australian*, 21 May 1997.
9. Lawrence Guntner & Peter Drexler. "Recycled film codes and the study of Shakespeare on film." *Deutsche Shakespeare*, 1993.
10. Antony Lane. "Insubstantial pageants." *Independent*, 30 Sep 1989.
11. I gathered comments from spectators mainly on the internet, including from the mailing list of the "2Bers" created by Kathryn Penote and organized by Ngoc Vu (ken-friends@uclink4.berkeley.edu).
12. Michael Pursell. "Playing the game: Branagh's *Henry V*." *Literature Film Quaterly* 20 (10 Jan 1992).
13. Chris Fitter. "A Tale of Two Branaghs: Henry V, Ideology and the Mekong Agincourt."
14. Kenneth Branagh. *Beginning*, p. 28.
15. Chris Fitter. "A Tale of Two Branaghs: Henry V, Ideology and the Mekong Agincourt."
16. Curtis Breight. "Branagh and the Prince, or a 'royal fellowship of death'."
17. Michael Pursell. "Playing the game: Branagh's *Henry V*."
18. Quoted in Anwar Brett, "Eternal Death." *X Posé*, May 1997.
19. Kenneth Branagh. *Beginning*, p. 225.
20. Kenneth Rothwell. "Kenneth Branagh's *Henry V*: The Gilt [Guilt] in the Crown Re-Examined." *Comparative Drama* 24 (1990–91).
21. Kenneth Branagh. *Hamlet: Screenplay, Introduction and Film Diary*, p. 2.
22. Kenneth Branagh. *In the Bleak Midwinter*, p. 33.
23. An interview with Charlie Rose, broadcast on "Charlie Rose," PBS, Dec 1995.

24. Steph Lady, Frank Darabont & Kenneth Branagh. *Mary Shelley's Frankenstein: The screenplay.* New York: Newmarket Press, 1994, p. 35.
25. "To See or Not to See—That is the Question as the Post-Modern Version of Hamlet comes to Town." *Australian*, 21 May 1997.
26. Donald Hedrick. "War is mud: Branagh's dirty *Henry V.*" *Shakespeare on Film Newsletter*, Apr 1991.
27. Frank Occhiogrosso. "Branagh's *Henry V*," a film review.
28. Michael Pursell. "Playing the game: Branagh's *Henry V.*"
29. Kenneth Branagh. *Hamlet: Screenplay, Introduction and Film Diary*, p. 162.
30. Pierre Berthomieu. *Kenneth Branagh: Traînes de feu, rosées de sang.*
31. Samuel Crowl. "*Much Ado About Nothing.*"
32. Quoted in H. R. Coursen. *Shakespeare in Production: Whose History?* Ohio: Ohio University Press, 1996, p. 112.
33. Adam Mars-Jones. "Much amiss." *Indépendant*, 27 Aug 1993.
34. Kenneth Branagh. *Much Ado About Nothing: Screenplay, Introduction and Notes on the Making of the Film*, p. 47.
35. Quoted in Ian Shuttleworth, *Ken & Em*, p. 160.
36. Quoted in Baz Bamigboye, "Once more unto the breach."
37. Kenneth Branagh. Liner notes to *Hamlet: Original Motion Picture Soundtrack.*
38. Quoted in James Fallon. "The Prince Returns." *W*, Nov 1996.

Kenneth Branagh's
Shakespearean Corpus

Henry V (Theatre, 1984)
Produced by the Royal Shakespeare Company at the Royal Shakespeare Theatre, Stratford-upon-Avon. Press Night: 22 March 1984.

Directed by Adrian Noble; design by Bob Crowley; music by Howard Blake.

Adam Bareham (GOWER), Brian Blessed (EXETER), Kenneth Branagh (HENRY V), Yvonne Coulette (ALICE), Derek Crewe (NYM), Richard Easton (CONSTABLE OF FRANCE), Dexter Fletcher (BOY), Paul Gregory (WESTMORELAND), Norman Henry (ERPINGHAM / GOVERNOR), Bernard Horsfall (PISTOL), Harold Innocent (CANTERBURY / BURGUNDY), Andrew Jarvis (COURT / CAMBRIDGE), Arthur Kohn (GREY / MACMORRIS), Ian McDiarmid (CHORUS), Ian MacKenzie (ORLEANS), Peter Miles (GRANDPRE), Cecile Paoli (KATHARINE), David Phelan (BEDFORD), Siân Probert (FLUELLEN), Christopher Ravenscroft (MONTJOY), Andy Readman (ENGLISH SOLDIER), John Rogan (BARDOLPH), Patricia Routledge (MISTRESS QUICKLY), Jonathan Scott-Taylor (GLOUCESTER), Sebastian Shaw (CHARLES VI / ELY), Stephen Simms (SCROOP / YORK), Malcolm Storry (WILLIAMS), Peter Theedom (BATES, JAMY), Nicholas Woodeson (DAUPHIN), Sarah Woodward (ENGLISH SOLDIER)

Love's Labour's Lost (Theatre, 1984)
Produced by Renaissance Theatre Company
Directed by Barry Kyle, with Kenneth Branagh as the King of Navarre.

Hamlet (Theatre, 1984)
Produced by the Royal Shakespeare Company at the Royal Shakespeare Theatre, Stratford-upon-Avon. Press Night: 9 August 1984.

Directed by Ron Daniels; design by Maria Bjornson; music by Nigel Hess.

Peter Theedom (FRANCISCO / NORWEGIAN CAPTAIN), Jimmy Yuill (BERNARDO / FIRST SAILOR), Paul Gregory (MARCELLUS / PRIEST), Nicholas Farrell (HORATIO), Richard Easton (GHOST), John Stride (CLAUDIUS), Virginia McKenna (GERTRUDE), Roger Rees (HAMLET), Raymond

Bowers (VOLTEMAND), Christopher Benjamin (POLONIUS), Kenneth Branagh (LAERTES), Frances Barber (OPHELIA), Martin Milman (ROSENCRANTZ), Myles Hoyle (GUILDENSTERN), Jim Hooper (REYNALDO), Bernard Horsfall (FIRST PLAYER), Philip Dupuy (SECOND PLAYER / COURTIER / SOLDIER), Stephen Simms (THIRD PLAYER / COURTIER / SOLDIER), Derek Crewe (FOURTH PLAYER / SECOND CLOWN), James Simmons (FORTINBRAS), Nicholas Bell (SECOND SAILOR / COURTIER / SOLDIER), Sebastian Shaw (FIRST CLOWN), Andrew Hall (OSRIC), James Newall (MESSENGER / COURTIER / SOLDIER), Sarah Woodward and Cathy Tyson (LADIES), Guy Fithen (COURTIER / SOLDIER)

Romeo and Juliet (Theatre, 1986)
Produced by Renaissance Theatre Company.
Directed by Kenneth Branagh.

Twelfth Night (Theatre, 1987)
Produced by Renaissance Theatre Company.
Directed by Kenneth Branagh.

As You Like It (Theatre, 1988)   .
Produced by Renaissance Theatre Company.
Directed by Geraldine McEwan, with Kenneth Branagh as Touchstone.

Much Ado About Nothing (Theatre, 1988)
Produced by the Renaissance Theatre Company at the Phoenix Theatre, London, as part of the Renaissance Shakespeare at the Phoenix series. Press Night: 25 August 1988. (And tour including Birmingham Rep, 8 March 1988.)

Directed by Dame Judi Dench; design by Jenny Tiramani; music by Patrick Doyle.

Samantha Bond (BEATRICE), Kenneth Branagh (BENEDICK), Richard Clifford (DON PEDRO), Patrick Doyle (BALTHAZAR / CONRAD), Richard Easton (LEONATO), Tam Hoskyns (HERO), Edward Jewesbury (ANTONIO / FIRST WATCH), James Larkin (CLAUDIO), David Lloyd Meredith (DOGBERRY), Dearbhla Molloy (URSULA), David Parfitt (SECOND WATCH / MESSENGER), Shaun Prendergast (DON JOHN), Sophie Thompson (MARGARET), Jay Villiers (BORACHIO), Jimmy Yuill (VERGES / FRIAR FRANCIS)

Hamlet (Theatre, 1988)
Produced by the Renaissance Theatre Company at the Phoenix Theatre, London, as part of the Renaissance Shakespeare at the Phoenix series. Press Night: 8 September 1988. (And tour including Birmingham Rep, 24 May 1988).

Directed by Derek Jacobi; set design by Jenny Tiramani; music by Patrick Doyle.

Kenneth Branagh (HAMLET), Samantha Bond (PLAYER / COURT LADY), Richard Clifford (HORATIO), Patrick Doyle (OSRIC), Richard Easton (CLAUDIUS), Tam Hoskyns (PLAYER / COURT LADY), Edward Jewesbury (POLONIUS), James Larkin (FORTINBRAS, VOLTEMAND / PLAYER KING), David Lloyd Meredith (GHOST / GRAVEDIGGER), Dearbhla Molloy (GERTRUDE), Sophie Thompson (OPHELIA), David Parfitt (ROSENCRANTZ / PRIEST / MARCELLUS), Shaun Prendergast (BARNARDO / LUCIANUS), Jay Villiers (LAERTES), Jimmy Yuill (GUILDENSTERN / SAILOR)

Hamlet (Theatre, 1988)

Produced by RennaissanceTheatre Company at the Tivoli Festival, Elsinore Castle, Denmark.

Directed by Derek Jacobi; set design by Jenny Tiramani; music by Patrick Doyle.

Kenneth Branagh (HAMLET), Samantha Bond (PLAYER / COURT LADY), Richard Clifford (HORATIO), Patrick Doyle (OSRIC), Richard Easton (CLAUDIUS), Tam Hoskyns (PLAYER / COURT LADY), Edward Jewesbury (POLONIUS), James Larkin (FORTINBRAS, VOLTEMAND / PLAYER KING), David Lloyd Meredith (GHOST / GRAVEDIGGER), Dearbhla Molloy (GERTRUDE), Sophie Thompson (OPHELIA), David Parfitt (ROSENCRANTZ / PRIEST / MARCELLUS), Shaun Prendergast (BARNARDO / LUCIANUS), Jay Villiers (LAERTES), Jimmy Yuill (GUILDENSTERN / SAILOR)

Henry V (Film, 1989)

Directed and adapted by Kenneth Branagh; director of photography: Kenneth McMillan; designed by Norman Dorme; costumes: Phyllis Dalton; edited by Mike Bradsell; music by Patrick Doyle; script: Anne Wotton; producer: Bruce Sharman; executive producer: Stephen Evans; associate producer: David Parfitt. A Renaissance Films production in association with BBC and Curzon Film distributors.

Kenneth Branagh (HENRY V), Derek Jacobi (CHORUS), Simon Sheperd (DUKE OF GLOUCESTER), James Larkin (DUKE OF BEDFORD), Brian Blessed (DUKE OF EXETER), James Simmons (DUKE OF YORK), Paul Gregory (WESTMORELAND), Charles Kay (CANTERBURY), Alec McCowen (ELY), Fabian Cartwright (CAMBRIDGE), Stephen Simms (LORD SCROOP), Jay Villiers (GREY), Ian Holm (FLUELLEN), Richard Briers (BARDOLPH), Geoffrey Hutchins (NYM), Robert Stephens (PISTOL), Robbie Coltrane (FALSTAFF), Judi Dench (MISTRESS QUICKLY), Christian Bale (BOY), Patrick Doyle (COURT), John Sessions (MACMORRIS), Jimmy Yuill (JAMY), Edward Jewesbury (ERPINGHAM), Paul Scofield (CHARLES VI), Michael Maloney (DAUPHIN), Harold Innocent (BOURGOGNE), Richard Clifford (ORLEANS), Emma Thompson (KATHERINE), Geraldine MacEwan (ALICE), Richard Easton (CONSTABLE), Christopher Ravenscroft (MONTJOY)

King Lear (Theatre, 1990)
Produced by Renaissance Theatre Company, World Tour.
Directed by Kenneth Branagh, and in the role of Edgar.

A Midsummer Night's Dream (Theatre, 1990)
Produced by Renaissance Theatre Company, World Tour.
Directed by Kenneth Branagh, and in the role of Peter Quince.

Hamlet (Radio, 1992)
Produced by the Renaissance Theatre Company and the BBC (Random Century Audiobooks). First aired on BBC Radio Drama on April 26, 1992.

Directed by Glyn Dearman; co-director: Kenneth Branagh; music by Patrick Doyle

Paul Gregory (BARNARDO / SECOND SAILOR / PRIEST / AMBASSADOR), Alex Lowe (FRANCISCO / MESSENGER), Michael Williams (HORATIO), Andrew Jarvis (MARCELLUS / LUCIANUS, FIRST SAILOR), Derek Jacobi (CLAUDIUS), Shaun Prendergast (VOLTEMAND / PROLOGUE / CAPTAIN / LORD), Mark Hadfield (CORNELIUS / REYNALDO / SERVANT / SECOND GRAVEDIGGER), James Wilby (LAERTES), Richard Briers (POLONIUS), Kenneth Branagh (HAMLET), Judi Dench (GERTRUDE), Sophie Thompson (OPHELIA), John Gielgud (GHOST), Gerard Horan (ROSENCRANTZ), Christopher Ravenscroft (GUILDENSTERN), Michael Hordern (PLAYER KING), Emma Thompson (PLAYER QUEEN), James Simmons (FORTINBRAS), Abigail Reynolds (COURT LADY), Michael Elphick (FIRST GRAVEDIGGER), Richard Clifford (OSRIC)

Coriolanus (Theatre, 1992)
Produced by Renaissance Theatre Company.
Directed by Tim Supple, with Kenneth Branagh as Coriolanus.

Hamlet (Theatre, 1992–93)
Produced by the Royal Shakespeare Company in collaboration with Renaissance Theatre Company at the Barbican Theatre, London. Press Night: 12 December 1992.

Directed by Adrian Noble; design by Bob Crowley; music by Guy Woolfenden.

David Birrell (FRANCISCO / LUCIANUS), Richard Bonneville (LAERTES), David Bradley (POLONIUS), Kenneth Branagh (HAMLET), Peter ByGott (VOLTEMAND), Richard Clothier (CORNELIUS), Howard Crossley (GRAVEDIGGER / PLAYER), Virginia Denham (PLAYER / GENTELWMN), Anthony Douse (BARNARDO / PRIEST), Rob Edwards (HORATIO), Michael Gould (ROSENCRANTZ), Guy Henry (OSRIC), Tim Hudson (MARCELLUS / PLAYER), Ian Hughes (FORTINBRAS / REYNALDO), Jane Lapotaire (GERTRUDE), Richard Moore (FIRST GRAVEDIGGER), Jonathan Newth

(PLAYER KING), Joanne Pearce (OPHELIA), Siân Radinger (PLAYER QUEEN), Clifford Rose (GHOST), Kenn Sabberton (NORWEGIAN CAPTAIN / PLAYER), John Shrapnel (CLAUDIUS), Nick Simons (ENGLISH AMBAS-SADOR), Angus Wright (GUILDENSTERN)

Romeo and Juliet (Radio, 1993)
Produced by BBC Radio.
Co-directed by Kenneth Branagh and Glyn Dearman, featuring Kenneth Branagh as Romeo.

Much Ado About Nothing (Film, 1993)
Directed and adapted by Kenneth Branagh; director of photography: Roger Lanser; music: Patrick Doyle; edited by Andrew Marcus; designed by Tim Harvey; costumes: Phyllis Dalton; script: Annie Wotton; produced by Stephen Evans, David Parfitt and Kenneth Branagh. A Renaissance Films production, presented by the Samuel Goldwyn Company.

Kenneth Branagh (BENEDICK), Emma Thompson (BEATRICE), Denzel Washington (DON PEDRO), Robert Sean Leonard (CLAUDIO), Kate Beckinsale (HERO), Richard Briers (LEONATO), Keanu Reaves (DON JOHN), Michael Keaton (DOGBERRY), Brian Blessed (ANTONIO), Ben Elton (VERGES), Imelda Staunton (MARGARET), Phyllida Law (URSULA), Patrick Doyle (BALTHASAR), Jimmy Yuill (FRIAR FRANCIS), Andy Hockley (GEORGE SEACOLE), Chris Barnes (FRANCES SEACOLE), Conrad Nelson (HUGH OATCOKE), Richard Clifford (CONRADE), Gerard Horan (BORRACHIO), Edward Jewesbury (SEXTON), Alex Lowe (MESSENGER)

King Lear (Radio, 1994)
Produced by BBC Radio and BDD.
Directed by Glyn Dearman, featuring Kenneth Branagh as Edmund.

In the Bleak Midwinter [English title] / A Midwinter's Tale [U.S. title] (Film, 1995)
Written and directed by Kenneth Branagh.

Othello (Film, 1995)
Directed by Oliver Parker, with Kenneth Branagh as Iago.

Hamlet (Film, 1996)
Directed and adapted by Kenneth Branagh; director of photography: Alex Thompson; edited by Neil Farrel; costumes: Alex Byrne; music: Patrick Doyle; designed by Tim Harvey; produced by David Barron. A co-production of Fishmonger Films Production, Castle Rock, and Turner.

Kenneth Branagh (HAMLET), Derek Jacobi (CLAUDIUS), Julie Christie (GERTRUDE), Richard Briers (POLONIUS), Brian Blessed (GHOST), Michael Maloney (LAERTES), Nicholas Farrell (HORATIO), Kate Winslet (OPHELIA), Charlton Heston (PLAYER KING), Rosemary Harris (PLAYER QUEEN), Rufus Sewell (FORTINBRAS), Billy Crystal (FIRST GRAVEDIGGER), Simon Russell Beale (SECOND GRAVEDIGGER), Tim Spall (ROSENCRANZ), Reece Dinsdale (GUILDENSTERN), Gerard Depardieu (REYNALDO), Robin Williams (OSRIC), Ian McElhinney (BARNARDO), Jack Lemmon (MARCELLUS), Ray Fearon (FRANCISCO), Ravil Isyanov (CORNELIUS), Don Warrington (VALTEMAND), Sir John Mills (OLD NORWAY), Jimmy Ellis (OLD FORTINBRAS), Sian Radinger (PROLOGUE), Rob Edwards (LUCIANUS), Charles Daish (STAGE MANAGER), Ben Thom (FIRST PLAYER), Perdita Weeks (SECOND PLAYER), Michael Bryant (PRIEST), Andrew Schofield (YOUNG LORD), Jeffery Kissoon (FORTINBRAS'S CAPTAIN), Melanie Ramsey (PROSTITUTE), Orlando Seale (BOATMAN), David Yip (FIRST SAILOR), Jimi Mistry (SECOND SAILOR), Jimmy Yuill (ALEXANDER), Frank Morgan (PYRRHUS), Sir John Gielgud (PRIAM), Dame Judi Dench (HECUBA), Tom Szekeres (YOUNG HAMLET), Ken Dodd (YORICK), Angela Douglas (ATTENDANT TO GERTRUDE), Sara Lam (ATTENDANT TO GERTRUDE), Rowena King (ATTENDANT TO GERTRUDE and MESSENGER), Peter Bygott (ATTENDANT TO CLAUDIUS), Riz Abbasi (ATTENDANT TO CLAUDIUS), David Blair (ATTENDANT TO CLAUDIUS and SERVANT), Yvonne Gidden (DOCTOR)

Other significant Theatre Productions

Another Country (Judd), Queen's Theatre, 1982
Francis (title role of St. Francis), Greenwitch Theatre, London, 1983
Golden Girls (Mike), RSC, 1984
Tell Me Honestly (playwright and director), Donmar Warehouse, London, 1985
Public Enemy (Tommy Black), RTC, 1987
John Sessions: Life of Napoleon (director), RTC, 1987
Much Ado About Nothing (Benedick), RTC, 1988
Look Back in Anger (Jimmy Porter), Lyric Theatre, London, 1989
Uncle Vanya (co-director), RTC, 1991

Other movies directed by Kenneth Branagh

Dead Again (Roman Strauss and Mike Church; director), 1991
Peter's Friends (Andrew; director), 1992
Swan Song (director), 1992
Mary Shelley's Frankenstein (Victor Frankenstein; director), 1995
In the Bleak Midwinter / A Midwinter's Tale (screenplay and director), 1996

Bibliography

Written works by Kenneth Branagh

Beginning. London: Chatto & Windus, 1989. (autobiography)
Hamlet: Screenplay, Introduction and Film Diary. London: Chatto & Windus, 1996.
Henry V: A Screen Adaptation. London: Chatto & Windus, 1989.
In the Bleak Midwinter: The Screenplay. London: Nick Hearn Books, 1995.
Introduction. *Mary Shelley's Frankenstein: The Classic Tale of Terror Reborn on Film.* London: Pan Books, 1994.
A Midwinter's Tale: Shooting Script. New York: New Market Press, 1996.
Much Ado About Nothing: Screenplay, Introduction and Notes on the Making of the Film. London: Chatto & Windus, 1993.
Public Enemy. London: Faber and Faber, 1988. (play; out of print)
Tell Me Honestly, 1985. (unpublished play)

Reviews and Articles on Kenneth Branagh's Shakespearean Movies

Henry V
Film by Kenneth Branagh, 1989

Aitken, Ian. "Formalism and realism: *Henry V.*" *Critical Survey* 3 (1991).
Appleyard, Brian. "Renaissance Man." *GQ,* Oct 1989.
Bamigboye, Baz. "Once more unto the breach." *Daily Mail,* 18 Nov 1988.
Bennett, Catherine. "Hyperbole's favourite son." *Sunday Correspondent Magazine,* 17 Sep 1989.
Billington, Michael. "A 'New Olivier' Is Taking On Henry V on the Screen." *New York Times,* 8 Jan 1989.
Branagh, Kenneth. "Cry 'Action' for Harry and friends." *Observer,* 24 Sep 1989.
———. "Hallowed Ground." *Vogue,* Sep 1989.
———. "Henry V." *Players of Shakespeare 2,* edited by Russell Jackson & Robert Smallwood. Cambridge: Cambridge University Press, 1988.
———. *Unpublished screenplay and storyboard of Henry V,* October 1998. Available at the Shakespeare Institute.
———. *Henry V: A Screen Adaptation.* London: Chatto & Windus, 1989.
———. "The Prince & the King." *Observer,* 19 Sep 1989.
Brent, Harry. "Versions of Henry V: Laurence Olivier versus Kenneth Branagh." *Teaching Shakespeare Today: Practical Approaches and Productive Strategies,*

170

edited by James E. Davis & Ronald E. Salomone. Urbana: National Council of Teachers of English, 1993.

Breight, Curtis. "Branagh and the Prince, or a 'royal fellowship of death'." *Critical Quarterly* 33.4 (1991).

Briggs, Julia. "Deep down and close up." *Times Literary Supplement,* 20–26 Oct 1989.

Bristol, Michael. "Crying all the way to the bank." *Big Time Shakespeare.* London: Routledge, 1996.

Brown, Geoff. "Larry's game is beyond our Ken." *London Times,* 2 Oct 1989.

Buckingham, Lisa. "CBS is in on the act." *Guardian,* 30 Jan 1990.

Buhler, Stephen. "Text, Eyes, and Videotape: Screening Shakespeare Scripts." *Shakespeare Quarterly,* Summer 1995.

Callaghan, Dympna. "Resistance and Recuperation: Branagh's *Henry V*." *Shakespeare On Film Newsletter,* Apr 1991.

Canby, Vincent. "A Down-to-Earth *Henry V* Discards Spectacle and Pomp." *New York Times,* 8 Nov 1989.

Cartmell, Deborah. "The *Henry V* Flashback: Kenneth Branagh's Shakespeare." *Pulping Fictions: Consuming Culture across the Literature/Media Divide,* edited by Deborah Cartmell, I. Q. Hunter, Heidi Kaye, & Imelda Whelehan. London and Chicago: Pluto, 1996.

Chevassu, François. "*Henry V*: Shakespeare pour tous." *La Revue du Cinéma,* Jan 1991.

Collier, Susanne. "Post-Falklands, Post-Colonial: Contextualizing Branagh as Henry V on Stage and on Film." *Essays in Theatre* 10.2 (May 1992).

Collins, David G. "Kenneth Branagh's *Henry V*: The Healing of Henry." *Publications of the Missouri Philological Association,* 1990.

Corliss, Richard. "Branagh the Conqueror." *Time International,* 13 Nov 1989.

———. "King Ken Comes to Conquer." *Time* (U.S. edition), 13 Nov 1989.

Coursen, H. R. "A Little Touch of Harry: The Making of *Henry V*." *Shakespeare on Film Newsletter,* Apr 1991.

———. "Sorting Well with Fierceness?" *Shakespeare in Production: Whose history?* Ohio: Ohio University Press, 1996.

———. *Shakespearean Performance as Interpretation.* Cranbury, London, and Mississauga: Associated University Presses, 1992.

Crowl, Samuel. "Fathers and Sons: Kenneth Branagh's Henry V." *Shakespeare Observed: Studies in Performance on Stage and Screen.* Ohio: Ohio University Press, 1992.

Davenport, Hugo. "Fire and steel from Branagh's Hal." *Daily Telegraph,* 5 Oct 1989.

Deats, Sara. "Rabbits and Ducks." *Literature Film Quarterly* 20 (1 Oct 1992).

Decurtis, Anthony. "Hail the New King on the Block." *Rolling Stone,* 8 Feb 1990.

Diaz Fernandez, José Ramón. "'This Star of England': Henry V, dirigido por Kenneth Branagh." *Investigaciones filológicas anglo-norteamericanas: Actas del I Congreso de lengua y literatura anglo-norteamericana,* edited by Lucía Mora González. Cuenca: Universidad de Castilla–La Mancha, 1994.

Dickstein, Morris. "War!" *Partisan Review* 4 (1990).

Donaldson, Peter. "Taking on Shakespeare: Kenneth Branagh's *Henry V*." *Shakespeare Quarterly,* Spring 1991.

Doyle, Patrick (composer). *Henry V: Original Soundtrack Recording.* EMI, CDC 7 49919 2.

Ebert, Roger. "*Henry V.*" *Chicago Sun-Times,* 15 Dec 1989.

Fabricius, Susanne. "The face of honour. On Kenneth Branagh's Screen Adaptation of *Henry V.*" *Screen Shakespeare,* edited by Michael Skovmand. Cambridge: Cambridge University Press, 1994.

Fitter, Chris. "A Tale of Two Branaghs: *Henry V,* Ideology and the Mekong Agincourt." *Shakespeare Left and Right,* edited by Ivo Kamps. New York, London: Routledge, 1991.

Flaumenhaft, Mera J. "Three Views of Henry V: Shakespeare, Olivier, and Branagh." *The Civic Spectacle: Essays on Drama and Community.* Lanham: Rowman & Littlefield, 1994.

Forbes, Jill. "*Henry V.*" *Sight and Sound,* Fall 1989.

Fortier, Mark. "Speculations on *2 Henry IV*: Theatre Historiography, the Strait Gate of History, and Kenneth Branagh." *Journal of Dramatic Theory and Criticism,* Fall 1992.

French, Philip. "Real Heroes are Spotty." *Observer,* 8 Oct 1989.

Frey, Charles H. "Branagh's *Henry V* / Abstract of an MMLA talk." *Shakespeare on Film Newsletter,* Apr 1991 (Original full paper sent by the author, 1 Jul 1998.)

Fuller, Graham. "Two Kings." *Film Comment,* Nov 1989.

Geguld, Harry M. "Royal Brotherhood of Death." *Humanist,* Jul 1990.

Genies, Bernard. "Le sacre de Kenneth." *Le Nouvel Observateur,* 31 Jan 1991.

Grassin, Sophie. "Et Shakespeare créa Kenneth Branagh." *L'Express,* 17 Jan 1991.

Griffin, C.W. "Henry V's Decision: Interrogative Texts." *Literature Film Quarterly* 25.2 (1997).

Grimley, Terry. "Branagh's boldness looks set to pay off." *Birmingham Post,* 6 Sep 1989.

Guntner, Lawrence & Peter Drexler. "Recycled film codes and the study of Shakespeare on film." *Deutsche Shakespeare,* 1993.

Hale, David G. "Video in the Shakespeare Class: *Henry V* 5.2." *Shakespeare and the Classroom,* Spring 1995.

Hattaway, Michael. "Shakespeare's Histories: The Politics of Recent British Productions." *Shakespeare in the New Europe,* edited by Michael Hattaway, Boika Sokolova, & Derek Roper. Sheffield: Sheffield Academic Press, 1994.

Healy, Thomas. "Remembering with Advantages: Nation and Ideology in *Henry V.*" *Shakespeare in the New Europe,* edited by Michael Hattaway, Boika Sokolova, & Derek Roper. Sheffield: Sheffield Academic Press, 1994.

Hedrick, Donald. "War is mud: Branagh's dirty *Henry V.*" *Shakespeare on Film Newsletter,* Apr 1991.

———. "War is mud: Branagh's dirty *Henry V* and the types of political ambiguity." *Shakespeare, The Movie,* edited by Lynda E. Boose & Richard Burt. London: Routledge, 1997.

Howard, Jean E. & Phyllis Rackin. *Engendering a Nation: a feminist account of Shakespeare's English Histories.* London, New York: Routledge, 1997.

Ingram, Raymond. "Video review: *Henry V.*" *Speech & Drama* 40.2 (Fall 1991).

Hinson, Hal. "*Henry V.*" *Washington Post,* 15 Dec 1989.

Holderness, Graham. "Reproductions: *Henry V.*" *Shakespeare Recycled: the Making of Historical Drama.* London, New York: Harvester Wheatsheaf, 1992.

————. "What ish my nation? Shakespeare and national identities." *Textual Practice* 5 (1991).

Howe, Desson. "*Henry V.*" *Washington Post,* 15 Dec 1989.

Jackson, Russell. "Two Films of *Henry V*: Frames and Stories." *Revue du Centre d'Etudes et de Recherche Elisabéthaine* 1.4 (1991). (Conférence internationale du 22 au 25 novembre 1990, edited by François Laroque. Presse de l'Université Paul Valéry Montpellier, 1991.)

Joffee, Linda. "'Next Olivier' Makes His Own Legacy." *Christian Science Monitor,* 30 Nov 1989.

Johnson, Brian. "Actor as conqueror." *Maclean's,* 20 Nov 1989.

Johnstone, Iain. "How to put hair on King Henry's chest." *Sunday Times,* 8 Oct 1989.

————. *A Little Touch of Harry: The Making of* Henry V. Mindseyes Films, 1989. Television documentary.

Jones, Winifred Maria. *Stage space to screen space: Kenneth Branagh's film of* Henry V *(1989) and Adrian Noble's stage production at Stratford-upon-Avon (1984).* Unpublished dissertation for the degree of Master of Arts in Shakespeare Studies of the University of Birmingham. The Shakespeare Institute, Sep 1991.

Kael, Pauline. "The current cinema." *New Yorker,* 27 Nov 1989.

Kauffmann, Stanley. "Claiming the Throne." *New Republic,* 4 Dec 1989.

Kilpatrick, Jacquelyn. "Kenneth Branagh's *Henry V.*" *Creative Screenwriting* 5.2 (1998).

Klawans, Stuart. "*Henry V.*" *Nation,* 11 Dec 1989.

Kliman, Bernice. "Branagh's Henry: Allusion and Illusion." *Shakespeare on Film Newsletter,* Dec 1989.

Kroll, Jack. "A Henry V for Our Time." *Newsweek,* 20 Nov 1989.

Lane, Anthony. "Insubstantial pageants." *Independent,* 30 Sep 1989.

Lane, Robert. "'When Blood is their argument': Class, Character, and Historymaking in Shakespeare's and Branagh's *Henry V.*" *ELH,* Spring 1994.

Lehmann, Courtney. "Kenneth Branagh at the Quilting Point: Shakespearean Adaptation, Postmodern Auteurism, and the (Schizophrenic) Fabric of 'Everyday Life'." *Post Script* 17.1 (Fall 1997).

Leith, William. "Acts of a nervous conqueror." *London Times,* 16 Sep 1989.

Lewis, Anthony. "*Henry V*: Two Films." *Past Imperfect: History According to the Movies.* London: Cassell, 1996.

Lewis, Peter. "Hal and high water." *7Days,* 24 Sep 1989.

————. "The man who would be Harry." *Sunday Times,* 10 Sep 1989.

Light, Alison. "The importance of being ordinary." *Sight and Sound,* Sep 1993.

Loehlin, James. "Let there be sung Non Nobis." *Shakespeare in Performance: Henry V.* Manchester: Manchester University Press, 1996.

Lord Hall, Joan. *Henry V: A Guide to the play.* London: Greenwood Press, 1997.

Malcolm, Derek. "Henry begins to clean up." *Guardian,* 12 Oct 1989.

————. "The king's a bastard." *Guardian,* 10 Oct 1989.

Manheim, Michael. "The English history play on screen." *Shakespeare and the Moving Image,* edited by Anthony Davies & Stanley Wells. Cambridge: Cambridge University Press, 1994.

————. "The Function of Battle Imagery in Kuroswa's Histories and the *Henry V* Films." *Film Literature Quarterly* 2 (1994).

174 Bibliography

Mantel, Hilary. "Mud and guts." *Spectator,* 21 Oct 1989.

Marienstras, Richard. "Epreuves et tourments de l'autorité, de la maturité." *Positif,* Apr 1991.

Mars-Jones, Adam. "Observing the breach." *Independent,* 5 Oct 1989.

Marsland, Elizabeth. "Updating Agincourt: The Battle Scenes in Two Film Versions of *Henry V.*" *Modern War on Stage and Screen/Der Moderne Krieg auf der Buhne.* Lewiston: Edwin Mellen, 1997.

McCombs, Gillian M. "'Once More unto the Breach, Dear Friends': Shakespeare's *Henry V* as a Primer for Leaders." *Journal of Academic Librarianship,* Sep 1992.

Mctear, Ian. "Why Henry V wants to play a baddie for Batman." *Birmingham Post,* 5 Oct 1989.

Neill, Heather. "Sentiment amid gore of battle." *Times Educational Supplement,* 15 Nov 1991.

Nightingale, Benedict. "Henry V Returns As a Monarch For This Era." *New York Times,* 5 Nov 1989.

Nokes, David. "Heroes of the hour." *Times Literary Supplement,* 20–26 Oct 1989.

O'Brien, Tom. "Heroism without glamour." *Commonweal,* 23 Feb 1990.

Occhiogrosso, Frank. "Branagh's *Henry V.*" *Shakespeare Bulletin,* Spring 1990.

Paller, Michael. "Kenneth Branagh: The Next Oliver?" *Theater Week,* 11 Dec 1989.

Patterson, Annabel. "A Political Thriller: The life and time of Henry V." *Teaching with Shakespeare—Critics in the classroom,* edited by Bruce McIver & Ruth Stevenson. Cranbury, London, and Mississauga: Associated University Presses, 1994.

Pearce, Jill. "*Henry V.*" *Cahiers Elisabéthains* 38 (Oct 1990).

Potter, Lois. "Bad and Good Authority Figures: Richard III and Henry V since 1945." *Deutsche Shakespeare,* 1992.

Pursell, Michael. "Playing the game: Branagh's *Henry V.*" *Literature Film Quarterly* 20 (10 Jan 1992).

Rainer, Peter. "*Henry V.*" *American Film,* Dec 1990.

Rathburn, Paul. "Branagh's Iconoclasm: Warriors for the Working Day." *Shakespeare on Film Newsletter,* Apr 1991.

Rauchut, E. A. "The Siege Oration in Branagh's *Henry V.*" *Shakespeare Bulletin,* Winter 1993.

Raymond, Ilene. "Adapting the Bard: An interview with Kenneth Branagh." *Creative Screenwriting* 5.2 (1998).

Richards, Bernard. "Reviews: Olivier's and Branagh's Henry V." *English Review* 1.1 (Sep 1990).

Robinson, David. "The Young Pretender." *London Times,* 5 Oct 1989.

Rothwell, Kenneth. "Kenneth Branagh's *Henry V*: The Gilt [Guilt] in the Crown Re-Examined." *Comparative Drama* 24 (1990–91).

Royal, Derek. "Shakespeare's Kingly Mirror: Figuring the Chorus in Olivier's and Branagh's *Henry V.*" *Literature Film Quarterly* 25.2 (1997).

Ryan, Desmond. "Beyond Olivier: A New Henry V." *Philadelphia Inquirer,* 13 Dec 1989.

Saada, Nicolas. "Le théâtre apprivoisé." *Cahiers du Cinéma,* Jan 1991.

Salomon, Patricia. "The Sentimentalizing of Communitas in Kenneth Branagh's *Henry V.*" *Shakespeare Bulletin,* Winter 1995.

Schwartz, Amy. "*Henry V.*" *Washington Post,* 6 Feb 1990.

Seidenberg, Robert. "*Henry V.*" *American Film*, Nov 1989.
Shaw, William. "Textual Ambiguities and Cinematic Certainties in *Henry V*." *Film Literature Quarterly* 2 (1994).
Sherrin, Ned. "First nights and last gulps." *London Times*, 30 Sep 1989.
Smith, Christopher. "History's Sir Thomas and Shakespeare's Erpingham." *Shakespeare Yearbook*, 1996.
Sotinel, Thomas. "Prendre les spectateurs au collet: Entretien avec Kenneth Branagh." *Le Monde: Dossiers & Documents Littéraires* 19 (Apr 1998).
Stephens, Robert & Michael Coveney. *Knight Errant*. London: Hodder & Stoughton, 1995.
Tatspaugh, Patricia. "Theatrical influences on Kenneth Branagh's film: *Henry V*." *Literature Film Quarterly* 20 (1 Oct 1992).
Thynne, Jane. "Branagh and Company plan films of *Henry V*." *Daily Telegraph*, 7 Oct 1988.
Tookey, Christopher. "Once more unto the breach." *Sunday Telegraph*, 8 Oct 1989.
Wade, Nicholas. "Henry V v. Henry V." *New York Times*, 6 Feb 1990.
Willson, Robert. "*Henry V*: Branagh's and Oliver's choruses." *Shakespeare on Film Newsletter*, Apr 1990.
Willson, Robert.. "War and Reflection on War: The Oliver and Branagh Films of *Henry V*." *Shakespeare Bulletin*, Summer 1991.
Wilmington, Michael. "A Blazing New *Henry V*." *Los Angeles Times*, 8 Nov 1989.

Much Ado About Nothing
Film by Kenneth Branagh, 1993

Alleva, Richard. "Beatrice Forever." *Commonweal*, 18 Jun 1993.
Barton, Anne. "Shakespeare in the Sun." *New York Review of Books*, 27 May 1993.
Bennett, Catherine. "Much too much ado." *Guardian Weekend*, 7 Aug 1993.
Billson, Anne. "With a hey nonny-nonny." *Sunday Telegraph*, 29 Aug 1993.
Branagh, Kenneth. "Beatrice and Benedick in close-up." *Sunday Telegraph*, 25 Jul 1993.
———. "Funny Shakespeare." *Studio*, Mar 1993.
———. *Much Ado About Nothing: Screenplay, Introduction and Notes on the Making of the Film*. London: Chatto & Windus, 1993.
Buck, Joan Juliet. "Costume frolics." *Vogue*, May 1993.
Canby, Vincent. "A House Party of Beatrice, Benedick and Friends." *New York Times*, 7 May 1993.
Castaldo, Annalisa. "Hold a Mirror up to Shakespeare: Reviews of Branagh's *Much Ado About Nothing*." Paper given at the Conference of the Shakespeare Association of America, Feb 1998.
Castell, David. *Chasing the Light: The Making of* Much Ado About Nothing. A Special Treats Production for Renaissance Films and The Samuel Goldwyn Company, 1993. Television documentary.
Chonez, Jennyfer. "*Much Ado About Nothing*: From Page, To Stage, To Screen." *Mémoire de Maîtrise d'anglais dirigé par Michèle Willems* (Université de Rouen), Jun 1998.
Coles, Joanna. "Branagh from heaven, cry tuned-in-hacks." *Guardian*, 22 May 1993.

Collins, Michael. "Sleepless in Messina: Kenneth Branagh's *Much Ado About Nothing*." *Shakespeare Bulletin*, Spring 1997.

Corliss, Richard. "Smiles of a Summer Night." *Time International*, 10 May 1993.

Coursen, H. R. "Branagh's *Much Ado*: II." *Shakespeare and the Classroom*, Spring 1994.

———. "The Critical Reception of Branagh's *Much Ado About Nothing*." *Shakespeare and the Classroom*, Fall 1993.

———. "Branagh's *Much Ado*: Art and Popular Culture?" *Shakespeare in Production: Whose history?*. Ohio: Ohio University Press, 1996.

Crowl, Samuel. "*Much Ado About Nothing*." *Shakespeare Bulletin*, Summer 1993.

Cox, John F. *Shakespeare in Production*: Much Ado About Nothing. Cambridge: Cambridge University Press, 1997.

Curtis, Quentin. "*Much Ado About Nothing*." *Independent On Sunday*, 29 Aug 1993.

Dawson, Jeff. "Healthy, Wealthy and Wise?" *Empire*, Sep 1993.

Deleyto, Celestino. "Men in Leather: Kenneth Branagh's *Much Ado About Nothing* and Romantic Comedy." *Cinema Journal* 36.3 (Spring 1997).

Denby, David. "Avon Calling." *New York*, 10 May 1993.

Doyle, Patrick (composer). *Much Ado About Nothing: Original Motion Picture Soundtrack*. Epic Soundtrax, 473989 2.

Ebert, Robert. "*Much Ado About Nothing*." *Chicago Sun-Times*, 21 May 1993.

Edgerton, Ellen. "Your Answer, Sir, Is Cinematical." *Shakespeare Bulletin*, Winter 1994.

Felperin Sharman, Leslie. "*Much Ado About Nothing*." *Sight and Sound*, Sep 1993.

Fowler, Rebecca. "Rounding up the usual luvvies." *Sunday Times*, 29 Aug 1993.

Friedman, Michael D. "Male bonds and marriage in *All's Well* and *Much Ado*." *Studies in English Literature*, 1 Apr 1995.

Grant, Steve. "A bit of ado." *Time Out*, 18–25 Aug 1993.

Gray, Malcom. "The populist bard." *Maclean's*, 17 May 1993.

Haeseker, Fred. "*Much Ado* just made to order." *Calgary Herald*, 14 May 1993.

Hale, David G. "Bibliography for Branagh's *Much Ado*." *Shakespeare and the Classroom*, Fall 1994.

Herbert, Susannah. "Ad-libber Emma puts on a bit of an act for the Cannes cabaret." *Daily Telegraph*, 22 May 1993.

Hinson, Hal. "*Much Ado About Nothing*." *Washington Post*, 21 May 1993.

Howe, Desson. "*Much Ado About Nothing*." *Washington Post*, 21 May 1993.

Jackson, Russell. "How do you coach film actors to speak Shakespeare's lines." *Sunday Times*, 29 Aug 1993.

———. "Shakespeare's comedies on film." *Shakespeare and the Moving Image*, edited by Anthony Davies & Stanley Wells. Cambridge: Cambridge University Press, 1994.

James, Caryn. "Why Branagh's Bard Glows on the Screen." *New York Times*, 16 May 1993.

Johnson, Brian. "*Much Ado About Nothing*." *Maclean's*, 10 May 1993.

Johnstone, Iain. "Branagh and the Bard." *Sunday Times*, 29 Aug 1993.

———. "The Ken film festival." *Sunday Times*, 23 May 1993.

Kauffmann, Stanley. "Familiar places, familiar faces." *New Republic*, 19 Jul 1993.

———. "Stars dance." *New Republic*, 10 May 1993.

Kennedy, Philippa. "Much Ado About Branagh." *Daily Express*, 8 May 1993.

Klawans, Stuart. "*Much Ado About Nothing*." *Nation*, 31 May 1993.

Klifa, Thierry. "Beaucoup de bruit pour rien." *Studio,* May 1993.

Kroll, Jack. "Shakespeare, As You Like It." *Newsweek,* 10 May 1993.

Lane, Anthony. "Too much ado." *New Yorker,* 10 May 1993.

Lehmann, Courtney. "Much Ado about Nothing? Shakespeare, Branagh, and the 'national-popular' in the age of multinational capital." *Textual Practice* 12.1 (Spring 1988).

Maguin, Angela. "*Much Ado About Nothing.*" *Cahiers Elisabéthains* 44 (Oct 1993).

Malcom, Derek. "*Much Ado About Nothing.*" *Guardian,* 26 Aug 1993.

———. "Sunny side up for the Bard." *Guardian,* 26 Aug 1993.

Manley, Will. "Something Out of Nothing." *Booklist,* 1 Sep 1993.

Mars-Jones, Adam. "Much amiss." *Independent,* 27 Aug 1993.

Maxwell, Glyn. "Reality and recreation." *Times Literary Supplement,* 3 Sep 1993.

Mazzetti, Katherine Andre. Uncluttered Shakespeare: The Renaissance Theatre Company's *Much Ado About Nothing* on Stage and Film. Unpublished dissertation for the degree of Master of Arts in Shakespeare Studies of the University of Birmingham. The Shakespeare Institute, Sep 1993.

Mondello, Bob. "Colorblind Casting a Rarity in Films." *All Things Considered* (NPR), 29 May 1993.

———. "Shakespeare's *Much Ado* now on film." *All Things Considered* (NPR), 7 May 1993.

Moses, Carol. "Kenneth Branagh's *Much Ado About Nothing*: Shakespearean Comedy as Shakespearean Romance." *Shakespeare Bulletin,* Winter 1996.

Munoz Valdivieso, Sofía. "'Silence is the perfectest herald of joy': The Claudio–Hero Plot in Kenneth Branagh's *Much Ado about Nothing.*" *SEDERI* 8 (1997).

Murat, Pierre. "Beaucoup de bruit pour rien." *Télérama,* 19 May 1993.

Naughton, John. "The Return of The Magnificent Eight?" *Premiere,* Sep 1993.

Navaro, Antonio José. "Luz, enredo y alegria: Mucho ruido y pocas nueces." *Dirigido,* Jan 1994.

Romine, Linda. "Branagh's *Much Ado* brings Shakespeare to life." *Memphis Business Journal,* 19 Jul 1993.

Rothenberg, Robert. "*Much Ado About Nothing.*" *USA Today,* 1 May 1994.

Ryan, Desmond. "Branagh's cinematic risks true in spirit to the bard." *Philadelphia Inquirer,* 19 May 1993.

Ryan, Richard. "Much Ado About Branagh." *Commentary,* Oct 1993.

Simon, John. "Shakespeare without tears." *National Review,* 7 Jun 1993.

Skovmand, Michael. "Introduction, with a discussion on Branagh and *Much Ado.*" *Screen Shakespeare,* edited by Michael Skovmand. Cambridge: Cambridge University Press, 1994.

Smith, Dinitia. "Much Ado About Branagh." *New York,* 24 May 1993.

Tanitch, Robert. "*Much Ado About Nothing.*" *Plays & Players,* Aug 1993.

Tebar, Juan. "Shakespeare, mucho ruido … y pocas nueces." *El Mundo* (*Cinelandia*), 26 Feb 1994.

Travers, Peter. "*Much Ado About Nothing.*" *Rolling Stone,* 27 May 1993.

Weinrihter, Antonio. "Entrevista: Kenneth Branagh." *Dirigido,* Feb 1994.

In The Bleak Midwinter [English title]
A Midwinter's Tale [U.S. title]
Film by Kenneth Branagh, 1995

Basco, Sharon. "Interview: Kenneth Branagh." *Christian Science Monitor,* 28 Feb 1996.

Billson, Anne. "Luvvies need luvving." *Sunday Telegraph,* 3 Dec 1995.

Boyar, Jay. "A Midwinter's tale." *Orlando Sentinel,* 4 Mar 1996.

Branagh, Kenneth. *In the Bleak Midwinter: The Screenplay.* London: Nick Hern Books, 1995.

Bucker, Park. "The 'Hope' Hamlet: Kenneth Branagh's comic use of Shakespeare's tragedy in *A Midwinter's Tale.*" *Shakespeare Yearbook,* 1997.

Coursen, H. R. "*A Midwinter's Tale.*" *Shakespeare Bulletin,* Summer 1996.

Curtis, Quentin. "Darlings, you weren't wonderful." *Independent On Sunday,* 3 Dec 1995.

Dowell, Pat. "Branagh's affectionate look at miscast misfits." *Army Times,* 1 Jan 1996.

Ebert, Roger. "*A Midwinter's Tale.*" *Chicago Sun-Times,* 23 Feb 1996.

Ellison, Mike. "Branagh's home comfort in Belfast." *Guardian,* 7 Nov 1995.

Garcin, Jérôme. "God save Branagh." *L'Express,* 23 Nov 1995.

Gritten, David. "Branagh's annus horribilis." *Daily Telegraph,* 29 Nov 1995.

———. "Kenneth Branagh on the rebound." *Los Angeles Times,* 3 Jun 1995.

Hinson, Hal. "*A Midwinter's Tale.*" *Washington Post,* 23 Feb 1996.

Holland, Mary. "Home is where Ken's art is." *Observer,* 5 Nov 1995.

Jays, David. "*In the Bleak Midwinter.*" *Sight and Sound,* Dec 1995.

Katelan, Jean-Yves. "Kenneth entre Hamlet & Hamlet." *Première,* Dec 1995.

Lasalle, Mike. "Shades of Woody Allen in *Midwinter's Tale.*" *San Francisco Chronicle,* 23 Feb 1996.

Lawson, Chris. "Melancholy Clowns: The Cult of *Hamlet* in *Withnail and I* and *In the Bleak Midwinter.*" *Shakespeare Bulletin,* Fall 1997.

Malcolm, Derek. "Now is the winter of our Ken." *Guardian,* 30 Nov 1995.

Mathews, Jack. "To laugh or not to laugh? You decide." *Newsday,* 9 Feb 1996.

Mondello, Bob. "A review of *A Midwinter's Tale.*" *All Things Considered (NPR),* 9 Feb 1996.

Murat, Pierre. "Au beau milieu de l'hiver." *Télérama,* 29 Nov 1995.

Naughton, John. "Interview with Kenneth Branagh." *Premiere,* Dec 1995.

Petrakis, John. "Clever *Midwinter* should redeem Branagh before critics." *Chicago Tribune,* 23 Feb 1996.

Rebichon, Michel. "Au beau milieu de l'hiver." *Studio,* Dec 1995.

Schickel, Richard. "Sweet Silliness." *Time,* 26 Feb 1996.

Shone, Tom. "Reeling from a charm offensive." *Sunday Times,* 3 Dec 1995.

Shulgasser, Barbara. "Branagh's screwball *Midwinter's Tale.*" *San Francisco Examiner,* 23 Feb 1996.

Siegel, Sol Louis. "*A Midwinter's Tale.*" *Philadelphia Business Journal,* 29 Mar 1996.

Stark, Susan. "To laugh or not to laugh." *Detroit News,* 1 Mar 1996.

Tranchant, Marie-Noëlle. "La thérapie de groupe de Kenneth Branagh." *Le Figaro,* 29 Nov 1995.

Othello
Film by Oliver Parker (Branagh as Iago), 1995

Anderson, John. "A tragic Moor for the '90s." *Newsday,* 14 Dec 1995.

Bates, Stephen. "Me, Ken and the Moor." *Guardian,* 1 Aug 1995.

Bowman, James. "Bard to death." *American Spectator,* 1 Mar 1996.

Corliss, Richard. "Pulp Elizabethan Fiction." *Time,* 15 Jan 1996.

Coulbourn. "Beware of jealousy ..." *Toronto Sun,* 28 Dec 1995.

Crowl, Samuel. *"Othello." Shakespeare Bulletin,* Winter 1996.

Curtis, Quentin. "A modest Moor, with much to be modest about." *Independent On Sunday,* 18 Feb 1996.

De Lisle, Tim. "Tim de Lisle visits the set of *Othello.*" *Independent On Sunday,* 21 Jan 1996.

Ebert, Roger. *"Othello." Chicago Sun-Times,* 29 Dec 1995.

Lamarr, Jake. "Actor Laurence Fishburne." *Premiere,* Mar 1996.

Larsen, Kristina. "Othello enfin noir!" *Première,* Sep 1995.

Mahoney, Martin. "Branagh and the Moor: Kenneth gives up the director's chair and comes up with a winner." *Irish Voice,* 9 Jan 1996.

Malkin, Marc. *"Othello." Premiere,* Nov 1995.

Mondello, Bob. "Shakespeare takes center stage in two new films." *All Things Considered (NPR),* 30 Dec 1995.

Peachment, Chris. "The soft core of the green-eyed monster." *Sunday Telegraph,* 18 Feb 1996.

Romine, Linda. "Don't miss this one: Othello has the right stuff." *Memphis Business Journal,* 1 Jan 1996.

Shone, Tom. "Moor is less." *Sunday Times,* 18 Feb 1996.

Stark, Susan. "Moor to the point." *Detroit News,* 29 Dec 1995.

Starks, Lisa S. "The Veiled (Hot) Bed of Race and Desire: Parker's *Othello* and the Stereotype as Screen Fetish." *Post Script* 17.1 (Fall 1997).

Stearns, David Patrick. "Producing Shakespeare as they like it." *USA Today,* 17 Dec 1995.

Stone, Alan. *"Othello." Boston Review,* 1996.

Werner, Laurie. "Playing Iago in *Othello* helps Branagh rebound from bad year." *Chicago Tribune,* 24 Dec 1995.

Hamlet
Film by Kenneth Branagh, 1996

Alleva, Richard. "A Sixteen-Wheeler: Branagh's *Hamlet.*" *Commonweal,* 28 Mar 1997.

Andrews, John F. "Kenneth Branagh's *Hamlet* launched at National Air and Space Museum." *Shakespeare Newsletter,* Fall 1996.

Annan, Vicky. *"Hamlet." What's On,* 12 Feb 1997.

Antony, Rick. "Kenneth Branagh." *Los Angeles Film & Music,* Feb 1997.

Arnold, Gary. "To film or not to film, that's the quest." *Insight on the News,* 17 Feb 1997.

Billard, Pierre. "Hamlet for Ever." *Le Point,* 10 May 1997.

Billson, Anne. "Blond bombshell can't keep his mouth shut." *Sunday Telegraph,* 16 Feb 1997.

Blake, Richard A. "Too, too solid." *America,* 17 May 1997.

Bowman, James. "Ken and Kolya." *American Spectator,* Mar 1997.

Brady, James. "In Step with Kenneth Branagh." *Parade Magazine,* 22 Dec 1996.

Branagh, Kenneth. *Hamlet: Screenplay, Introduction and Film Diary.* London: Chatto & Windus, 1996.

Brooks, Richard. "To cut or not to cut Ken's film." *Observer,* 13 Oct 1996.

Brown, Geoff. "Ken's lust action hero." *London Times,* 13 Feb 1997.

Buhler, Stephen M. "Double Takes: Branagh Gets to Hamlet." *Post Script* 17.1 (Fall 1997).

Burnett, Mark Thornton. "The 'Very Cunning of the Scene': Kenneth Branagh's *Hamlet*." *Literature Film Quarterly* 25.2 (1997).

Bush, Lyall. "Fighting the Good Fight with Kenneth Branagh." *MovieMaker,* Mar 1997.

Carr, Jay. "Full-length *Hamlet* still swift." *Boston Globe,* 21 Jan 1997.

Cartmell, Deborah. "Reading and Screening Ophelia." *Shakespeare Yearbook,* 1997.

Case, Brian. "Fraught in the act." *Time Out,* 12–19 Feb 1997.

Clark, David. "Blond Ambition." *What's On,* 12 Feb 1997.

Clark, Mike. "Branagh's *Hamlet* overflows with visual splendors." *USA Today,* 22 Dec 1996.

Clergeat, Romain. "Hamlet—Entretien avec Kenneth Branagh." *Paris Match,* 15 May 1997.

Cohen, Clélia. "Derrière le miroir." *Cahiers du Cinéma,* Jun 1997.

Corliss, Richard. "The Whole Dane Thing." *Time,* 13 Jan 1997.

Costa, J. R. "Fortinbras and the Englishman, Take Three." To see or not to see: The Inclusion and Exclusion of Fortinbras in Five Film Productions of Hamlet. Unpublished dissertation for the degree of Master of Arts in Shakespeare Studies of the University of Birmingham. The Shakespeare Institute, Sep 1997.

Coursen, H. R. "The Critical Reception of Branagh's Complete *Hamlet* in the U.S. Popular Press." *Shakespeare and the Classroom,* Fall 1997.

———. "Words, words, words: Searching for Hamlet." *Shakespeare Yearbook,* 1997.

Crowdus, Gary. "Recent Shakespearean Films." *Cineaste* 23.4 (1998).

Crowl, Samuel. "*Hamlet*." *Shakespeare Bulletin,* Winter 1997.

Crunelle-Vanrigh, Anny. "All the world's a screen: Transcoding in Branagh's *Hamlet*." *Shakespeare Yearbook,* 1997.

Da Vinci Nichols, Nina. "Branagh's *Hamlet* Redux." *Shakespeare Bulletin,* Summer 1997.

Davenport, Hugo. "Don't get mad, play Hamlet." *Electronic Telegraph Article,* 15 Feb 1997.

Davenport, Hugo. "Hugo Davenport talks to Kenneth Branagh." *Cinema Electronic Telegraph,* 15 Feb 1997.

De Bruyn, Olivier. "Cannes, festival du théâtre filmé?" *L'Evénement du Jeudi,* 15 May 1997.

Deitch Rohrer, Trish. "An Englishwoman abroad." *Premiere,* Feb 1997.

Dickson, Jane, Jill Poppy, and Ian Wall. *To Cut or Not To Cut: The Making of Hamlet.* Film Education (BBC 2), 1997. Television documentary.

Doyle, Patrick (composer). *Hamlet: Original Motion Picture Soundtrack.* Sony Classical, SK 62857.

D'silva, Beverley. "The Film's the Thing." *Independant on Sunday,* 12 Jan 1997.

Dudek, Duane. "Branagh's epic-length *Hamlet* keeps its grip." *Milwaukee Journal Sentinel,* 14 Feb 1997.

Duncan, Andrew. "To be or not to be happy." *Radio Times,* 15–21 Feb 1997.

Fallon, James. "The Prince Returns." *W,* Nov 1996.

Felperin, Leslie. "*Hamlet.*" *Sight and Sound,* Feb 1997.

Film Education. Screening Shakespeares: *Hamlet.* Accompanying leaflet to the BBC2 Learning Zone program To Cut or not to Cut.

Fine, Marshall. "Kenneth Branagh brings a brilliant, human *Hamlet* to life." *Courier Journal Weekend,* 7 Mar 1997.

Fisher, Bob. "Tragedy of Epic Proportions." *American Cinematographer,* Jan 1997.

French, Philip. "A hit, a very palpable hit." *Observer,* 16 Feb 1997.

French, Philip. "There ain't nothing like a Dane." *Electronic Mail & Guardian,* 30 May 1997.

Gabrenya, Frank. "*Hamlet:* to cut or not to cut." *Weekend Movie Guide and Show Times,* 19 Feb 1997.

Garner, Jack. "First full-length filmed version of Shakespeare's tragedy is a triumph." *Rochester Democrat and Chronicle,* 13 Feb 1997.

Geier, Thom. "Branagh creates a very palpable hit." *US News & World Report,* 13 Jan 1997.

Gelber, Alexis. "Hamlet at the Millennium: He's Under Our Skin." *Newsweek,* 23 Dec 1996.

Gleiberman, Owen. "A Very Palpable Hit." *Entertainment Weekly,* 24 Jan 1997.

Gold, Sylviane. "To see or not to see." *Newsday,* 22 Dec 1996.

Gomez, Lourdes. "Shakespeare, el mejor guionista del mundo." *El Pais,* 28 Apr 1996.

Goodridge, Mike. "*Hamlet.*" *Screen International,* 20 Dec 1996.

Goodwin, Christopher. "A culture divide." *Sunday Times,* 19 Jan 1997.

Gorman, Ann. "Citizen Ken: Hamlet." *Ekrano Magazine,* 13 Feb 1997.

Grant, Steve. "*Hamlet.*" *Time Out,* 13–19 Feb 1997.

Gray, Marianne. "*Hamlet.*" *Film Review,* Mar 1997.

Gritten, David. "Why is Kenneth Branagh starring in and directing a 3-hour version of *Hamlet*?" *Los Angeles Times,* 2 Jun 1996.

Gritten, David. "The Film's the Thing." *Daily Telegraph,* 11 Jan 1997.

Groen, Rick. "The grand swagger of Branagh's *Hamlet.*" *Globe and Mail,* 24 Dec 1996.

Hartl, John. "An epic *Hamlet.*" *Seattle Times,* 19 Jan 1997.

Hicks, Chris. "*Hamlet.*" *Deseret News,* 14 Feb 1997.

Hinson, Mark. "Star-studded *Hamlet* falls short of engrossing." *Tallahassee Democrat,* 28 Feb 1997.

Hirschhorn, Clive. "The Man Who Shot Shakespeare." *Applause,* Feb 1997.

Hobson, Louis. "Branagh and the bard." *Express,* 19 Jan 1997.

Howe, Desson. "Branagh's *Hamlet:* Not to Be." *Washington Post,* 24 Jan 1997.

Hunter, Patrick. "Hamlet's Ghost on Screen." *Shakespeare Yearbook,* 1997.

Hutchinson, Tom. "Once More Unto the Snore, Dear Friends." *Guardian,* Feb 1997.

Jackson, Kevin. "Four hours, and a star every minute." *Independent on Sunday,* 16 Feb 1997.

Jackson, Russell. "Kenneth Branagh's Film of *Hamlet*: The Textual Choices." *Shakespeare Bulletin,* Spring 1997.

Janusonis, Michael. "Branagh's *Hamlet* is a truly tragic film." *Journal-Bulletin Arts,* 30 May 1997.

Jensen, Michael. "Review of Branagh's screenplay of *Hamlet*." *Shakespeare Bulletin,* Fall 1997.

Johnstone, Iain. "Will Hamlet cheer him up?" *Sunday Times,* 19 Nov 1995.

Kaiden, Elizabeth. "Shortening Branagh's masterpiece is a tragedy." *Straits Times (Singapore),* 29 Aug 1997.

Katelan, Jean-Yves. "To Be or not Mister B." *Première,* Jun 1997.

Kauffmann, Stanley. "On films: At Elsinore." *New Republic,* 27 Jan 1997.

Kaye, Elizabeth. "Alas, poor Kenneth!" *Esquire,* Jan 1997.

Kennedy Sauer, David. "Suiting the word to the action: Kenneth Branagh's interpolations in *Hamlet*." *Shakespeare Yearbook,* 1997.

Keough, Peter. "Almost great Dane." *Boston Phoenix,* 23–30 Jan 1997.

Keyishian, Harry. "'Shakespeare Films' and the Question of Genre." Paper given at the Conference of the Shakespeare Association of America, Feb 1998.

Kirkland, Bruce. "The Shakespeare guy." *Toronto Sun,* 23 Dec 1996.

Kirkland, Bruce. "Branagh makes superb *Hamlet*." *Toronto Sun,* 24 Dec 1996.

Lacey, Liam. "Bringing Shakespeare to the masses." *Globe and Mail,* 24 Dec 1996.

Lamassoure, Patrick. "Kenneth Branagh." *Le Film Français,* 12 May 1997.

Lasalle, Mick. "Branagh gives *Hamlet* a good shake." *San Francisco Chronicle,* 24 Jan 1997.

Lasalle, Mick. "The Reigning Prince of Shakespeare." *San Francisco Chronicle,* 19 Jan 1997.

Lerman, Gabriel. "Entrevista: Kenneth Branagh." *Dirigido,* Feb 1997.

Levin, Bernard. "*Hamlet*—the bottom line." *London Times,* 18 Feb 1997.

Lomonico, Michael. "Branagh's *Hamlet*—Power and Opulence." *Shakespeare Magazine* 1 (1996).

Mandelbaum, Jacques. "Hélas, cher Prince." *Le Monde,* 14 May 1997.

Manuelo, Nicole. "Kenneth Branagh: *Hamlet* a changé sa vie." *Figaro,* 10 May 1997.

Mars-Jones, Adam. "A winter's tale?" *Independent,* 13 Feb 1997.

Maslin, Janet. "*Hamlet*." *Guardian,* 27 Dec 1996.

Maslin, Janet. "More Things in *Hamlet* Than Are Dreamt of in Other Adaptations." *New York Times,* 25 Dec 1996.

McCabe, Bob. "Alas, poor Doddy, I knew him well." *Express On Sunday,* 15 Dec 1996.

McCarthy, Todd. "*Hamlet*." *Variety,* 9–15 Dec 1996.

Means, Sean. "Branagh's *Hamlet* a crowning achievement." *Salt Lake Tribune,* 14 Feb 1997.

Moore, Roger. "Brilliant Bad: Branagh's *Hamlet* triumphs." *Journal Arts,* 14 Feb 1997.

Mullan, John. "Ken, Al and Will, too." *Times Literary Supplement,* 21 Feb 1997.

Multeau, Norbert. "Un scénariste nommé Shakespeare." *Le Spectacle du Monde,* Jun 1997.

Murat, Pierre. "De nos jours, Hamlet dirigerait l'ONU." *Télérama,* 14 May 1997.

Nathan, Ian. "As happy as Larry." *Empire,* Mar 1997.

———. "*Hamlet*." *Empire,* Mar 1997.

Nechak, Paula. "What happened to Kenneth Branagh on the way to his *Hamlet*?" *Chicago Tribune*, 28 Mar 1997.

Neubourg, Monique. "*Hamlet* à Cannes." *Eurostar*, May 1997.

Novak, Ralph. "*Hamlet*." *People*, 2 Mar 1997.

O'Brien, Geoffrey. "The Ghost at the Feast." *New York Review*, 6 Feb 1997.

Olshaker, Mark. *Discovering Hamlet: The Making of* Hamlet. Unicorn Projects, 1988. Television documentary.

Ottenhoff, John. "Hamlet and the Kiss." *Shakespeare Yearbook*, 1997.

Pliskin, Fabrice. "Branagh: Moi, Hamlet." *Nouvel Observateur*, 7–13 May 1997.

Quinn, Anthony. "The long and winding road to Elsinore." *Mail on Sunday*, 16 Feb 1997.

Rafferty, Terrence. "Solid Flesh." *New Yorker*, 13 Jan 1997.

Raymond, Ilene. "Adapting the Bard: An interview with Kenneth Branagh." *Creative Screenwriting* 5.2 (1998).

Rayner, Richard. "*Hamlet*." *Harper's Bazaar*, 1997.

Reams, Patrick. *The Readiness Is All: The Making of* Hamlet. BBC Education, 1997. Television documentary.

Robbins, Mark. "*Hamlet*: La actualidad de los clasicos." *Dirigido*, Feb 1997.

Robinson, Anna. "Anna Robinson haunts the cinema and routs the ghosts out of her past." *Trinity (Oxford Student Publications)* 3 (1997).

Rose, Lloyd. "*Hamlet*: Kenneth Branagh's Inaction Flick." *Washington Post*, 24 Jan 1997.

Rosenberg, Scott. "In Branagh's full-length *Hamlet*, cheesy showmanship gradually wins out over good diction." *Salon*, Jan 1997.

Ross, Bob. "New *Hamlet* fills gaps with spectacle." *Tampa Tribune*, 2 Dec 1996.

Ryan, Desmond. "Branagh's complete and compelling *Hamlet*." *Philadelphia Inquirer*, 24 Jan 1997.

Sartori, Beatrice. "Kenneth Branagh—Hamlet." *La Espera (Cinelandia)*, 17 May 1997.

Scola, Gloria. "Kenneth Branagh: 'Shakespeare es el mejor guionista de cine'." CAMBIO16, 19 May 1997.

Shulgasser, Barbara. "*Hamlet*: Elsinore, 90210: Branagh is superb on both sides of the camera." *San Francisco Examiner*, 24 Jan 1997.

Sinden, Peter. "Do the Bard man!" *Film Review*, Mar 1997.

Smith, Liz. "Branagh's *Hamlet*." *Newsday*, 13 Dec 1996.

Sterritt, David. "Hamlet No. 47: Less Could Be More." *Christian Science Monitor*, 6 Jan 1997.

Stone, Alan. "*Hamlet*." *Boston Review*, 1996.

Stringer, Robin. "Branagh's epic worth the wait." *Evening Standard*, 17 Jan 1997.

Tanitch, Robert. "*Hamlet*." *Plays & Players*, Mar 1997.

Theobald, Frédéric. "Hamlet fait du cinéma." *La Vie*, 22 May 1997.

Thomas, Kevin. "Unwrapped: A Guide to Christmas Day Releases: Branagh Acts *Hamlet* as the Bard Wrote It." *Los Angeles Times*, 25 Dec 1996.

Thompson, Gary. "Kenneth Branagh rediscovers the *Hamlet* of his youth." *Buffalo News*, 23 Nov 1997.

Thorsell, William. "The many joys of bard-watching." *Globe and Mail*, 26 Dec 1996.

Tookey, Christopher. "Much Ado at the Movies." *Applause*, Feb 1997.

Topman, Lawrence. "Nothing rotten in Branagh's big, bodacious *Hamlet*." *Charlotte Observer*, 24 Jan 1997.

Tutti, Emma. "The Great Dane." *Screen International*, 15 Mar 1996.

Tuttle, Nancye. "Branagh fires up *Hamlet*." *Lowell Sun*, Jan 1997.

Weisel, Al. "Idol chatter: Kenneth Branagh." *Premiere*, Dec 1996.

Welsh, Jim. "Branagh's Enlarged *Hamlet*." *Literature Film Quarterly* 25.2 (1997).

Willson, Robert. "Kenneth Branagh's *Hamlet* or The Revenge of Fortinbras." *Shakespeare Newsletter*, Spring 1997.

Wilmeth, Thomas. "Fortinbras on Film: Safe passage for the prince." *Shakespeare Yearbook*, 1997.

Wilmington, Michael. "A noble *Hamlet*." *Tribune*, 24 Jan 1997.

Wolf, Matt. "Hamlet? Branagh knows him well." *Newsday*, 1 Jan 1997.

———. "Branagh follows in Olivier's footsteps." *Reuters*, 26 Dec 1996.

———. "Following in Olivier's footsteps." *Variety*, 16 Dec 1996.

Articles and Reviews of
Kenneth Branagh's Shakespearean Plays

Henry V
Play directed by Adrian Noble, RSC, 1984

Asquith, Rob. "Hooray Henry." *Observer*, 19 May 1985.

Barber, John. "A King from Belfast." *Daily Telegraph*, 29 Mar 1984.

Billington, Michael. "*Henry V*." *Guardian*, 30 Mar 1984.

———. "Unto the breach again." *Guardian*, 18 May 1985.

Collier, Susanne. "Post-Falklands, Post-Colonial: Contextualizing Branagh as Henry V on Stage and on Film." *Essays in Theatre* 10.2 (May 1992).

Cropper, Martin. "Patriotic to a fault: Henry V." *London Times*, 18 May 1985.

Evans, Gareth Lloyd. "Plays in performance: *Henry V*." *Drama*, Fall 1984.

Features, Rex. "A young actor is chosen to peel layer after layer off Henry V." *Sunday Telegraph Magazine*, 15 Mar 1984.

Hebert, Hugh. "The Hal of fame." *Guardian*, 23 Mar 1984.

Hoyle, Martin. "*Henry V* in Stratford." *Plays & Players* 378 (1985).

Jones, Winifred Maria. Stage space to screen space: Kenneth Branagh's film of *Henry V* (1989) and Adrian Noble's stage production at Stratford-upon-Avon (1984). Unpublished dissertation for the degree of Master of Arts in Shakespeare Studies of the University of Birmingham. The Shakespeare Institute, Sep 1991.

Loehlin, James. "Rainy marching in the painful field." *Shakespeare in Performance: Henry V*. Manchester: Manchester University Press, 1996.

Shaughnessy, Robert. *Representing Shakespeare: England, History and the RSC*. New York & London: Harvester Wheatsheaf, 1994.

Shrimpton, Nicholas. "Shakespeare performances in Stratford-upon-Avon, 1983–84." *Shakespeare Survey* 38 (1985).

Trewin, John. "*Henry V*." *Birmingham Post*, 29 Mar 1984.

Wardle, Irving. "The history man." *London Times*, 30 Mar 1984.

Warren, Roger. "Shakespeare at Stratford-upon-Avon." *Shakespeare Quarterly*, Spring 1985.

Whitebrook, Peter. "Branagh's bugbear." *Plays & Players* 378 (1985).

Reviews from the Theatre Record, Mar 26–Apr 8, 1984.
Allen, Paul. *New Statesman,* 6 Apr 1984.
Barber, John. *Daily Telegraph,* 29 Mar 1984.
Billington, Michael. *Guardian,* 29 Mar 1984.
Chaillet, Ned. *Wall Street Journal,* 6 Apr 1984.
Coveney, Michael. *Financial Times,* 29 Mar 1984.
Hurren, Kenneth. *Mail on Sunday,* 1 Apr 1984.
Ratcliffe, Michael. *Observer,* 1 Apr 1984.
Say, Rosemary. *Sunday Telegraph,* 1 Apr 1984.
Tinker, Jack. *Daily Mail,* 29 Mar 1984.

Love's Labour's Lost
Play directed par Barry Kyle (Branagh as the King of Navarre), RSC, 1984

Gilbert, Miriam. *Shakespeare in Performance:* Love's Labours Lost. Manchester. Manchester University Press, 1996.

Reviews from the Theatre Record, 8–21 Oct 1984.
Barber, John. *Daily Telegraph,* 11 Oct 1984.
Billington, Michael. *Guardian,* 12 Oct 1984.
Chaillet, Ned. *Wall Street Journal,* 19 Oct 1984.
Edwards, Christopher. *Spectator,* 27 Oct 1984.
Hurren, Kenneth. *Mail on Sunday,* 14 Oct 1984.
Morley, Sheridan. *Punch,* 24 Oct 1984.
Ratcliffe, Michael. *Observer,* 14 Oct 1984.
Tinker, Jack. *Daily Mail,* 11 Oct 1984.

Romeo and Juliet
Play directed by Kenneth Branagh, RTC, 1986

De Jongh, Nicholas. "Head not heart." *Guardian,* 15 Aug 1986.
Edwards, Christopher. "Tasty Morsels." *Spectator,* 30 Aug 1986.
Jackson, Russell. "Beginning with Branagh: *Romeo and Juliet,* Hammersmith, 1986." *Shakespeare: Text and Theater, Essays in honor of Jay L. Halro.* University of Delaware, 1999.
Rissik, Andrew. "Theatre in London: *Romeo and Juliet.*" *London Times,* 16 Aug 1988.
Roper, David. "*Romeo and Juliet.*" *Plays & Players,* Oct 1986.

Reviews from the Theatre Record, 13–26 Aug 1986.
Edwardes, Jane. *Time Out,* 20 Aug 1986.
Hoyle, Martin. *Financial Times,* 15 Aug 1986.
Khan, Naseem. *City Limits,* 21 Aug 1986.
Shannon, David. *Today,* 15 Aug 1986.
Shorter, Eric. *Daily Telegraph,* 16 Aug 1986.
Shulman, Milton. *London Standard,* 18 Aug 1986.
Wheen, Francis. *Sunday Today,* 24 Aug 1986.

Twelfth Night
Play directed by Kenneth Branagh, RTC, 1987

Billington, Michael. "Shakespeare in a flurry." *Guardian,* 5 Dec 1987.

Brown, Georgina. "Malvolio and The Good Life." *Independent,* 2 Dec 1987.

Coursen, H. R. "The Renaissance Theatre's Television *Twelfth Night.*" *Shakespeare on Film Newsletter,* Apr 1989.

Edwards, Christopher. "In festive spirit." *Spectator,* 12 Dec 1987.

Eyres, Harry. "Inspired acting." *London Times,* 5 Dec 1987.

Hurren, Kenneth. "*Twelfth Night.*" *Plays & Players,* Feb 1988.

James, John. "*Twelfth Night.*" *Times Educational Supplement,* 18 Dec 1987.

Jones, D. A. N. "Illyria in winter." *Sunday Telegraph,* 6 Dec 1987.

Kellaway, Kate. "Frosty Festivity." *Observer,* 6 Dec 1987.

Morley, Sheridan. "Coming up to Rosie." *London Times,* 2 Dec 1987.

Osborne, Laurie. "The videotexts of *Twelfth Night.*" *Shakespeare on Film Newsletter,* Apr 1992.

Pearce, Jill. "*Twelfth Night.*" *Cahiers Elisabéthains* 33 (Apr 1988).

Peter, John. "Acting in a new-found spirit of enterprise." *Sunday Times,* 13 Dec 1987.

Spencer, Charles. "Feeling the chill." *Daily Telegraph,* 5 Dec 1987.

Woudhuysen, H. R. "Melancholy pleasures." *Times Literary Supplement,* 18–24 Dec 1987.

Reviews from the Theatre Record, 3–16 Dec 1987.

Battersby, Kate. *Today,* 4 Dec 1987.

Hiley, Jim. *Listener,* 31 Dec 1987.

Hirschhorn, Clive. *Sunday Express,* 13 Dec 1987.

Hoyle, Martin. *Financial Times,* 5 Dec 1987.

Hurren, Kenneth. *Mail on Sunday,* 6 Dec 1987.

Jameson, Sue. *London Broadcasting,* 4 Dec 1987.

Kemp, Peter. *Independent,* 5 Dec 1987.

Morley, Sheridan. *Punch,* 16 Dec 1987.

Pascal, Julia. *Jewish Chronicle,* 11 Dec 1987.

Paton, Maureen. *Daily Express,* 4 Dec 1987.

Rose, Helen. *Time Out,* 9 Dec 1987.

Shulman, Milton. *Evening Standard,* 4 Dec 1987.

Tinker, Jack. *Daily Mail,* 7 Dec 1987.

Wolf, Matt. *City Limits,* 10 Dec 1987.

Much Ado About Nothing, As You Like It, Hamlet
Plays respectively directed by Judi Dench, Geraldine McEwan, and Derek Jacobi, RTC, 1988

Billington, Michael. "*Hamlet* without a quandary." *Guardian,* 27 May 1988.

———. "Sweet and simple." *Guardian,* 5 May 1988.

———. "The cry and the shudder." *Guardian,* 9 Sep 1988.

Branagh, Kenneth & Derek Jacobi. "Two Great Danes." *Telegraph Sunday Magazine,* 28 Aug 1988.

Cochrane, Claire. "*Much Ado About Nothing, As You Liket It, Hamlet.*" *Cahiers Elisabéthains* 34 (Oct 1988).

De jongh, Nicholas. "A raw kind of loving." *Guardian,* 27 Aug 1988.
———. "Paradise regained." *Guardian,* 2 Sep 1988.
Dench, Judi. "A life in the theatre." *Shakespeare: An Illustrated Stage History,* edited by Russell Jackson. Ohio: Ohio University Press, 1996.
Duncan-Jones, Katherine. "Much Ado About Nothing, As You Like It." *Times Literary Supplement,* 16–22 Aug 1988.
Edmonds, Richard. "Much Ado About Nothing." *Birmingham Post,* 9 Mar 1988.
Edwards, Christopher. "Too too solid performance." *Spectator,* 17 Sep 1988.
Eyres, Harry. "Ophelia's night." *London Times,* 9 Sep 1988.
Gordon, Giles. "Much Ado About Nothing." *Plays & Players,* Oct 1988.
Gore-Langton, Robert. "Hamlet." *Plays & Players,* Oct 1988.
———. "Sound Stage: Hamlet without the castle." *Listener,* 25 Aug 1988.
Grimley, Terry. "Hamlet." *Birmingham Post,* 25 May 1988.
Jones, D. A. N. "As You Like It." *Sunday Telegraph,* 4 Sep 1988.
Kemp, Peter. "Amusing arcadia." *Independent,* 2 Sep 1988.
———. "The police state of Denmark." *Independent,* 30 May 1988.
Kingston, Jeremy. "In the addicts' Arden." *London Times,* 2 Sep 1988.
Morley, Sheridan. "A change of direction." *London Times,* 27 Aug 1988.
Osborne, Charles. "A young man's Hamlet." *Daily Telegraph,* 9 Sep 1988.
———. "Trumpeting virtues." *Daily Telegraph,* 27 Aug 1988.
Peter, John. "How to make a virtue of bare necessity." *Sunday Times,* 8 May 1988.
Potter, Lois. "In the name of action." *Times Literary Supplement,* 10–16 Jun 1988.
Ratcliffe, Michael. "Love ever green." *Observer,* 8 May 1988.
Sherrin, Ned. "Directing debs have a bash at the Bard." *Sunday Times,* 28 Aug 1988.
Shorter, Eric. "Renaissance of the invisible art." *Daily Telegraph,* 9 May 1988.
Spencer, Charles. "Holiday in a comic realm." *Daily Telegraph,* 2 Sep 1988.
Taylor, Paul. "A version of pastoral." *Guardian,* 7 Mar 1988.
———. "Methods of madness." *Independent,* 10 Sep 1988.
Wardle, Irving. "A touch of fine romance." *London Times,* 6 May 1988.
———. "Pressure-cooker prince." *London Times,* 27 May 1988.
———. "Women, romance—and Archie Rice." *London Times,* 5 May 1988.
Wells, Stanley. "Shakespeare Performances in England, 1987–88." *Shakespeare Survey,* 1990.

Reviews from the Theatre Record, 20 May 1988.
Billington, Michael. *Guardian,* 7 May 1988.
Coveney, Michael. *Financial Times,* 26 May 1988.
Dungate, Rod. *Tribune,* 10 Jun 1988.
Hoyle, Martin. *Financial Times,* 5 May 1988.
———. *Financial Times,* 7 May 1988.
Marriot, John. *Daily Mail,* 31 May 1988.
Paton, Maureen. *Daily Express,* 17 May 1988.
Ratcliffe, Michael. *Observer,* 29 May 1988.
Sampson, Val. *Today,* 6 May 1988.
Taylor, Paul. *Independent,* 5 May 1988.
———. *Independent,* 6 May 1988.

King Lear / A Midsummer Night's Dream
Plays directed by Kenneth Branagh, RTC, 1990

Bevington, David. "Singing in the Rain." *Shakespeare Quarterly*, Winter 1990.

Billington, Michael. "The Janus face of Renaissance." *Guardian*, 13 Aug 1990.

Coursen, H. R. "The Summer of *King Lear*." *Reading Shakespeare On Stage*. London: Associated University Presses, 1995.

Donahue, Patricia. "*A Midsummer Night's Dream* and *King Lear*." *Shakespeare Bulletin*, Spring 1990.

Gross, John. "The real Lear stands up at last." *Sunday Telegraph*, 19 Aug 1990.

Kellaway, Kate. "Let Me not be Mad, not Mad, Sweet Heaven: Three productions of King Lear." *Literary Review*, Dec 1990.

Kingstion, Jeremy. "Charmless dream redeemed." *London Times*, 10 Aug 1990.

Kroll, Jack. "And Now, Live From L.A. ..." *Newsweek*, 19 Feb 1990.

Logan, Robert A. "Kenneth Branagh's *A Midsummer Night's Dream*." *A Midsummer Night's Dream: Critical Essays*, edited by Dorothea Kehler. New York: Garland Publishing, 1998.

Marowitz, Charles. "Is that all there is?" *London Times*, 29 Jan 1990.

————. "Shakespeare for Schools." *Theater Week*, 12 Feb 1990.

McCulloh, T. H. "Kenneth Branagh's 'Gift of Certainty'." *Los Angeles Times*, 14 Jan 1990.

Morgenstern, Joe. "Branagh does Shakespeare his way." *Wall Street Journal*, 29 Jan 1990.

Morris, Steven. "Los Angeles in performance." *Drama* 174 (1989).

Morris, Tom. "*King Lear* and *A Midsummer Night's Dream*." *Times Literary Supplement*, 24–30 Aug 1990.

O'Steen, Kathleen. "Headaches, rewards follow Branagh troupe's international tour." *Variety*, 7 Feb 1990.

Pollack, Joe. "Branagh and the Bard." *St Louis Post-Dispatch*, 27 May 1990.

Russell, Thomas W. "The Renaissance Theatre Company in Los Angeles, 1990." *Shakespeare Quarterly*, Winter 1990.

Simon, John. "International Theatre Festival." *New York*, 25 Jun 1990.

Stanfill, Francesca. "To the mantle born?" *New York*, 12 Feb 1990.

Taylor, Paul. "Driest summer on record." *Independent*, 15 Aug 1990.

Taylor, Paul. "One in the eye for tradition." *Independent*, 17 Aug 1990.

Weiss, Alfred. "The Edinburgh International Festival, 1990." *Shakespeare Quarterly*, Winter 1990.

Coriolanus
Play directed by Tim Supple (Branagh as Coriolanus), RTC, 1992

Billington, Michael. "Mobbing the star." *Guardian*, 15 May 1992.

Coveney, Michael. "The head boy must settle for a B-plus." *Observer*, 17 May 1992.

Gross, John. "Flaws fatal and otherwise." *Sunday Telegraph*, 17 May 1992.

Hassell, Graham. "Star-spangled Branagh." *Plays & Players*, May 1992.

McCauley, Janie. "*Coriolanus*." *Shakespeare Bulletin*, Spring 1993.

Morgan, Gwyn. "*Coriolanus*." *Plays & Players*, Jul 1992.

Nightingale, Benedict. "Every inch his macho mother's son." *London Times*, 15 May 1992.

Peter, John. "Titanic tour de force." *Sunday Times*, 17 May 1992.

Smith, Peter. "*Coriolanus*." *Cahiers Elisabéthains* 42 (Oct 1992).

Spencer, Charles. "The crying killer." *Daily Telegraph*, 15 May 1992.

Taylor, Paul. "Smalltime heroism." *Independent*, 15 May 1992.

Wardle, Irving. "Ken and John's shows." *Independent on Sunday*, 17 May 1992.

Hamlet
BBC Radio, co-directed by Glean Dearman and Kenneth Branagh, 1992

Crunelle-Vanrigh, Anny. "*Hamlet & Romeo and Juliet*." *Cahiers Elisabéthains* 45 (Apr 1994).

Curtis, Nick. "*Hamlet*." *Plays & Players*, Jun 1992.

Hay, Malcolm. "Sight and Sound: Malcom Hay on the Month's TV and Radio." *Plays & Players*, Jun 1992.

Jackson, Russell. "Two Radio Shakespeares: Staging and text." *Shakespeare: Cosmopolisme et Insularité—Actes du Congrès la Société Française Shakespeare 1993*. Paris: Les Belles Lettres, 1994.

Neill, Heather. "*Hamlet* takes to the air." *Times Educational Supplement*, 24 Apr 1992.

Purves, Libby. "The King and I." *Radio Times*, 25 Apr 1992.

Reynolds, Gillian. "Hamlet, prince of airwaves." *Daily Telegraph*, 25 Apr 1992.

Stoddart, Patrick. "Branagh scores a palpable hit." *London Times*, 27 Apr 1992.

Whitley, John. "Mrs Dale and the Prince of Denmark." *London Times*, 23 Apr 1992.

Hamlet
Play directed by Adrian Noble, RSC/RTC, 1992–1993

Andrews, David. "*Hamlet*." *Plays & Players*, Feb 1993.

Brustein, Robert. "Architectural barriers." *New Republic*, 29 Mar 1993.

Coursen, H. R. "Hamlet." *Shakespeare Bulletin*, Spring 1993.

———. "London: February 1993." *Reading Shakespeare On Stage*. London: Associated University Presses, 1995.

Crowl, Samuel. "Hamlet 'Most Royal': An Interview with Kenneth Branagh." *Shakespeare Bulletin*, Fall 1994.

Crunelle-Vanrigh, Anny. "A conversation about *Hamlet*." *Cahiers Elisabéthains* 44 (Oct 1993).

———. "A detailed account of *Hamlet*." *Cahiers Elisabéthains* 44 (Oct 1993).

Dawson, Antony. *Shakespeare in Performance*: Hamlet. Manchester: Manchester University Press, 1995.

Delingpole, James. "Branagh heads star-studded line-up at RSC." *Daily Telegraph*, 16 Jan 1992.

Dougary, Ginny. "Oh, what a roguish and peasant slave." *Times Saturday Review*, 21 Nov 1992.

Gross, John. "Stronger on action than introspection." *Sunday Telegraph*, 27 Dec 1992.

Hirshhorn, Clive. "Lucid *Hamlet* is a triumph for Branagh." *Sunday Express,* 27 Dec 1992.

Holland, Peter. "Shakespeare performances in England, 1992–1993." *Shakespeare Survey* 47 (1994).

Jackson, Russell. "Shakespeare at Stratford-upon-Avon, 1993–94." *Shakespeare Quarterly,* Fall 1994.

Lapworth, Paul. "Most royal … and noble too." *Sun Herald,* 26 Mar 1993.

Lavender, Andy. "The power behind the scene: A talk with designer Bob Crowley." *London Times,* 16 Dec 1992.

Nelsen, Paul. "Noble Thoughts on Mighty Experiences: An Interview with Adrian Noble." *Shakespeare Bulletin,* Summer 1993.

Nightingale, Benedict."Princely noble in lunacy." *London Times,* 21 Dec 1992.

Peter, John. "What a piece of work." *Sunday Times,* 27 Dec 1992.

Pope, Harvey. "Prince of theatre packs them in." *Observer,* 18 Mar 1993.

Rich, Frank. "Branagh's Hamlet as a Young Conservative." *New York Times,* 24 Dec 1992.

Spencer, Charles. "A *Hamlet* of hidden mysteries." *Daily Telegraph,* 21 Dec 1992.

Tait, Simon. "Branagh leads return to RSC." *London Times,* 16 Jan 1992.

Reviews from the Theatre Record, 2–31 Dec 1992.

Billington, Michael. *Guardian,* 19 Dec 1992.

Coveney, Michael. *Observer,* 20 Dec 1992.

De Jongh, Nicholas. *Evening Standard,* 21 Dec 1992.

Dunn, Tony. *Tribune,* 1 Jan 1993.

Edwardes, Jane. *Time Out,* 30 Dec 1992.

Hurren, Kenneth. *Mail on Sunday,* 20 Dec 1992.

Morley, Sheridan. *Herald Tribune,* 23 Dec 1992.

Nathan, David. *Jewish Chronicle,* 1 Jan 1993.

Paton, Maureen. *Daily Express,* 19 Dec 1992.

Rutherford, Malcolm. *Financial Times,* 21 Dec 1992.

Shuttleworth, Ian. *City Limits,* 7 Jan 1993.

Smith, Neil. *What's On,* 30 Dec 1992.

Taylor, Paul. *Independent,* 21 Dec 1992.

Tinker, Jack. *Daily Mail,* 19 Dec 1992.

Wardle, Irving. *Independent on Sunday,* 20 Dec 1992.

Books and Profiles on Kenneth Branagh

Appleyard, Bryan. "Enter the outsider." *London Times,* 8 Aug 1987.

Bardsley, Barney. "Waiting for the renaissance of the actor." *Drama,* Winter 1984.

Berthomieu, Pierre. *Kenneth Branagh: Traînes de Feu, Rosées de Sang.* Paris: Editions Jean-Michel Place, 1998.

Billington, Michael. "Formidable force." *Interview,* Oct 1989.

Branagh, Kenneth. "An actor's London." *Evening Standard Magazine,* Dec 1988.

———. "Renaissance Men." *Drama* 165 (1987).

———. *Beginning.* London: Chatto & Windus, 1989.

———. Foreword. *Parallel Realities of Northern Ireland.* Belfast: The Blackstaff Press, 1994.

———. Foreword. *Shakespeare and Mabeth: The story behind the play.* Stewart Ross. London: David Bennett Books, 1994.

Burt, Paddy. "A Life in the Day of Kenneth Branagh." *Sunday Times,* 10 Jul 1988.

Cameron, James. "Kenneth Branagh: Hero or luvvie?" *Midlands Now,* Nov 1994.

Christiansen, Richard. "A role model: *Beginning.*" *Chicago Tribune,* 20 May 1990.

Cowley, Deborah. "Kenneth Branagh: Theatre's New Young King." *Readers Digest,* Feb 1990.

Crowdus, Gary. "Sharing an Enthusiasm for Shakespeare: An Interview with Kenneth Branagh." *Cineaste* 24.1 (1998).

Cushman, Robert. "My brilliant career." *Sunday Times,* 1 Oct 1989.

Cushman, Robert. "Renaissance company closes." *Daily Telegraph,* 6 Apr 1994.

Daneman, Paul. "Free the theatre." *Drama* 171 (1989).

Davenport, Hugo. "Branagh: A talent eclipsed." *Daily Telegraph,* 2 Oct 1995.

Davison, John. "Directing a regional renaissance." *Sunday Times,* 5 Jul 1987.

Day, Carol. "Not So Melancholy, Baby." *Madison,* Dec 1998.

De Jongh, Nicholas. "The Branagh business." *Guardian,* 9 Oct 1989.

Diamond, Jamie. "There is (Sexy) Life After Shakespeare." *Cosmopolitan,* Sep 1991.

Ezard, John. "Branagh joins BFI board." *Guardian,* 1 Sep 1993.

Fallowell, Duncan. "High street Ken." *ES,* May 1992.

Fernandez Valenti, Tomas. "Kenneth Branagh: Entre Shakespeare y Mary Shelley (1)." *Dirigido,* Jan 1995.

———. "Kenneth Branagh: Entre Shakespeare y Mary Shelley (2)." *Dirigido,* Feb 1995.

Grimley, Terry. "Actor who gained control of his work." *Birmingham Post,* 16 Sep 1989.

Gristwood, Sarah. "My brilliant career." *Money,* Jun 1984.

Groult, Florent. "*Hamlet.*" *Cine Scores,* Jan 1997.

Hatchuel, Sarah. "Kenneth Branagh: When a Theatre Actor Blossoms Into a Movie Director." *Shakespeare Newsletter,* Winter 1997.

Hatchuel, Sarah. "Making Melodies for Branagh's films: An interview with Patrick Doyle." *Shakespeare,* Winter 1998.

Hill, Rosemary. "Renaissance Man." *Telegraph Sunday Magazine,* 28 Jun 1987.

Hubbard, Kim. "The Man Who Would Be King: Rising Star Kenneth Branagh." *People,* 12 Feb 1990.

Jackson, Russell. "Working with Shakespeare: Confessions of an Adviser." *Cineaste* 24.1 (1998).

Langan, Sean. "Star-spangled Branagh." *Mail on Sunday,* 15 Aug 1993.

Lawson, Mark. "More than an actor." *Independent,* 9 May 1987.

Leech, Michael. "The Young Contender." *Woman & Home,* Feb 1986.

Lovell, Glenn. "Oh horror! Branagh loves old scary film." *Calgary Herald,* 21 May 1993.

Meier, Paul. "Kenneth Branagh: With Utter Clarity." *Drama Review,* Summer 1997.

Melia, Amparo. "*Hamlet.*" *Rosebud Banda Sonora,* Mar 1997.

Morley, Sheridan. "The company directors." *London Times,* 12 Mar 1988.

Petty, Moira. "Kenneth Branagh's burning question." *Daily Express,* 25 Nov 1995.

Renton, Alex. "Renaissance Man." *Plays & Players,* Jul 1987.

Rix, Brian. *Tour de Farce: A tale of touring theatres and strolling players (from Thespic to Branagh).* London, Sydney, & Auckland: Hodder & Stoughton, 1992.

Roberts, Diane. "Renaissance Man." *Southwark Globe,* Spring 1988.

Robinson, Lucy. "Prize Guy." *Daily Mirror,* 23 Oct 1987.

Stewart, Andrew. "Settling Hamlet's score." *Classic FM Magazine,* Feb 1997.

Shuttleworth, Ian. *Ken & Em: A Biography of Kenneth Branagh and Emma Thompson.* London: Headline Book Publishing, 1994.

Taylor, Paul. "Love him, loathe him: Ken divides us all." *Sunday Times,* 19 Jan 1997.

Thornber, Robin. "Fortunes of fame." *Guardian,* 7 Mar 1988.

Tirard, Laurent. "Branagh Côté Jardin." *Studio* (Cannes) [May], 1997.

Tyler, Rod. "Renaissance Man." *Sunday Express Magazine,* 10 Sep 1989.

Wolf, Matt. "Hard Act to Follow: *Beginning.*" *Listener,* 28 Sep 1989.

————. "Too Much Ado Over New Oliver." *Wall Street Journal,* 23 Sep 1988.

Woods, Vicki. "The Observer Interview: Kenneth Branagh." *Observer/Life,* 1 Dec 1996.

Woodward, Ian. "Branagh, Frances Barber and Samantha Bond." *Sunday Express,* 12 Feb 1989.

Worsthorne, Peregrine. "More deserving of heckle than of hype." *Sunday Telegraph,* 17 Sep 1989.

Yakir, Dan. "King Ken." *US,* Apr 1990.

Internet sites on Kenneth Branagh

<www.bbc.co.uk/education/archive/hamlet/> (BBC site on Branagh's *Hamlet*)

<www.branaghcompendium.com> (Unofficial site on Kenneth Branagh, maintained by Ngoc Vu)

<www.geocities.com/Athens/Parthenon/6261/hamlet.html> (a compendium of more than 100 critics' reviews of Branagh's *Hamlet*)

<www3.nbnet.nb.ca/mosherm> (Branagh FAQ maintained by Marilyn Mosher)

Works Cited

Alleva, Richard. "Beatrice Forever." *Commonweal*, 18 Jun 1993.

Andrews, David. Review of *Hamlet*, Royal Shakespeare Company, London. *Plays & Players*, Feb 1993.

Bamigboye, Baz. "Once more unto the breach." *Daily Mail*, 18 Nov 1988.

Berthomieu, Pierre. *Kenneth Branagh: Traînes de feu, rosées de sang*. Paris: Editions Jean-Michel Place, 1998.

Billington, Michael. "A 'New Olivier' Is Taking On Henry V on the Screen," review of *Henry V*. *New York Times*, 8 Jan 1989.

———. "Hamlet without a quandary." *Guardian*, 27 May 1988.

———. "Sweet and simple." *Guardian*, 5 May 1988.

Bilson, Anne. "Blond bombshell can't keep his mouth shut." *Sunday Telegraph*, 16 Feb 1997.

Branagh, Kenneth. *Beginning*. London: Chatto & Windus, 1989.

———. "Funny Shakespeare." *Studio*, Mar 1993.

———. "Henry V." In *Players of Shakespeare 2*, edited by Russell Jackson and Robert Smallwood. Cambridge: Cambridge University Press, 1988.

———. *Hamlet: Screenplay, Introduction and Film Diary*. London: Chatto & Windus, 1996.

———. Liner notes to *Hamlet*, Renaissance Theatre in association with BBC Radio. Random Century Audiobooks, RC 100 (1992).

———. Liner notes to *Hamlet: Original Motion Picture Soundtrack*. Sony Classical, SK 62857.

———. *Henry V: A Screen Adaptation*. London: Chatto & Windus, 1989.

———. "Henry V." *Players of Shakespeare 2*, edited by Russell Jackson & Robert Smallwood. Cambridge: Cambridge University Press, 1988.

———. Liner notes to *Henry V: Original Soundtrack Recording*. EMI, CDC 7 49919 2.

———. *In the Bleak Midwinter: The Screenplay*. London: Nick Hern Books, 1995.

———. Interview by Susanne Stamberg at the "Smithsonian's Stellar Shakespeare Weekend," 21 Dec 1996. Folger Library of Washington, DC. A summary of it can be found in the *Shakespeare Newsletter*, Fall 1996.

———. Interview on the set of *Hamlet*, 6 Feb 1997. "Kaleidoscope." BBC Radio 4.

———. Interview by Charlie Rose, broadcast on "Charlie Rose," PBS, Dec 1995. Available from *Journal Graphics Video*.

———. Interview by Charlie Rose, broadcast on "Charlie Rose," PBS, May 1993. Available from *Journal Graphics Video*.

————. Interviewed by Isabelle Giordanno on Canal+ (in French), Cannes, May 1993.

————. Interviewed by Samuel Crowl, Stratford, 19 Apr 1993.

————. Interviewed on Canal+ (in French), Jan 1993.

————. Interviewed on CBC Radio (Canada) at *Hamlet*'s release.

————. *Much Ado About Nothing: Screenplay, Introduction and Notes on the Making of the Film.* London: Chatto & Windus, 1993.

————. *Public Enemy.* London and Boston: Faber and Faber, 1988.

————. A meeting between Kenneth Branagh and Gerard Depardieu, organized by *Studio*, Jan 1991.

————. Interviewed for Movie Show at the release of *Dead Again* in 1991.

Breight, Curtis. "Branagh and the Prince, or a 'royal fellowship of death,'" *Critical Quarterly* 33.4 (1991).

Brett, Anwar. "Eternal Death." *X Posé*, May 1997.

Briers, Richard. Liner notes to *Hamlet,* Renaissance Theatre in association with BBC Radio. Random Century Audiobooks, RC 100 (1992).

British Broadcasting Corporation (BBC). Leaflet accompanying the BBC2 documentary *To Cut or Not to Cut: The Making of* Hamlet, *1996.* Broadcast on "Learning Zone," Feb 1997.

Brustein, Robert. "Architectural barriers." *New Republic*, 29 Mar 1993.

Canby, Vincent. "A House Party of Beatrice, Benedick and Friends." *New York Times*, 7 May 1993.

Clark, David. "Blond Ambition." *What's On*, 12 Feb 1997.

Corliss, Richard. "Branagh the Conqueror." *Time International*, 13 Nov 1989.

Coursen, H. R. Review of *Hamlet*, Royal Shakespeare Company, London. *Shakespeare Bulletin*, Spring 1993.

————. *Shakespeare in Production: Whose History?* Ohio: Ohio University Press, 1996.

Crowl, Samuel. "Hamlet 'Most Royal': An Interview with Kenneth Branagh." *Shakespeare Bulletin*, Fall 1994.

————. "Much Ado About Nothing." *Shakespeare Bulletin*, Summer 1993.

Crunelle-Vanrigh, Anny. "A conversation about Hamlet." *Cahiers Elisabéthains* 44 (Oct 1993).

————. "A detailed account of Hamlet." *Cahiers Elisabéthains* 44 (Oct 1993).

Dawson, Antony. *Shakespeare in Performance:* Hamlet. Manchester: Manchester University Press, 1995.

Dawson, Jeff. "Healthy, Wealthy and Wise?" *Empire*, Sep 1993.

de Jongh, Nicholas. "A raw kind of loving." *Guardian*, 27 Aug 1988.

Dench, Judi. "A life in the theatre." In *Shakespeare: An Illustrated Stage History*, edited by Russell Jackson. Ohio: Ohio University Press, 1996.

Discovering Hamlet. Alexandria, Virginia: PBS Home Video, 1998. A4078-WEBHV.

Donaldson, Peter. "Taking on Shakespeare: Kenneth Branagh's *Henry V.*" *Shakespeare Quaterly*, Spring 1991.

Dougary, Ginny. "Oh, what a roguish and peasant slave." *London Times Saturday Review*, 21 Nov 1992.

Doyle, Patrick. Liner notes to *Hamlet,* Renaissance Theatre in association with BBC Radio. Random Century Audiobooks, RC 100 (1992).

————. Liner notes to *Henry V: Original Soundtrack Recording.* EMI, CDC 7 49919 2.

————. Interviewed by the author, Apr 10 1997.

Ebert, Roger. Review of *Henry V*. *Chicago Sun-Times*, 15 Dec 1989.

Edgerton, Ellen. "'Your Answer, Sir, Is Cinematical': Kenneth Branagh's *Much Ado About Nothing*." *Shakespeare Bulletin*, Winter 1994.

Eyres, Harry. "Ophelia's night." *London Times*, 9 Sep 1988.

Fabricius, Susanne. "The face of honour: On Kenneth Branagh's Screen Adaptation of *Henry V*." In *Screen Shakespeare*, edited by Michael Skovmand. Cambridge: Cambridge University Press, 1994.

Fallon, James. "The Prince Returns." *W*, Nov 1996.

Fisher, Bob. "Tragedy of Epic Proportions." *American Cinematographer*, Jan 1997.

Fitter, Chris. "A Tale of Two Branaghs: Henry V, Ideology and the Mekong Agincourt." In *Shakespeare Left and Right*, edited by Ivo Kamps. London: Routledge, 1991.

French, Philip. "A hit, a very palpable hit." *Observer*, 16 Feb 1997.

Fuller, Graham. "Interview with Kenneth Branagh." *Interview*, Nov 1994.

————. *Film Comment* 25 (1989).

Gordon, Giles. Review of *Much Ado About Nothing*, Renaissance Theatre Company, London. *Plays & Players*, Oct 1988.

Grimley, Terry. "Ken slows down for fourth Dane." *Birmingham Post*, 18 Mar 1993.

Gritten, David. "Why is Kenneth Branagh starring in and directing a 3-hour version of Hamlet?" *Los Angeles Times*, 2 Jun 1996.

Guntner, Lawrence, & Peter Drexler. "Recycled film codes and the study of Shakespeare on film." *Deutsche Shakespeare*, 1993.

Hedrick, Donald. "War is mud: Branagh's dirty *Henry V*." *Shakespeare on Film Newsletter*, Apr 1991.

Hirschhorn, Clive. "The Man who shot Shakespeare." *Applause*, Feb 1997.

Hoyle, Martin. Review of *Much Ado About Nothing*, Renaissance Theatre Company, London. *Financial Times*, 5 May 1988.

Iselin, Pierre, ed. "Hamlet and the 'curious perspective,' or the uncertainties of the gaze." In *Hamlet: Essays*. Paris: Didier Eruditions—CNED, 1997.

Jackson, Russell. "How do you coach film actors to speak Shakespeare's lines." *Sunday Times*, 29 Aug 1993.

————. Interviewed by the author in Stratford-upon-Avon, 10 Mar 1997.

————. "Shakespeare at Stratford-upon-Avon 1993—94." *Shakespeare Quarterly*, Fall 1994.

Jacobi, Derek. Interview by Susan Stamberg at the "Smithsonian's Stellar Shakespeare Weekend," 21 Dec 1996. Folger Library of Washington, DC. A summary of it can be found in the *Shakespeare Newsletter*, Fall 1996.

————. Liner notes to *Hamlet*, Renaissance Theatre in association with BBC Radio. Random Century Audiobooks, RC 100 (1992).

Klawans, Stuart. "Films." *Nation*, 11 Dec 1989.

Klifa, Thierry. "Beaucoup de bruit pour rien." *Studio*, May 1993.

Kliman, Bernice. "Branagh's Henry: Allusion and Illusion." *Shakespeare on Film Newsletter*, Dec 1989.

Lady, Steph, Frank Darabont & Kenneth Branagh. *Mary Shelley's Frankenstein: The Screenplay*. New York: Newmarket Press, 1994.

Lane, Antony. "Insubstantial pageants." *Independent*, 30 Sep 1989.

Lauliac, Christian. "Interview: Patrick Doyle." *Ciné Scores*, Jan 1996.

Lawson, Mark. "More than an actor." *Independent*, 9 May 1987.

Loehlin, James. *Shakespeare in Performance:* Henry V. Manchester: Manchester University Press, 1996.

Manheim, Michael. "The English history play on screen." In *Shakespeare and the Moving Image*, edited by Anthony Davies and Stanley Wells. Cambridge: Cambridge University Press, 1994.

Mars-Jones, Adam. "Much amiss." *Independent*, 27 Aug 1993.

Munsn Deats, Sara. "Rabbits and ducks." *Literature Film Quaterly* 20.1 (Oct 1992).

Naughton, John. "The Return of The Magnificent Eight?" *Premiere*, Sep 1993.

Nelsen, Paul. "Noble Thoughts on Mighty Experiences: An Interview with Adrian Noble." *Shakespeare Bulletin*, 1993.

Nightingale, Benedict. "Princely noble in lunacy." *London Times*, 21 Dec 1992.

Occhiogrosso, Frank. "Branagh's *Henry V*," a film review. *Shakespeare Bulletin*, Spring 1990.

Paton, Maureen. Review of *Hamlet*, Renaissance Theatre Company, London. *Daily Express*, 17 May 1988.

Peter, John. "What a piece of work." *Sunday Times*, 27 Dec 1992.

Pursell, Michael. "Playing the game: Branagh's *Henry V*." *Literature Film Quaterly* 20 (Jan 1992).

Rabkin, Norman. *Shakespeare and the Problem of Meaning*. Chicago: Chicago University Press, 1981.

Rafferty, Terrence. "Solid Flesh." *New Yorker*, 13 Jan 1997.

Ratcliffe, Michael. "Love ever green." *Observer*, 8 May 1988.

———. Review of *Hamlet*, Renaissance Theatre Company, London. *Observer*, 29 May 1988.

Rathburn, Paul. "Branagh's Iconoclasm: Warriors for the Working Day." *Shakespeare on Film Newsletter*, Apr 1991.

Rennaissance Theatre Company in association with BBC Radio. Introduction to brochure notes for *Hamlet*. London: Random Century Audiobooks, 1992.

Rothwell, Kenneth. "Kenneth Branagh's *Henry V*: The Gilt [Guilt] in the Crown Re-Examined." *Comparative Drama* 24 (1990—91).

Saada, Nicolas. "Le théâtre apprivoisé. "*Les Cahiers du Cinéma*, Jan 1991.

Salomon, Patricia. "The Sentimentalizing of Communitas in Kenneth Branagh's *Henry V*." *Shakespeare Bulletin*, Winter 1995.

Sampson, Val. Review of *Much Ado About Nothing*, Renaissance Theatre Company, London. *Today*, 6 May 1988.

Shaw, William. "Textual Ambiguities and Cinematic Certainties in *Henry V*." *Film Literature Quaterly* 2 (1994).

Shuttleworth, Ian. *Ken & Em: A Biography of Kenneth Branagh and Emma Thomson*. London: Headline Book Publishing, 1994.

Sinden, Peter. "Do the Bard man!" *Film Review*, Mar 1997.

Skovmand, Michael, ed. Introduction. *Screen Shakespeare*. Cambridge: Cambridge University Press, 1994.

Smith, Dinitia. "Much Ado About Branagh." *New York*, 24 May 1993.

Snead, Elizabeth. "For Kate Winslet, the past provides the perfect roles." *USA Today*, 12 Apr 1996.

So, Mark. "Patrick Doyle." *Film Score Monthly*, Jun 1994.

Spencer, Charles. "A Hamlet of hidden mysteries." *Daily Telegraph*, 21 Dec 1992.

Stearns, David Patrick. "He unveils epic visions of Hamlet." *USA Today*, 7 Jan
    1997.

Talouarn, Bruno. "Interview with Patrick Doyle." *Main Title*, Jun 1993.

Taylor, Paul. Review of *Much Ado About Nothing*, Renaissance Theatre Company,
    London. *Indépendant*, 5 May 1988.

"To See or Not to See—That is the Question as the Post-Modern Version of
    Hamlet comes to Town." *Australian*, 21 May 1997. (author unknown)

Wardle, Irving. Review of *Henry V*, Royal Shakespeare Company, London. *London
    Times*, 30 Mar 1984.

Weisel, Al. "Idol Chatter: Kenneth Branagh." *Premiere*, Dec 1996.

Whitebrook, Peter. "Branagh's bugbear." *Plays & Players* 378 (1985).

Whitley, John. "Mrs Dale and the Prince of Denmark." *London Times*, 23 Apr
    1992.

Wilmington, Michael. "A noble Hamlet." *Chicago Tribune*, 24 Jan 1997.